William Burt Pope

The Person of Christ

Dogmatic, Scriptural, Historical

William Burt Pope

The Person of Christ
Dogmatic, Scriptural, Historical

ISBN/EAN: 9783337720834

Printed in Europe, USA, Canada, Australia, Japan

Cover: Foto ©Lupo / pixelio.de

More available books at **www.hansebooks.com**

THE PERSON OF CHRIST:

DOGMATIC, SCRIPTURAL, HISTORICAL.

THE PERSON OF CHRIST:
DOGMATIC, SCRIPTURAL, HISTORICAL.

The Fernley Lecture

OF

1871,

WITH TWO ADDITIONAL ESSAYS ON THE
BIBLICAL AND ECCLESIASTICAL DEVELOPMENT
OF THE DOCTRINE,

AND ILLUSTRATIVE NOTES.

SECOND EDITION.

BY THE REV. W. B. POPE,
THEOLOGICAL TUTOR, DIDSBURY COLLEGE.

LONDON:
WESLEYAN CONFERENCE OFFICE,
2, CASTLE-STREET, CITY-ROAD;
SOLD AT 66, PATERNOSTER-ROW.

1875.

ERRATA.

Page 97, line 8, for " ANGEL JEHOVAH," read "ANGEL OF JEHOVAH."
Page 99, line 15, for " distinctly," read " certainly."
Page 121, line 9 from below, for " imparted," read " imported."
Page 141, line 3 from below, place a " period " instead of a " semicolon.

PREFACE TO SECOND EDITION.

THE present Edition is enlarged by an Essay on the Development of the Revelation of Christ's Person in Scripture, together with a few additional Illustrative Notes. The Writer's original design is now accomplished: that of exhibiting consecutively the Dogmatic, Biblical, and Historical elements of this fundamental doctrine. The whole is only an outline for the guidance of the student. May the Lord give it His blessing!

Didsbury College,
Christmas, 1874.

ANALYSIS.

THE PERSON OF CHRIST.

	PAGE
The Holy Ghost the Revealer of Christ	1
The Saviour the Revealer of Himself	2
In the Unity of His Divine and Human Natures	2

I. The Constitution of the Incarnate Person.
    The Vocabulary of the Doctrine in Scripture and in Theology   3
I. The PERSONALITY only Divine.
    In what Personality consists .   6
    1. That of the Eternal Son 6
        (1.) This viewed in relation to Himself and His other
            names, especially the "Word" and the "Image"   7
        (2.) In its aspect towards the Incarnation.
            Why the Son, and only the Son, incarnate .   8
            His special affinity with our race   9
    2. This Personality unchangeable .   10
        (1.) No second Person added to it.
            The Testimony of Scripture   11
            The necessity of redemption   11
        (2.) The Human nature Impersonal.
            How this is to be understood . .   12
            Incarnation-phrases, specially St. John's   13

II. The Divine-human PERSON.
    1. Two Natures to be united, each perfect . . . 15
        (1.) Christ "truly" God in opposition to Gnostics and
            Arians . . .   16
        (2.) Christ "perfectly" Man.
            "Only" man: a theory excluded .   17
            "Real" man as against Docetism . . . 18
            Without defect or addition, as against Apollinaris   19

	PAGE
2. No Change through the Incarnation.	
(1.) None in the Divine Nature .	21
Change only in manifestation .	21
Modern Theories of Depotentiation	22
(2.) None in the Human Nature .	24
(3.) None as the result of the Union .	25
Eutychianism . .	26
3. Hence Christ is God and man.	
(1.) Christological Watchwords . .	28
(2.) Scriptural Guarantees for them .	29
(3.) Athanasian Summing-up . .	30
The Hypostatic Union . .	31

III. The Mystery and Glory of Christian Faith.

1. The Mystery in two senses . .	31
(1.) As once hidden now revealed .	31
The Mystery of Ages . .	32
The Mystery of Eternity	33
(2.) As still unsearchable .	33
Testimony of Scripture	34
This an essential element in the study of the doctrine	35
Consequences of undue speculation	35
2. The Glory of Theology . .	36
(1.) The Perfection of its revelations .	37
(2.) The Centre of its doctrine . .	37

II. Relation of the Indivisible Person to Christian Theology.

General View .	38

I. Revelation.

1. Christ the Revealer absolutely, and to man	39
Not through man, to man but in our nature	39
2. Application of this.	
(1.) To Philosophy.	
That which requires all revelation to be within	41
That which limits knowledge of God	41

	PAGE
(2.) To the Written Word.	
Christ a living Person infallibly speaking	42
To those who understand His speech .	42

II. Mediation.
Its three senses in relation to Christ   43
1. As union of God and man in Him.
  (1.) Pledge of Reconciliation of God and the Race   44
  (2.) Presupposes the coming Atonement.
      Speculative error of necessary incarnation independently of sin 44
      Practical error of Latitudinarians on the one hand, and Sacramentarians on the other . . . 45
2. Intervention of a Reconciler between God and man   46
  (1.) The Two Natures necessary.
      Divinity for the worth . .   46
      Manhood for the appropriateness .   47
  (2.) One Person necessary.
      A Living Sacrifice .   48
      Hence objections obviated . .   49
  (3.) As to the full doctrine of Atonement.
      One Person Vicarious for the Race .   49
      One Person Representative of His Church   51
      One Person centre of Union to Individuals . .   51
  (4.) Hence Redemption necessary and not an experiment   52
3. The Mediatorial Ministry.
  (1.) Generally.
      The Humiliation of the God-man only .   53
      Under guidance of the Holy Ghost in all   54
  (2.) The Twofold Estate.
      Unity of Person in the great Obedience   55
      Unity of Person in the Exaltation   57
  (3.) The Final End of it.
      The Judgment . .   58
      The authority laid down . .   59
      Son in His Indivisible Person subject for ever   59

	PAGE
III. Real Presence	60
1. In His One Person Present and Absent	61
2. His Person represented by the Holy Ghost	62
3. Theories of Sacramental Presence.	
Transubstantiation (the Whole Person)	64
Consubstantiation (the Manhood) .	65
Anglican Real Presence	66
The true Real Presence	67
IV. Personal Religion.	
General View	69
1. One Person claims personal Submission .	69
2. Object of Christian Faith and Trust .	71
3. Union with Christ's Person	72
The true Mysticism .	72
4. Divine-human Lawgiver:	
As Man; as God; as God-man .	73
5. Divine-human Pattern:	
Necessarily Divine and necessarily human	75
The Two Natures not to be divided . .	75
Consequences of regarding either nature alone	76
6. Object of Worship and Devotion	79
Prayer to Jesus	79
7. Disposer of man's destiny as God-man	80
V. The Divine-human Head of the Church . .	81
1. His Person test of Orthodoxy in the visible Church .	82
Application to Christian Communities, and to Methodism	83
2. Head of the Mystical Body	84
3. Eternal Centre of the visible and invisible Churches	
made one	86
From the Doctrine to the Person .	87
From the Person to the Doctrine .	88

SCRIPTURAL DEVELOPMENT.

	PAGE
Principle of Arrangement and Exhibition	91
I. THE OLD TESTAMENT:	
Referred to by Christ	92
Measure and Limitation or Development	93
I. The Future SEED as Human . .	95
1. Of the Woman	95
2. Of Abraham	96
3. Of David	96
II. The Angel of Jehovah as Divine.	97
1. In Historical Books .	97
2. In the Prophets	98
III. Divine-human in Later Old Testament.	99
1. Psalms:	
(1.) Psalm ii.	100
(2.) Psalm cx.	101
(3.) Psalm xlv.	102
2. The Prophets .	103
(1.) Isaiah and Micah	103
(2.) Jeremiah	104
(3.) Zechariah . .	105
(4.) Daniel : Son of God and Son of Man .	105
(5.) Malachi	106
IV. This Divine-human Person subordinate as Mediator	107
1. The Servant of God and the Anointed .	107
2. The Angel and the Word and the Wisdom of God	108
I. Measure of Old-Testament Revelation .	109
Future Incarnation Veiled, and dimly anticipated .	109
1. Internal Character of the Predictions	109
2. Theology of Later Jewish Church	110
3. Testimony of the New Testament .	110
The Person of Christ the Mystery of Ages	110

	PAGE
II. OUR LORD'S TESTIMONY:	
As Distinct from that of the Evangelists	. 111
Methods of His Testimony	. 112

I. While on Earth: His Names.
  1. Son of God .   113
    (1.) Preexistent.   115
    (2.) Consubstantial with the Father .   . 116
      α His Sonship distinguished from ours .   . 116
      β Assertions of His Divinity as Son   117
      γ Acceptance of Ascriptions of Divinity   . 118
      δ Occasional Testimonies of His Divinity   119
  2. Son of Man.
    Origin of Term.   . 121
    Our Lord's Reason for using it .   . 122
  3. The Son in His One and Indivisible Person   . 123
    (1.) Personality without distinction of Natures .   . 124
    (2.) Divine Personality .   . 125
    (3.) Subordination .   . 126
      Rigorous Limitation of the Term.   127
      Voluntary Subordination; not explained   . 127
      α Our Lord's General Abstinence from Highest Titles.   . 128
      β Expressions of Mediatorial Inferiority.   . 128
      γ Sent under a Commission partly Reserved .   . 131
      δ Subjection to Infirmity and Temptation and Death   131
      ε Emphasis laid on the Human Side of His Person.   132

II. Testimony from Heaven   . 133
  1. In the Acts .   . 134
  2. In the Apocalypse .   . 135
  Our Lord's Testimony on Earth with Reservations   . 137
  It contains the Germ of all Future Doctrine   137

III. APOSTOLIC TESTIMONY:

I. The Evangelists .   . 138
  1. The Synoptists: St. Matthew and St. Luke; St. Mark   139
  2. Compared with St. John .   . 141

ANALYSIS. xiii.

	PAGE
II. The Apostles	141
1. Common Element : Doctrine of Mediatorial Trinity	142
2. Their Independence	145
3. Various Types	145
α St. Peter : as Preacher and Writer	145
Harmony of these Separate Testimonies	146
β St. James	147
γ St. Jude	148
δ St. Paul : Peculiarity of his Testimony	148
Epistle to the Romans : the Two Natures United	150
Epistles to the Corinthians : the Subordination	152
Epistles of Imprisonment : their Peculiar Testimony	156
The Colossian Epistle : the Eternal Sonship	157
The Ephesian Epistle : the Mediatorial Trinity	159
St. Paul in the Acts	161
The Philippian Epistle : the Exinanition	161
The Epistle to the Hebrews : Christ God in the Temple	164
The One Undivided Mediator	166
The Pastoral Epistles	167
ε St. John : his Personal Testimony in Prologue	170
His Testimony in his Epistles	176
In the Apocalypse	179
SUMMARY	179

HISTORY OF THE DOGMA.

Testimony to the Truth through all Ages	183
I. Anti-Nicene Age	183
1. Apostolical Fathers	184
2. Ebionism, Gnosticism, Docetism	184
3. The Logos-Doctrine	186
4. Patripassianism	187
5. Unitarianism	187
6. The Union of the Two Natures : Origen	188

	PAGE
II. The Christological Controversies :	
1. Arianism . .	. 188
2. Apollinarianism	. 189
3. Schools of Thought underlying Subsequent Controversies	. 191
4. Nestorianism	192
5. Eutychianism	. 193
6. Chalcedonian Formula and Quicunque	. 194
III. Later Reproductions of Error :	
1. Monophysite Eutychianism	. 196
2. Monothelitism . . .	. 197
3. Adoptianist Nestorianism .	. 199
IV. Mediæval Speculation . . .	. 200
1. The Schoolmen . .	. 201
2. Pantheistic Christology	. 201
3. Nihilianism . . .	. 202
4. The Incarnation apart from Sin	. 202
5. Mysticism	. 204
V. The Reformation :	
1. The Lutheran Communicatio Idiomatum	. 206
2. The Two Estates in Lutheranism	. 207
3. The Reformed Christology .	. 208
4. Tendencies of the Two Systems	. 209
5. The Various Confessions . .	. 210
VI. Modern Arianism and Socinianism	. 212
1. Socinianism : its History .	. 213
2. Arianism	. 215
3. Subordinationism . . .	216
4. Humanitarianism or Unitarianism	216
5. Illuminism and Infidelity .	. 217
VII. Modern Development . .	. 218
1. Transcendental Philosophy .	. 218
2. Decline of Rationalism : Schleiermacher .	. 220

	PAGE
3. The Tendencies of Unitarianism	222
4. German Theories of Depotentiation	224
5. Conclusion	226

NOTES.

I. Nature and Person	231
II. The Son Incarnate	233
III. Reasons for the Incarnation of the Son	234
IV. The Son of God and the Son of Man	237
V. Impersonality of the Human Nature	239
VI. St. John's Incarnation-Phrases	242
VII. Apollinarianism in Modern Theology	245
VIII. "The Exinanition"	249
IX. Depotentiation	250
X. The Unchanged Manhood	254
XI. Biblical Theology	254
XII. Revelation	256
XIII. Latitudinarian Theories	257
XIV. Modern Theopaschitism	258
XV. and XIX. The Sinlessness of Jesus	261
XVI. The Exinanition Incomprehensible	264
XVII. The Sacramental Presence	264
XVIII. The Real Presence by the Spirit	274
XIX. The Controversy on the Eternal Sonship	279
XX. The Angel of Jehovah	280
XXI. The Son of God in the Gospels	286
XXII. The Son of Man in the Gospels	291
XXIII. St. Paul's Testimony to the Two Natures	293

THE PERSON OF CHRIST.

THE opening discourse of last year, on the Office of the Holy Ghost, was a fit introduction to every theological doctrine that shall be discussed in this place; but I may refer to it as specifically the prelude of my present theme. That exposition was in no part more luminous than where it was occupied with the Spirit's testimony to Jesus. Evidently the lecturer found it hard to respect the limits of his subject, and to keep his Master in the subordinate place which its treatment required. My duty is to exhibit, in its supreme importance, the Christian doctrine of the Person of our Lord as the subject of the Spirit's testimony, and especially in relation to the unity and indivisibility of His Person. Leaving behind, therefore, though not forgetting, the question which the inaugural lecture left lingering in our ears, " Have ye received the Holy Ghost since ye believed?" I have to illustrate and enforce that earlier and all-essential test of the Gospels, " Whom say ye that I am?"

The central and the chief of the Redeemer's final announcements concerning the Comforter is, " He shall glorify Me." The Spirit's other offices, of showing the things of Christ to the disciples, bringing His words to their remembrance, guiding them into further truth, all were based upon this—the revelation of Christ Himself. The Spirit was to be the guardian of the mystery of the Lord's indivisible Person in the union of His two natures: of that mystery which governs all His own utterances, as from the unity of a double consciousness He bears testimony to His one undivided Self, speaking of Himself as departing and yet abiding for ever, humanly remembering His Divine coming forth from the Father and humanly anticipating His going back to the Father, whilst uniting that past and future in one such present as can belong only to God.

While I essay to speak of that one undivided and indivisible Person whose "I" unites two natures, fills heaven and earth, and is the glory of the Christian faith, the Holy Ghost will be my sole Teacher, the whole Bible will be my text. All the Bible, I say: for no one passage, no one apostle or prophet, no single book, neither of the Testaments alone, can suffice. Of this the Lord Himself has set the example. When He opened the individual branches of His Messianic commission, He quoted the lawgiver, the prophet, and the psalmist; as in Nazareth, and the temple, and the mountain in Galilee. But when He spoke of His wonderful Self, of that ME which overarches both natures, all offices, and is a manifestation at once temporal and eternal, He appealed to all the Bible that then was. "Search the Scriptures: they are they which testify of Me." "Beginning at Moses and all the prophets, He expounded unto them" out of "all the Scriptures the things concerning Himself." This was the ME which the Spirit should glorify: not the Divine nature, for the restoration of the Divine glory was asked of the Father; not the human nature, for the glorification of that was also the Father's gift in the ascension. But it was what we may term the Divine-human Person of the Christ. The indivisible unity of that Person, of Jesus our Lord as ONE LORD, will be the governing thought of the present Essay: first as established in the constitution of the Person of the God-man; and, secondly, as stamping its impress upon the fundamental doctrines of Christian theology.

I.

The constitution of the Redeeming Mediator may be viewed, first, with reference to the eternal ground of His Divine personality; that being determined, we may regard the Person which results from the hypostatic union of two natures in that unchanged personality. It will then be our task to dwell upon the unity of the Sacred Person as the glory and mystery of the Christian faith: a glory which is beheld and acknowledged only by those who humbly submit to receive the mystery.

I. The Personality which, as distinct from the Person, of the Christ, constitutes the ground of His eternal unity, and identity as one Redeeming Agent, is Divine: it is that of the only-begotten Son of the Father, whose conscious personality in the Triune Essence is of necessity unchangeable. Before discussing these two topics, however, a few words must be devoted to the adjustment of our phraseology.

Generally speaking, the vocabulary of Divine mysteries, whether as to the internal relations or the external manifestation of the Godhead, is governed by laws of its own. There is a sense in which, as Luther was never weary of saying, Christian theology speaks with new tongues; it must do so, for it makes familiar to man new and transcendent subjects. The language of the Holy Ghost, who alone searcheth the deep things of God and His Christ, is perfectly simple and unambiguous; and, if we adhered solely to His words, our task would be relieved of much difficulty. But however diligently we attempt this, however fervently we may desire a return in the future to the simplicity of Scripture, it is at present a thing impossible. Theology, as including Christology, is a science humanly constructed out of Divine elements. It is a science which yields to none in the subtilty of its analysis, the grandeur of its synthesis, and the perfection of its inductive processes. It must speak to the men of this world in their own language. But, while bound by this necessity, it stipulates for a reverent construction of its terms, and for a certain tolerance which its high subject-matter demands. Bringing the incomprehensible mysteries of faith down to the region of logical definition, it requires that allowance be made for the essential inadequacy of the most carefully pondered formulas. Its analogies, and illustrations, and suggestions, rising from the earthly to the heavenly things, must receive a liberal and candid interpretation. With those who reject the Scripture, and count theology a bewildering aberration of the human intellect, it of course has no further contention: of them it has no hope. To those who receive the Bible as God's oracle among men, theological science vindicates its terminology by showing that it is as close a reproduction of inspired thought as can be made in uninspired language. Our boldness could indeed scarcely be charged with irreverence were we to say, remembering the Lord's promise, that much of the established and sanctified phraseology of our science is only the reflection of Holy Writ, and little less than the words of a secondary inspiration.

This principle may be applied to a wide field of topics in systematic theology. From the word Trinity, the most august creation of human speech, with its assemblage of terms defining the hypostatical relations of the Persons of the Triune nature, down through the whole compass of mediatorial theology to the ordinary phrases of Christian intercourse, there is an abundant vocabulary which finds no precise representatives in the language of Scripture, although it is perfectly faithful to that language as its developed synonymous expression. But we must limit ourselves to the vocabulary of our present subject. Christology has its own distinct range of theological coinage. Its highest achievement here is the term Θεάνθρωπος, *Deus-homo*, God-man; and with this it boldly utters the secret of the whole Bible. It long faltered and hesitated in the choice of a word that should express the holy bond between the Divinity and the Manhood: after many experiments it rested on the word Incarnation, which is the slightest possible deviation from the very word of the Holy Ghost through St. John: "He was made flesh." It then defined the two natures in Christ: Scripture still consenting, for it speaks constantly of what the Redeemer is "according to the flesh," and of what He is declared to be as the Son of God, Himself "God blessed for ever." The distinction of natures is only not declared in such language as this: an essential difference in absolute unity. So also is it with the one Person. The New Testament represents our Lord as a conscious, intelligent Agent, who preserves from eternity into time and onward to eternity His own unbroken identity. And this we not inaptly or unreasonably term His undivided personality. It is true that there is a wide difference between personality in us, individuals of a species, and personality in Him of whose Person it may be said that "there is none like unto Him." In Christ, for instance, a new nature adds a new organ of consciousness, without impairing the essential unity of the Self: of this we find in our own being scarcely any analogy. In Christ two distinct wills, the human and the Divine, blend in one Divine-human and supreme purpose: here also analogy affords us only a precarious help. In Christ a new becoming, a dawning sense of existence, grows up within an eternal unchangeable being: in this, analogy all but entirely fails us. Difficulties might be multiplied; and it cannot be said that our theological language does more than defend the doctrine from error. When it speaks of one indivisible personality in the Redeemer, it does not profess to use a word that is shielded from censure; it only avows that, in Christ all things that are twofold, all the double elements of being, are gathered up into a higher unity, and that He is one Person in the simple meaning of the term: one in supreme intelligence, consciousness of identity, and all the operations of an agent who wills and acts. [1.]

Hence, in conclusion, the term Person as applied to our Lord has a conventional meaning, which is not amenable to science, but not inconsistent with it. In the true philosophy personality is not nature: it is that in which the nature, with its various developments and forms of exhibition, inheres. The person of a man is the substratum of all that belongs to his nature, as consciously his own and distinguished from every other. The Person of Christ is Himself, the substratum of all that belongs to the twofold manner of existence.

1. When it is said that the ground of the Saviour's one personality is Divine, we must be understood to mean specifically that of the eternal Son. This is a point of far-reaching importance to the entire doctrine concerning Christ, and we cannot be led astray in pursuing it, provided our thoughts are kept rigidly within the limits of revelation.

In the essence of the Godhead there are three Persons, consubstantial, co-eternal, and co-equal, one of whom is revealed to man as God's "own Son" (Romans viii. 3), as the "only-begotten Son, which is in the bosom of the Father" (John i. 18, iii. 16), and as "the First-begotten" who was brought "into the world" (Hebrews i. 6, Colossians i. 15). These are the only three designations that are certainly given in Scripture to the Person who became incarnate. Theology, led by Origen, introduced the paraphrase of the "Eternal Son;" and with strict propriety, since all the interior relations of the Godhead are of necessity eternal. But these three stand out as the elect terms of Holy Writ: generation is common to all; and the Son is the own and only-begotten as it respects the Father, and the first-begotten as it respects us in His incarnation. Let us briefly consider these in their order; but only so far as concerns our present object, to show that the ground of the personality of the God-man is the eternal Sonship.

(1.) It is in the Person of His Son that God unites again our race to Himself. The Son is the one name that belongs to the Redeemer both in heaven and on earth, in time and in eternity. In the personal subsistences of the Trinity it is His personal distinction to receive eternally His personality from the Father: "as the Father hath life in Himself, so hath He given to the Son to have life in Himself" (John v. 26). Two other names are indeed assigned to the pre-existent Mediator. St. John terms Him "the Word," and St. Paul the "Image" of God; both with the same meaning, and both with express reference to the incarnation. He is the reflection to the universe of the invisible God in the one, and in the other the Revealer of the silent God. But it must be remembered that these terms are introduced only as sublime figures that illustrate the greater name of "Son." They are never used save in connection with that greater name, which gives them their personal character and, so to speak, hypostatises them. "The Word was made flesh," St. John tells us; but the glory which was beheld was that of the "only-begotten of the Father," that of the "only-begotten Son" (John i. 18). His first epistle is not an exception; for the opening paragraph concerning the "Word of Life" finds no pause till it reaches " His Son Jesus Christ " (1 John i. 1—3). St. Paul to the Colossians also makes the " Image of the invisible God " only a secondary attribution to Him who is "the Son of " the Father's "love" (Colossians i. 13—15); and his language is precisely echoed, whether by himself or not, in the epistle to the Hebrews (chap. i. 1, 2). Hence, as it is our Lord's Sonship which constitutes His personality in the Divine essence, so it is His Sonship which continues that personality in the flesh. And, in this sense also, "the Son abideth ever." [2.]

(2.) Viewed more expressly with reference to His incarnation, the subject leads to the question which forces itself irresistibly on our minds, and is seconded by our hearts, as to the reason why it was the Son of God who took our nature. Doubtless this question is one of many that the Scripture leaves to the silent pondering of meditation : yet not altogether to silent pondering; for some hints as to the reason, both in Him and in us, are given, which may be shaped into words.

No other Person in the Godhead was incarnate than the Son. Each of the sacred Persons has His propriety, in eternal truth to which the language of Scripture is faithful, with reference to mediatorial redemption; but this pre-eminence is His, that the assumption of our nature, with all its concomitants of sorrow and of joy, belongs only and for ever to Him. The style of Scripture is not that God became incarnate : rather, with unswerving precision, that " the Word, the only-begotten Son, was made flesh and dwelt among us." That the Second Person should or could, apart from the Father and the Holy Ghost, take our nature into union with Himself is an unfathomable mystery. But the very word " Son " points to the direction at least where the solution lies. Co-eternal and consubstantial with the

Father, the Son is yet "God of God;" and, in His eternal subordination to the Father as the Fountain of the Deity—a subordination without inferiority—lies the possibility of His mission to our race, and of His acceptance of that mission. "Let Us make man," and "Lo I come," are fragments of heavenly language which fall upon prepared ears with profound meaning. But between this derived Sonship, which the Scripture avows, and the Arian generation in time and for a special purpose of the Father's will, which the Scripture denies, there is a literally measureless difference. The Son of God is the eternal Son of an eternal Father; but He is an eternal "Son," and in that truth our redemption has its profound pre-requisite. "All Mine are Thine," are words of our Lord Himself which forbid further speculation; but they do not relinquish His original property in us.

The special relation of the eternal Son to the race of mankind may suggest another reason, or rather another aspect of the same reason. There are not wanting intimations in Holy Writ of an essential affinity between the Son, the express Image of the Person of God, and man created also in the Divine image. "All things," says St. Paul, referring however primarily to man, "were created by Him and for Him" (Colossians i. 16): words upon which meditation may inexhaustibly dwell. "For Him" were we created, even as He redeemed us "for Himself:" the image of God in us, all the greatness of our nature, being a reflection, distant yet true, of His eternal mind. He is the "First-born before every creature:" again we must understand that man is pre-eminently meant; and the apostle signifies, not simply that the Son was begotten before the creature—a declaration that is included but does not fully explain this most unusual phrase—but that the intelligent creation, and especially man, the elect creature of God, was made after the image and likeness of the Son, with the elements of a nature capable of being partaker of the Divine, to be afterwards crowned and redeemed by Him, when He should "come to His own." Hence we may dare to believe, magnifying the distinction of our birthright, that we had received His nature before He assumed ours. [3.]

To sum up what has been said, and at the same time to anticipate what follows, the abiding personality of the Son gives unity to the entire manifestation of the Divine-human Person. "The Son" absolutely is His supreme name, assumed by Himself and given to Him by His apostles (John iii. 35, Hebrews i. 1—8). Becoming the "Son of man," the name in which He most delighted, He ceased not to be the "Son of God," the name which He permitted His servants to use (Matthew xvi. 16). As He goes onward from strength to strength in His earthly development, He is declared at every new crisis to be the Son. With most solemn emphasis St. Paul tells us He was finally marked out as such in His resurrection, when His human nature had vanquished death and reached perfection (Romans i. 4). But this was only the last of a series of defining crises, of which we can allude to only three :—His introduction to the world in His incarnation (Hebrews i. 2—6, Luke i. 35); His baptism, which visibly sealed the secret of His birth (Matthew iii. 17); and His death, when the voice of the Centurion was chosen to close the long series of angelic, Divine, and human testimonies—" Truly this was the Son of God" (Matthew xxvii. 54). [4.]

2. The ground of our Lord's indivisible personality being His Divine Sonship, it must be steadfastly maintained that it knows no change. In His voluntary manifestation in this world of phenomena, where He underwent vicissitudes that have and can have no parallel, He in His essential Self

preserved that Divine immutability which is "without variableness or shadow of turning."

(1.) He did not surrender His personality, nor divide it with another, nor even add to it a second Person. In other words, the Son of God did not join to Himself an individual man, begotten and born after the manner of men, sanctified from his mother's womb, educated and trained to the highest perfection of which our nature is capable. Such a union with a second First-born of humanity, especially when regarded as created anew of the Holy Ghost, is not in itself inconceivable. We can imagine this most highly favoured among men, born of this most highly favoured among women, made by the inhabitation of the Son of God the "fairest among ten thousand and the altogether lovely;" with such grace poured upon his lips that he should speak "as never man spake;" and so replenished by that Divine fellowship as to leave the memory of a life and death that should eclipse all other excellence. But, fair as this ideal is, it is only a vision. The Scripture knows no such alliance. The First-begotten is brought into the world in quite another way. The Father sends His Son and receives Him again in the flesh,—Him, and not a son of man whom He brings with Him. The Holy Spirit prepares for Him the elements of our nature, "that holy thing," to be His body; and the Son takes the body thus prepared, and becomes partaker of our flesh and blood (Luke i. 35; Hebrews x. 5, ii. 14). In the sacred record there occurs no expression that can be pressed into the service of a double personality in Christ. He never speaks of a second Self, nor even of a higher or lower nature. The necessity of doctrine, when He left it to the more systematic teaching of His apostles, required that they should make this latter distinction; but it will be found that they invariably guard, and by a phraseology chosen for the purpose, the unity of His indivisible Person. [5.]

This only pays its tribute to the necessity of our redemption. Our salvation could not come from a brother of our race, however richly endowed with the Spirit, however high in the fellowship of God. Enough that one so greatly beloved should save himself; that indeed must needs follow: but others he could not save. At the utmost, such a union of the Son of God with a man would simply have exhibited a higher degree of what in kind was seen in Adam. That holy man would only have been the vehicle or sphere of a nobler Divine theophany, and more like one of the judges or prophets than we dare to think. He could not, in the sense which Scripture always teaches, represent our nature; and the link between that Christ Jesus— supposing him to be then Christ Jesus—and the Son of God, would have been one which, though forged in heaven, might be strained and broken upon earth. Such an alliance, in very deed, Satan suspected between God and the Holy One led up to him in the wilderness. He remembered one great breach, when the Third Person of the Trinity was separated by the Fall from a man in whom God was well pleased. He essayed his craft a second time; but, as the fathers used to say, he was cheated by his own devices; and, this time hopelessly baffled, held his error in reserve for the Nestorian heresy.

(2.) To be more particular, modern theology has sometimes expressed the sense of the scriptural statements on this subject by the affirmation that the Redeemer assumed our impersonal nature. It is not a happy expression, and we turn from it with more satisfaction to a summary of those Scriptures which it professes to explain.

No clear idea can be conceived of an impersonal intelligent nature. But the phrase may perform good service if it only guards the truth that when our Lord became incarnate He took our nature, with all its personal capacities and powers, into such a union with Himself as forbade its personality to be for a single instant distinct. Nothing in His entire human development but became part of the Self of the Divine Son. The dawning consciousness of the Infant belonged to the God-man. This Child never had the "knowledge to cry, My father, and my mother" (Isaiah viii. 4), to human parents: His first incarnate word speaks of one Father, common to His Divine and human natures (Luke ii. 49), and from that moment to the end there is but one Divine "I" spoken through human lips. There is no communion indicated between the lower nature and the higher; only between the one Christ and His Father. The perfect human will remained; yet in such necessary though free harmony with His Divine will that the Scripture never distinguishes between the two. But when the absolute personality, that which gives unity of operation to an agent, is concerned, the simple truth is forced upon us that the Redeemer's human nature does not inhere in a human person. He formed for Himself in the incarnation a new embodiment of our nature; and in such an unspeakable manner that He became man while He continued to be God. To every created eye that beheld Him He was very man; but angels and men learned to acknowledge, when taught of the Spirit, that He was God manifest in the flesh, and that there did not exist, and could not exist, a human person in Christ apart from the Personal Son. Thus understood, His manhood may be said to be impersonal.

It is a relief to turn to the sayings of the Word. I take three from St. John, he being pre-eminently the evangelist of the incarnation: three which individually and in the union of their mutual lights declare without definition all that man labours to define.

First in order, though last in time—in fact, the last saying of Scripture concerning the incarnation—is the testimony that Jesus Christ, the Son of God, came in the flesh (1 John iv. 2, 3). Not now to dwell on other purposes for which this striking expression was adopted, it is obvious that the Lord Jesus is said to have come, not into, but "in," the verity of our flesh: "the flesh" here, paradoxical as it may seem, meaning both the matter of our earthly organization and the whole nature of which it is the visible frame. The second phrase, "the Word was made flesh" (John i. 14)—the most wonderful of all the incarnation sayings—utters the same truth. It has been exaggerated into a meaning which will hereafter be condemned; but no perversion must blind us to the doctrine here plainly taught, that the Logos, the Son, so came in the flesh as to make that flesh His own, part of Himself, nay, His very Self. He assumed our nature with as much reality of possession as that by which He held His Divine Being of the Father, with such a perfect identification indeed as leaves St. Paul's assumption-terms far behind. The third phrase, He "dwelt among us" (John i. 14), a phrase which represents many other variations of the idea, expands the same truth. "Among us," or in us, or in the essential elements of our nature, He dwelt and still dwells: not sharing our human conditions for a season, as a stranger tarrying but for a night. He appeared in us, in our nature as a temple, to inhabit it with His glory, and pour the light of His grace and truth into the souls of all who enter into His fellowship as He has entered into theirs. He has made of our nature a new sanctuary, filled with the Spirit of holiness which all who are one with Him receive, and thereby become "partakers of His holiness" (Hebrews xii. 10). But that temple is still Himself.

Uniting the three phrases, it will be found that, while they carry the full meaning of what is understood by an impersonal human nature, they so qualify each other as to rescue that truth from every kind of perversion. The strongest and boldest word, "was made flesh," has on either side its meet corrective : He "came" in the flesh, and still continues therefore to be the Son of God in the flesh which He enters. On the other hand, that flesh is the shrine in which He dwells : He who dwells in the temple is greater than the temple, and the natures are therefore distinct. The central text gives its strength to the other two, while by them it is in some sense softened and explained. The doctrine taught by these three gradational sayings—"He came in flesh," "He became flesh," "He dwelt in flesh,"— is precisely the same which the other apostles declare in other almost equally emphatic terms: that is, by His taking "on Him the seed of Abraham" (Hebrews ii. 16), by His partaking of the children's "flesh and blood" (Hebrews ii. 14), and by His being "made of a woman" (Galatians iv. 4). And all is confirmed by Him who gives these other witnesses their testimony, and who best knows the secrets of His own being. He calls Himself "the Son of man," meaning far more than Ezekiel or than Daniel knew : He is the Son and Representative of the kind or race of man. [6.]

II. We are thus led to consider the Divine-human Person of our Lord, His personality being only Divine. The distinction here established, and the terms employed to establish it, are not found in Scripture ; but the tenour of Scripture cannot be understood without bearing it generally in mind. Nor has it been current in systematic theology, which has hovered about some such expedient without venturing to settle upon it as a principle of interpretation. How far it is justified will appear as we proceed to show that the two natures in Christ's Person are distinct and perfect; that neither of them undergoes any change in consequence of the union; and that the One Person may be regarded as God or as man interchangeably.

1. The Person of Christ is the result of the indivisible and abiding union of the Divine and human natures. This is perhaps the most wonderful proposition that theology has to affirm : a stumbling-block to the unbeliever, it is a sore offence to a certain philosophy, but the very rejoicing of the heart to Christian faith.

(1.) The term "truly" (the Centurion's ἀληθῶς, Mark xv. 39) was employed by the fathers of antiquity to declare their faith in the supreme Divinity of the Son. The specific protest of this word was not needed in apostolic times. But the apostles predicted the coming of those who should deny "the only Lord God" (2 Peter ii. 1, Jude 4); and the second century witnessed the beginning of heresies which assailed, not so much the Divinity of our Lord, as, so to speak, the integrity of His Divine nature. The Gnostic sects united in asserting that the better part of the Christ was an emanation from God which descended upon the man Jesus, or rather, as will be seen, upon what seemed to be such,—thus an imaginary God upon an imaginary man. Sabellius did not indeed impair His Godhead, but, if the paradox be allowed, abolished it nevertheless by denying the Son's distinct subsistence. Arius at a later time gathered up the scattered hints of many heresies into the fatal affirmation that the Son of God was Divine, but not of the Divine essence, not co-eternal, and not strictly consubstantial, with the Father ; begotten before the world, but yet in time; and being, before all human computation begins, among the things that were not. This ancient error, after which for one melancholy age the whole world went out, was rebuked by the Nicene Creed, in a formula that precisely reflects the spirit of Scripture without using its language. The Arian delusion has never since overspread the earth, nor taken a formal place among the heresies. It has indeed continued to fascinate individual thinkers, has entangled many honest speculatists, and coloured too much of the poetry of our own and other Christian nations. But the Nicene theology, especially as represented by the somewhat chastised confession used in our services, has on the whole ruled the church of Christ. "Very God of very God" has been the avowal of a faith that there is nothing essential to the nature Divine that is not in the Person of our Lord. When the Father sent His Son He gave His other, equal Self: nothing Divine that did not with Him leave, so far as He left, the bosom of the Father: ascending once more from the streams of human theology to the absolutely undefiled fountain, "God was manifest in the flesh." The Old Testament, paying its first tribute to the human nature, announces that the Seed of the woman should save the world; and the New Testament opens with the revelation that that Seed of the woman is Immanuel, God with us.

(2.) So also the term "perfectly" was anciently used to express the church's faith in the veritable manhood of the Christ. He is Man without defect, without superfluity, in the perfect integrity of human nature.

To the theory that Jesus of Nazareth is *only* man, it hardly enters into our design to make more than passing reference. It denies the very first postulate of that doctrine of the Person of Christ which is the object of our exposition. With the other heresies to which allusion has been or will be made, we may hold controversy: they have their several more or less consistent hypotheses concerning both the Person and the work of Christ. The Humanitarians, as they may be called, teach indeed something of His work; but His Person, in the sense we assign, is to them an idle term. The Ebionites of antiquity, and their modern descendants the Socinians,—descendants, but with few links of any intermediate lineage,—simply oppose the full living current of Scripture, the plainest sayings of which they either torture or trifle with or suppress. By making the Author of the Christian faith only a man of like passions with ourselves, they destroy the very foundations of the truth. Redemption has no meaning; the Bible has lost its living soul; and the gulf between God and man remains impassable. Upon this in every sense *human* theory—it deserves no better name—we can only look down with pity.

The manhood of Christ is without defect. The first assault of heresy on our Lord's Person was aimed at His human nature. The oriental heretics who troubled the old age of St. John, whom St. Paul also had more casually encountered, denied that the man in Christ was more than a mere semblance. In their horror of matter as the seat of all evil, from which therefore the spiritual Christ came to deliver us, they invented a thousand expedients to make the redeeming work effectual through a merely phantastic or delusive union of God's Messenger with our flesh. The Church condemned them as Docetics. The last writer of the Bible, in its final document, was not so tolerant. He called the holder of this error, which robbed the Redeemer of His veritable manhood, "Antichrist;" and language has, to the true discernment of the Christian ear, no more terrible anathema than that. But it was not St. John alone who spoke : it was Christ Himself who thus declared to the race of His adoption, that He "counts that man *His enemy*" who violates the reality of His human flesh and blood.

In the course of ages another error arose, not anticipated in Scripture; an error which, held loosely by Arius, was shaped into consistency by Apollinaris, and impaired the integrity of our Lord's manhood by taking from Him His intellectual nature, His rational soul. On this theory the Divine Logos literally took flesh and blood, informing the sensitive nature of Christ with the Divinity instead of a thinking mind. This perversion of St. John's words, "Jesus Christ came in flesh," was rebuked in the second Œcumenical Council held at Constantinople in 381; but the formula of condemnation appears only in the Athanasian Creed: "Perfect God, perfect man, subsisting of a rational soul and human flesh." Thus, we may believe, did the Holy Ghost, who prepared for the Lord His human nature, vindicate the integrity of that nature, and defend the holy vesture from those who would rend it. And we may be sure that the condemnation was just. If the resolution of Christ's flesh and blood into mere semblance was Antichrist, much more was the annihilation of the nobler part, the essential part, of the nature which Christ came to redeem. The Lord rebuked Simon Peter for standing between Himself and His human passion. And in that rebuke Apollinaris was condemned: "Get thee behind Me, Satan!" For it was through His human spirit, in which He sometimes is heard "rejoicing," through His human soul, which "was exceeding sorrowful, even unto death," through His human mind, on which was imprinted anew the violated law, and the verity of which is proved by innumerable tokens of positive exercise and negative limitation, that He redeemed the spirit, soul, and body of mankind.

Our Lord's manhood is also without superfluity. The

error of Apollinaris was one of excess as well as of defect. It not only robbed the Christ of the human mind in which to think, and learn, and teach, and suffer; it also gave Him the Divine Logos as an excessive and exaggerated intellect. There is a certain grotesque grandeur in the conception of this heresy, the most imposing, and perhaps the most enduring, the traces of which are found in Christological history. Modified in Eutychianism and its Monothelite sequel, it has recently appeared in the Exinanition-theories of Germany and France as well as in some well-known American speculations; and has infected the popular thought and speech where the doctrine has not been dreamt of. Its influence may be detected wherever the Lord Jesus is regarded as thinking, feeling, and acting, directly as God without the intermediation of a finite rational soul. It is an error which does not generally reveal its evil effect; but it commits an irreparable breach in theology. The splendid gift it seems to bestow in return for what it takes from Christ is a pure unreality. And its practical influence removes from Christian life the human example of the Lord. [7.]

Hence the manhood of our Lord was simply and only perfect in its integrity: not more, not less, than the realized ideal of human nature as in the mind of God, in the mind of the Son, it existed at the creation. But it must be remembered that its very perfection made this manhood a new thing; a new thing, and yet only the restoration of the old which we had from the beginning. The second Head of the human race was in mind, soul, flesh, perfect; in Him was the goodliness of man's beautiful form as unmarred by man's sin. In Him was no germ of evil that might by any possibility find development: with the grief that may be felt for sin, as also with the grief that sin entails, He became vicariously acquainted, beyond all experience of the most wretched of its victims. But in Him was no sin, nor the possibility of sin. In all that belongs of right to man He is perfect: nothing is in Him that man had not at the first. Apart from its union with the Son, our human nature had no new element of strength or capacity added: the very utmost that human mind in human flesh can do or endure was in its resources: no less, no more. St. John's word may be borrowed to sum up all: "Which thing is true in Him and in us,"—that "Holy Thing" (Luke i. 35).

2. It must now be shown that the two natures of our Lord undergo no change in consequence of the Incarnation. Any such imaginable change may be assumed to refer to the Divinity, or to the manhood, or to both, through some undefinable result of the union.

(1.) There could be no change in the Divine nature, by the very terms of the statement; though an opposite theory has been very popular both in ancient and in modern times, but especially on the continent during the present century. Speculative theology has made St. John's sentence, "The Word was made flesh," its starting-point; and has found the basis of its exposition in St. Paul's words to the Philippians (chap. ii. 8), "but made Himself of no reputation," or, literally, "emptied Himself." These words are capable of two connections with the context: one of these being chosen, they mean that He who existed in the form of God thought not, when human redemption demanded, His manifest equality with God a thing to be eagerly retained—had He so thought, a descent to the sphere of our salvation would have been impossible—but emptied Himself, assuming and being found in the form of a servant. This undoubtedly signifies that the Eternal Son voluntarily divested Himself of something when He became man. A great prize He seized, (adhering to the phraseology,) but much He gave up. What

He surrendered He Himself has told us (John xvii. 5): it was "the glory which He had with the Father before the world was." Hence He consented "for a season, if need be"—and there was infinite need—to take the fashion of man upon Him, to make that lower nature the main vehicle of His self-manifestation, and thus to become the minister of human redemption. He emptied Himself, or voluntarily gave up His repute, and kept Himself down in this lower sphere: otherwise He must have ascended "where He was before" too soon. He underwent the whole process of human development: including the assault of Satanic temptation, both as *common to man* and as *proper to Christ*. Making His Divinity during His humiliation (ὀλίγον ἄρτι) secondary and not supreme, He surrendered Himself to the disposal of the Holy Spirit,—the Spirit both of His Divine and of His human nature. In nothing that concerned redemption did He as yet act as "Master and Lord," but as "he that serveth." He received His knowledge through human faculties. During the course of His humbled estate, He spake as a man, He understood as a man, He thought as a man,—He, that is, the Divine-human Son; and, save at occasional periods when the irrepressible community with the Father burst through every restraint, and beholders "were greatly amazed" (Mark ix. 15), He made His human life of submission the law of His manifestation, limiting Himself as none but Himself could limit Him. [8.]

But this self-humiliation or self-sacrifice is very different from that of the modern theories of the exinanition of Christ. These theories — they are many — unite in one common principle, that the Eternal Son, as an energy or potency of the Divine nature, contracted Himself voluntarily within finite conditions of existence; sank, if such language without meaning may be tolerated for a moment, from the Absolute into the Relative; and passed through a mysterious zero as touching the Divine into the beginning of a human consciousness in which the Divine would again gradually resume its glory. This would appear to many advocates of the doctrine an exaggeration; but it is honest as an exposition of what their sentiments appear to all but themselves. This is the legitimate account of the common element in their various interpretations of "the Word was made flesh." It may be enough, in addition, to state without any argument the consequences of this hypothesis. It tends to confound variations in the Divine glory or manifestation with variations in His essential existence. It robs God of His power as well as of the display of His power; and puts no difference between His arm and the stretching out of His arm. It makes the human nature unduly "capable of God," and abolishes, which is a thing inconceivable, the distinction between the finite and the Infinite. It not only takes His "reputation" from the Son of God, but for a season His very existence as Divine. It disturbs the Holy Trinity by removing the Second Person, perhaps for ever, from His place and throne; and, by a miracle before which Joshua's pales, withdraws the Son from the heavens that He may reappear in man's sphere with healing in His beams. Instead of a Son of God in the flesh who is still in the bosom of the Father, it gives us a new Being whose development on earth is a kind of Platonic reminiscence of a glorious estate in the past eternity. It takes no account of the many passages in which the Redeemer reveals the secret of a Divine consciousness: soliloquising as it were as God, while His ministerial language is that of man; declaring Himself to be in heaven, while speaking upon earth; assuming the incommunicable "I AM" as His own; and making known some at least of the mysteries of the universe as Himself the "Door opened in heaven." This theory, like many other false theories concerning Christ, is full of a strange and imposing grandeur, and has thrown its spell over some of the profoundest theologians of the day. But it is essentially misleading: it sins against the first rudiments of our notion of the Divine nature; and does not by its fatal travesty of the incarnation solve the difficulties which it promises to solve. The God who sinks so low is God no longer. It is needless to speak with asperity of an error that sprang from the purest desire to save the consistency of truth. But there are not wanting signs that English theology needs to be warned against a speculation which perhaps will bear more noxious fruit in a foreign soil than in that which gave it birth. [9.]

(2.) There was no change through the incarnation in our Lord's human nature. Here indeed it might well be supposed to have been otherwise. A lower nature like ours, thus embraced and upheld and sublimed, might well be expected to rise at the touch of God. But the Scripture assures us that it was not so, and confirms our thought concerning the reason why it could not be so. The same necessity—the same ever-recurring "must"—which required Him to be made like unto His brethren, required Him also to continue like them to the end. In every possible way, and by every beautiful artifice of language, has the Holy Ghost obviated our misconception on this subject. One entire chapter (the second to the Hebrews, namely) has been written as it were of set purpose: in exceedingly emphatic terms, as the student of the original knows, it is declared that "He Himself likewise took part of the same nature with the children:" "likewise," in a sense that admits of no suspicion. And as He and His brethren, the Sanctifier and the sanctified, are originally "of one," so in continuance

He abides the same; no change passed upon Him that might cause Him ever to "be ashamed to call us brethren," even in the heavenly places where we see Him in glory (Hebrews ii. 14, 11, 9). So far does the Word of God go in this direction that it might seem sometimes to ally our Lord with much in our nature from which we ourselves, with Simon Peter's uninstructed zeal, might wish to exempt Him. With jealous precision guarding His holy manhood from the taint of our sin, it nevertheless so draws the picture of the Sufferer in His solitary way as to show that it is the same Jesus, the Man of sorrows, throughout. Here and there it leads us to see what we cannot understand, and to hear what it is a trial of faith to hear; and all to prove to us that the incarnation which puts on man's nature infinite honour has not a whit altered the elements of its character. He is still Man unchanged, even in glory: the first word of the angels after the ascension tells us so: "This same Jesus" (Acts i. 11). [10.]

(3.) Nor is there any mysterious result of the union that may be regarded as involving a change in both natures at once. To use a subtile distinction made by men of old: Christ is one Person "in" the two natures, without being a new Person formed "of" the two natures. As Nestorius was condemned at the Council of Ephesus, A.D. 431, for keeping the Saviour's Godhead and manhood so widely apart as to make Him two persons, so Eutyches was condemned at Chalcedon, A.D. 451, for confusing the two natures into one composite being, neither God nor man. It will be obvious to every one that recoil from one error would lead towards its direct opposite. Neither Nestorius nor Eutyches would have accepted the definition just given of their respective errors; they had the purest desire, the one to preserve the reality of our Lord's human nature, the other to guard the unity of His person; but they both and perhaps equally misled their followers. Eutyches, in particular, with whom we have now to do, so suffered his theological thinking to be overwhelmed by the majesty of Christ's Divinity that he lost the manhood almost entirely, and let it be absorbed into the Godhead as a drop in the ocean. Both in his own and in his followers' hands, the heresy degenerated into the assertion of a certain composite being, between Divine and human. The God in Christ was depressed by the very fact of this blending with the human, albeit the human element was infinitesimally small; whilst the man in Christ was elevated into an unnatural union with the Godhead, if such a word may be allowed. The result was a conglomerate, against which the decision of the Council defended the church by demanding that the two natures of Christ should be held as unchanged and unconfused. Of all the errors that haunt this Immanuel's land of theology the Eutychian is perhaps the most obvious and at the same time the most unreasonable. The more steadily it is regarded, the more repulsive does it appear in itself; and almost every precious doctrine of the Gospel withers at its touch. It literally takes away our Representative from the incarnate Person, especially after the ascension : it is not true on this theory that "there is one mediator, the man Christ Jesus." The man Christ Jesus is for ever gone. Much as we need, and struggle to secure, the unity of Christ's Person, it is not to be maintained in any such way as this. That unity is in a higher region, into which no human mind save His own can enter: a region where two wills, if indeed we say rightly two "wills," two consciousnesses, two processes of intelligence, two personalities also if rightly understood, are found belonging to one Subject, "who is over all, God blessed for ever."

3. Christian theology is shut up, therefore, to the confes-

sion of a belief that the Lord Christ is both God and man: not indeed God in part, and man in part, but both, and each, and either, together and interchangeably. It has always been the effort of scientific theologians to provide formulæ that should express and regulate this truth; and the result is one of the richest, and, perhaps, the most satisfactory departments of the Christian vocabulary. Here again the Scripture gives but little direct help; though it never fails to point the way to the truth, and its express statements are so clear on every side that careful attention to them all will infallibly protect our definitions from error. Certain well-known regulative hints are there which abundantly justify the decisions of the earliest Councils: giving their sure warrant to what we may term the Nicene theology concerning the Lord's Divine Sonship, to the Ephesine theology concerning His manhood, and to what may perhaps most appropriately be called the Chalcedonian theology concerning His one Person.

(1.) The four leading terms or definitive watchwords, which like a quaternion guard the sacred Person of the Lord, are simply the plain teachings of Scripture classified and condensed into single defensive terms: Christ is " truly " God, " perfectly " man, " indivisibly " one Person, " unconfusedly " two natures. Again, with more express reference to the union of the two natures in one personal agent, these last two adverbs in the Chalcedonian Council became four: the natures are said to be united (I must give the almost untranslatable Greek of words that have done more service than any other four): ἀσυγχύτως, without any commixture such as would produce a third nature unknown to God or man; ἀτρέπτως, without transmutation or the turning of one nature into the other; ἀδιαιρέτως, undividedly, so as not to permit two distinct personal subsistences;

ἀχωρίστως, inseparably, so that the union shall never be dissolved, being indeed incapable of dissolution. So far, mainly against the Eutychian tendency, though dealing with every side of the question. Turning its battery of exquisite terms against Nestorius in particular—our chief enemy in the present discussion—the Council, or rather the Divines who represented its doctrine, asserted that the mysterious union of the two natures was not by a "junction" or link, however subtily conceived, by assistance however plenary and perfect, by "inhabitation" however intimate, by "relation" however close and logically defensible, by "estimation" or repute however true in some respects that might be, by "conformity of will" however certain that also was, or indeed by anything but a union in which the one part united is created by that which unites it to itself, so that the same Person shall be God and man at once, always, and for ever: one Mediatorial Agent, to will, and to act, and to be responsible for all His own most wonderful works.

(2.) Some more advanced formulæ may be noted, which have not so satisfactorily succeeded in seizing and fixing the pervading spirit of Scripture. The Lutheran theory, which indeed descended from antiquity, but like many others received a new and more vivid stamp in Luther's bold hands, was expressed by the phrase "*Communicatio idiomatum*," implying no less than that the properties of one nature belong also to the other. "In reality," said the defenders of the Lutheran doctrine of the ubiquity of Christ's human nature; "in figure only," said Zwingli and other theological opponents of Luther. Neither of these views is faithful to the record, which is content with exhibiting to the eye and to the faith of the church One Redeemer, who unites in Himself the attributes of the Divine and human natures, silently forbidding us to ascribe anything belonging to the Divinity to the manhood, or anything belonging to the manhood to the Divinity, but encouraging us to assign both spheres of attributes to the one common central Person.

A long and glorious series of New Testament witnesses rise to confirm this truth. "Immanuel" on its first page—that most holy compound and unresolvable name—unites the two Testaments, and is the very superscription of the whole doctrine of the Person of Christ. His witness to Himself throughout the Gospels is faithful to the same law. His "I" dwells in eternity as well as in time, in time within eternity. He is "the Son of man which is in heaven," while He is instructing as a Master "the master of Israel," and making him His own disciple (John iii. 13). This was His first recorded testimony while on earth; His last to the same effect is not one sentence only, but the whole tenour of His discourse and prayer on the eve of His passion. Not indeed the last: for His revelation to St. John in Patmos carries the evidence to the highest point. There He stands before His servant with every human lineament, the glory of which He strengthens him to behold and describe; and uses language which belongs to both natures, but is bound into perfect unity by the "I" and the "Me:" I am Alpha and Omega; the Beginning and the End; the First and the Last. I was dead and am alive again; and I live for evermore (Revelation i. 8, 18). And all His apostles know His secret: only one high theory gives meaning to their words. "The Lord"—not His Divine nature, not His Human nature —purchased the church with His blood (Acts xx. 28). The princes of this world "crucified the Lord of glory" (1 Corinthians ii. 8): they crucified as to His passible flesh Him whose Person is the Lord of glory. "In Him dwelleth all the fulness of the Godhead bodily" (Colossians

ii. 9): not dwelleth in His body, but "in Him bodily." In the epistle to the Hebrews, which in relation to the doctrine of Christ's Person is the parallel of St. John's gospel, "Jesus Christ" is "the same yesterday, to-day, and for ever:" a declaration which derives much emphasis from the fact that in it the epistle revolves back to its earliest statement, "Thy throne, O God, is for ever and ever" (chaps. i. 8, xiii. 8). It may seem strange to wind up the testimonies of Christ and His apostles by the word of a heathen; but no better language can be found than that into which the reverent Roman was surprised, under the cross: "Truly THIS MAN was THE SON OF GOD" (Mark xv. 39).

(3.) The ancient creed called the Athanasian sums up all in the expression " One Christ." Whatever exception may be taken to this marvellous structure of symmetrical statements in other parts, these sentences are without fear and without reproach: " It is therefore true faith that we believe and confess that our Lord Jesus Christ is both God and man. He is God, generated from eternity from the substance of the Father; man, born in time from the substance of His mother. Perfect God, perfect man, subsisting of a rational soul and human flesh. Equal to the Father in respect to His Divinity, less than the Father in respect to His humanity. Who, although He is God and man, is not two, but one Christ. But one, not from the conversion of His Divinity into flesh, but from the assumption of His humanity into God. One not at all from confusion of substance, but from unity of Person." The conventional language of Christian theology speaks of One essence in Three Persons, as the definition of the Holy Trinity: it speaks, conversely, of One Person in two natures, as the definition of Christ. He is one as the Agent in our salvation, One as the Object of our trust, One as the Head of the Church. This is termed the Hypostatic Union : the two natures are hypostatically united in Christ's Person as the Three Persons are hypostatically united in the Triune essence. This signifies that it is not a Theophany, or manifestation of God in and through a human person; that it is not the union of a Representative of the Godhead with a representative of mankind; but that it is an unspeakable union, the substratum, issue, and result of which is one Hypostasis or Person.

III. The Divine-human Person of our Lord is the mystery and the glory of the Christian faith. And this I dwell upon, not for the sake of loyal expatiation on the Object which Christian faith adores, but as a most important element in the study of the doctrine itself.

1. The word "mystery" in the New Testament has one meaning: it is the unfolding of what had long been promised but kept hidden. But another meaning springs out of this: it is the revelation to faith of what the understanding cannot fathom, but believes on Divine authority.

In the former sense the Person of Christ is a mystery revealed. "The glory of this mystery," says St. Paul to the Colossians (chap. i. 27), is " Christ in you," or among you, " the Hope of Glory : " that is, the Christ Immanuel. Ages and generations had waited for it, with light enough to quicken desire, but not enough to make expectation definite. One Deliverer, sometimes as in the first prediction human, sometimes as in the psalms and prophets Divine, had been always coming. The incarnation was prefigured and anticipated throughout the Old Testament: it inspired its songs and prophecies, gave a wonderful humanness to its Divine appearances, and moulded almost everywhere its phraseology. The dawning mystery of the

ancient Scriptures is the Three-One God and His Christ. As
the Divine glory behind the veil sometimes seems to dispart
into a triple radiance, blending while we behold into one
again; so also the Form of the Fourth, like the Son of
God become the Son of man, is seen elsewhere than in the
fiery furnace. The deepest secret released from the Old Testament is the Person of Christ. We must not think of the
Gospel scheme, and its publication among the Gentiles,
as the "mystery which hath been hid from ages and
generations," apart from Himself who is far above His
works and more wonderful than all. The great atonement is to be offered in the sanctuary, and the Gentiles
are to be called from their outer court into the "fellowship
of the mystery;" but the mystery itself is the Revelation of
Christ. A greater than the atonement, than the temple
itself, is here. It is the Lord who "suddenly comes to His
temple."

We go higher than the ages and the generations. The
mystery of the Divine-human had been hid with Christ in
God before the world was. Speculation is lost when it
passes beyond finite relations; but we cannot close our eyes
to evident hints that the purpose of the incarnation was
bound up with the first idea of our race—if such language
may be used—in the mind of the Word. Those who assert
that the union of God with man in the Son was a
necessity apart from the fall are so far right as that
man was never contemplated save in connection with the
Divine-human Person as his Head and Crown. They
agitate a needless question when they ask if the Son would
have been given to us without the plea of our sin. To us
there can be, alas! no idea of our race dissociated from
sin, and the redemption which is coeval with sin. And
sure we are that, as man was contemplated as falling

through transgression, so in the Divine provision he was to rise again in Christ. Time, with all its redeeming wonders is only the revelation of the mystery of eternity. And that mystery is the Christ of God (Colossians ii. 2).

In the second meaning of the term, the Person of Christ, the unity of God and man—of the Divine essence in the person of the Son with the human nature as impersonally assumed—will be for ever the mystery of mysteries. The nature of God is incomprehensible, human life is a marvel understood only by its Creator; but here we have the wonder of Divinity superadded to the wonder of humanity, and both if it be possible made unspeakably more wonderful by an eternal union in one Person. The Scripture is everywhere conscious of this its most profound and unsearchable secret: and it is its highest glory that it can bear the weight with such sublime ease. So is it with our Lord Himself. He maintained no reserve as to His Divine origin, yet He showed Himself always alive to the offence which His claim would excite in human reason, unenlightened from above. "How will ye believe if I tell you of heavenly things!" was an appeal that had direct reference to this subject. When He asked again "Whose son is He?" and "How is He His son?" and "What think ye of Christ?" it was not merely to embarrass the Pharisees, but to show to any remnant of vision that lingered in them how deep were the teachings of their Scriptures concerning Himself. And so when He asked His own disciples "Whom say ye that I am?" it was, as we gather, to teach them that only a special revelation, sent for that very purpose, could enable them to give the right answer. The true light began even then to shine around Him, but He promised when He departed that it should more fully shine: "at that day ye shall know that I am in My Father!" (John xiv. 20; compare verse 10.) But

He did not thereby signify that the mystery would become plain to His friends, nor that the offence of the incarnation should cease to His foes. Simeon's prediction over the Infant—the "sign which shall be spoken against; that the thoughts of many hearts may be revealed" (Luke ii. 34, 35) —had its range far beyond the Resurrection. The Pentecostal sun of revelation, which lighted up the things of Christ and Christ Himself with more than transfiguration glory, has not taken away the mysteriousness of this mystery. But it gave the apostles strength to bear it, and courage to glory in it; it raised them to that noblest posture of the human mind, repose in the assurance of what it cannot understand. St. Paul is never more elevated than when he is in the presence of " the mystery of God, and of the Father, and of Christ " (Colossians ii. 2); or, as he perhaps wrote, " the mystery of the God Christ." Nor has he any nobler prayer than that in which he supplicates for the Colossians in an agony that they might rejoice in " the full assurance " of " the acknowledgment of the mystery " (Colossians ii. 2), in such a full plerophory of conviction as should carry before it every trace of doubt, and silence every thought of unhallowed curiosity. His final testimony is, " Great confessedly is the mystery of godliness: God was manifest in the flesh " (1 Timothy iii. 16). St. John, writing long after the other organs of revelation had finished their task, St. John, who came from the bosom of Christ as Christ came from the bosom of the Father, who, if any man, might have done something to simplify this truth, has no such thought in his mind. His saying, " The Word was made flesh," beyond any other rebukes human impatience of the incomprehensible. And this is in his didactic gospel. In the Apocalypse, with its wonderful visions of Christ's Person and work, the seer shows that Paradise itself has given him no new light. His last record is perhaps the most instructive, as a summary of truth and an end of all controversy: "The testimony of Jesus is the Spirit of prophecy." " On His head were many crowns; and He had a name written, that *no man knew but He Himself:* and He was clothed with a vesture dipped in blood: and His name is called The Word of God" (Revelation xix. 10, 12, 13). Here we have the most holy Trinity; God, the Word, and the Spirit. But let us see that we receive the full meaning of that saying in the centre: no man knoweth His name but Himself!

Are we then forbidden to ask concerning this mystery? Does the Saviour say to us, as He said to Manoah, when His hour was not yet come: " Why askest thou thus after My name, seeing it is secret?" Most certainly not. I appeal again to His words, " At that day ye shall know that I am in My Father!" The thoughts of individual believers, and the labours of the church, have never been discouraged by the Lord Himself. But the study must be pursued with reverence and restraint, and with the assurance that some residual difficulties will always remain. This has been too often forgotten. Many who speak very fluently about the subordination of reason to faith forget their own principles when speculation tempts them, or when the flippant scepticism of the day suggests its calm dilemmas. But it must be remembered; it is one of the first elements of the question: —the question of our Lord's two natures, His one Person, and an union between them which, though we give it that name, has nothing analogous nor parallel in human things.

Theology has suffered much from the desperate determination of speculatists to sound the depths of the hypostatic union. Three times has the whole strength of the Christian intellect been spent on the subject: first, in the age which followed the Nicene testimony, when the church was entirely occupied with Christology; secondly, in the days of Scholasticism, when the subtilty of the schoolmen began afresh a study which the Lutheran divines received from them and pursued with a subtilty almost equal to their own; and thirdly, in the present century when, in Germany especially, the discussion of the Person of Christ has started afresh, with new and most ambitious aims, and a tranquil perseverance which no difficulty can daunt. The results of the Christological investigations of this last period are in some respects to be rejoiced over, in some respects to be deplored. It would be ungrateful to deny the value of labours which have given birth to noble creations of Christian theology. But they teach the necessity of caution and theological self-restraint. The various theories that have been constructed to explain the self-exinanition of the Son (Philippians ii. 8), the revived discussions of the ancient questions discussed by the Kryptists and the Kenotics as to whether the Son of God only hid the Divine attributes which He possessed, or really was for a season without both their possession and their use; the hypotheses that seek to reconcile a Divine-human personality with the possibility of sin in Him and His real victory over real temptation; the schemes that have been constructed to establish a gradual incarnation, a progressive interpenetration of the human person of Christ by the Divine Son:—all these departments of Christological study are teeming with writers the tendency of whose works shows that speculation is trying to lift a veil which is not to be lifted till the great day, or which, if rent at all, must be rent "from the top downwards." Probably it will never be removed, and the Person of Christ will be pondered as an unrevealed mystery for ever. Be that as it may, it is certain that, after all we can do, difficulties will remain for the exercise of our humility and patience. There are a few texts that will always remain knots, however polished knots, in the fair stem of our doctrine concerning the Incarnate Son. For His own life, like ours, is " hid with Christ in God."

The issue of all this is, that whatever may be done to defend the doctrine from perversion on the right hand and the left, the terms of the union of Divinity and Manhood in the Redeemer cannot be scientifically stated.

2. But to those who receive the mystery it is the centre of all truth. This doctrine is at once the cross and the crown of Christian theology: the burden it has to bear, the truth in which it glories. The unity of our Saviour's Person as the God-man, in whom the Divine and the human natures meet for ever, is in itself the supreme truth of the new Christian revelation, and in its bearing on all points of Christian theology is of the most vital importance.

I will not say that alone of all the doctrines of our most holy Faith it was absolutely new to the mind of man. They err who strive to prove that neither in the Bible nor out of it was there any clear pre-intimation of this glorious wonder. No great truth belonging to the relations of God and man has ever been left altogether without a witness: there is nothing absolutely new under the sun of revelation from the time it first arose. As the Holy Trinity, redemption by atonement, the entrance of the Spirit of inspiration into the human mind, and other teachings of Christianity, had all their dimmer foreshadowings in Heathenism and their brighter pre-intimations among the Jews; so was it with the doctrine of the Incarnation. The periodic and transitory avatars in the East, the descent of the gods to men in the West, and the more authentic theophanies of the ancient revelation, all prepared the way for that awful truth. Still, when it became fact in what was therefore the fulness of time, when the mystery of ages and of eternity was an accomplished reality, it was so wonderful that it seemed as if no sign had ever brought it or could have brought it near to the human mind.

And in its relations to the compass of Christian theology this doctrine of the Indivisible Person is of the most commanding importance. It is the basis at once and the superstructure and the topstone of the whole. A needless jealousy for the atonement, as if it were a counterpart of the incarnation that we are tempted to neglect, has sometimes obscured this truth. No fruit of theological controversy is more deplorable than that there should be rivalry between Bethlehem and Calvary in the minds of Christian men. Neither is the incarnation without the atonement, nor the atonement without the incarnation, " in the Lord." In Him and with Him all things are freely given us (Romans viii. 32). All that man needs, and all that God has for the supply of man's need, the whole sum of human destiny and hope, is contained in the Person of Christ, " who for us men, and for our salvation, came down from heaven, and was incarnate by the Holy Ghost of the Virgin Mary, and was made man, and was crucified for us." "It pleased the Father that in Him should all fulness dwell " (Colossians i. 19), " and of His fulness have all we received " (John i. 16). Christian theology, like the Christian believer, is "complete in Him," in whom "are hid all the treasures of wisdom and knowledge" (Colossians ii. 10, 3).

II.

The relation of the one and indivisible Person of Christ—of His Person as one and indivisible—to the circle of Christian doctrine is no less than fundamental. Any the slightest error that touches the unity of the one Christ, both God and man, leads directly either to a subversal of the Christian Faith or to such a perversion of its leading tenets as leaves but little worth defending. It would be useful to trace the bearings of this dogma through the whole domain of theology, in all its branches, whether Biblical, or Dogmatic, or Historical. But this would require a treatise, and a bare analysis of what might be attempted is all that time will admit now. I shall endeavour to attain the same end by showing the connection of our dogma with all the main principles of evangelical doctrine. For instance, its vital importance may be traced in connection with the following five watchwords of Christian theology: first, with the truth and reality of Revelation generally; secondly, with the essential meaning of Mediation between God and man; then with the doctrine of Christ's presence in His church; then with the evangelical privilege of personal union between Christ and the believer; and, lastly, with the Christian doctrine of Christ's Church, its character, and development, and destiny. It will be found that the truth amidst conflicting errors in each of these essential subjects of Christian theology depends upon, is saved by, a true statement of its relation to the Indivisible Person of Christ, which alone gives to each its strength and their harmony to all. [11.]

I. At the basis of the Christian Faith lies the idea of a Revelation of God to man, to his mind and in His nature. In His incarnate Person our Lord is not only the medium of that revelation, He is the revelation itself; not only the "Apostle of our profession" (Hebrews iii. 1), He is also "the Way, THE TRUTH, and the Life" (John xiv. 6).

1. It has been seen that the only names given to the Son, when His incarnation is spoken of, are such as define Him to be the eternal and essential Revealer of the Being of God to the universe. The absolute God becomes relative to His creatures through Him who is the "Brightness of His glory,"

"the express Image of His Person," "the Word" of His eternal thought. By maintaining the unity of Christ's Person in the flesh we bring the communication of "that which may be known of God" (Romans i. 19) into our very nature. To "know God *and* Jesus Christ whom He hath sent" is to know God *in* Jesus Christ. In these last days He hath spoken to us in His Son (Hebrews i. 1): whereby we are to understand, not that the earlier fragments of truth were given without the Son—for it was the "Spirit of Christ" who was in the prophets—but that the glorious Source of all our knowledge has now become manifest as such. "No man hath seen God at any time; the only-begotten Son, which is in the bosom of the Father, He hath declared Him" (John i. 18). Here is the great distinction. No knowledge of God can come to us through the report of an observer from without; it must come from within, from the bosom of the Father Himself. "None by searching can find out God," we are told in the Old Testament; in the New Testament no man can even "approach" to search (1 Timothy vi. 16). Nothing is more certain than that all revelation is most absolutely shut up to Christ. And as we have the only Revealer of God, so His revelation is in the indivisible unity of His Person brought nigh to us, "in our mouth and in our heart." It is our own, and a light within ourselves. The Son does not instruct a human person with whom He is united, that He again as a prophet may instruct us. He is in our nature; and we receive through union with Him out of His fulness of grace and truth (John i. 14, 16). He makes the knowledge of God in some sense "common to man," unveiling the Father through our own faculties and "in our own language wherein we were born" as "the light that lighteth every man that cometh into the world," or that cometh into the nature that He has made His own. But out of His fulness only we receive who have first received power to become the sons of God (John i. 12, 16).

2. The applications of this truth can be only indicated: first, in its relation to human philosophy, and, secondly, in its bearing upon the written Scripture.

Philosophy assumes a twofold attitude to this question. In one of its moods it lays great emphasis, and with reason, on the impossibility that any revelation of God to man should exist save in man's own consciousness. Our doctrine responds by saying that it is even so: whatever means, media, or instrumentalities the Revealer employs, He is within our nature—generally in every man who shares it, specially in every regenerate soul—the living internal "Word of life" (1 John i. 1). In another of its moods, philosophy rejects the idea that the absolute God can be brought within the cognisance of a finite mind. Christ in the flesh denies this. He does not indeed manifest in our nature all the essence of the Godhead: only τό γνωστὸν τοῦ Θεοῦ, that which is known or knowable of God (Romans i. 19). An infinite reserve of knowledge is His, in the unity of His Person, that will never be ours; but "all things that I have heard of the Father"—in contradistinction to that eternal and absolutely personal knowledge which He claims in Matthew xi. 27,—"I have made known unto you" (John xv. 15). "Christ in us" is a guarantee that we have as our high prerogative a true, real, and sufficient knowledge of God: perfect, so far as it is possible to man; real, and corresponding to His true nature; and sufficient for every human need in time and in eternity. Let not philosophy, therefore, either by too much pride or by too much humility, deny the possibility that the finite should know the Infinite.

In its relation to the written Scripture this truth is of great importance. No man can be a genuine disciple of Christ who does not receive the Holy Oracles at His hands as a testimony to Himself given by His own Spirit to the prophets before He came, and by His own Spirit to the apostles after He departed. It is not too much to say that the whole Book —the rich word of Christ (Colossians iii. 16)—must be brought with the disciple when he comes to his Master, must continue with him through all his discipleship, and never cease to be his guide at least while he is a student on earth. Now, if it be true that our Lord makes the Volume—and it is a perilous thing to doubt this—the voice running through all ages of His own Divine-human personality, certain conclusions flow rapidly, surely, and blessedly, from that principle. We may safely grant that the true Bible is Christ in the Bible: as the life is more than meat, so the Word is more than all His words; and it is the Living Truth Himself whom we seek for in the letter. But then that letter is as it were the vesture in which He with His truth is clothed; and it must needs be worthy of Him, a "seamless garment woven from the top throughout." "Let us not rend it." Admitting that the teaching of Scripture is progressive, and limited, and committed to a form that is liable to the fluctuations of human literature, it is nevertheless the teaching of One whose words cannot betray us, will never teach us error, and shall not even the lightest of them fall to the ground. Best of all, we have Christ with us in His word: God incarnate, speaking from heaven, and yet the human Oracle of mankind. "It is the voice of a God," but "it is in the speech of man;" and if we would hold communion with His Person it is needful that we "understand His speech" (John viii. 43). We must remember that His Spirit alone can make the words His to our hearts which our minds may receive as His. We must have that same preparation which the Lord required in those to whom He spake on earth, the presence of which made Him an embodied manifestation of the Father, the absence of which deprived Him of all His dignity and power to the souls of the unbelieving, so that He who "spake as never man spake" was contradicted as never man was contradicted (Hebrews xii. 3). To him who takes the word of God as the record of Jesus, and reads, or rather "searches,"—for there is great force in that solitary command given by Christ concerning the Bible (John v. 39),—with a mind submissive to the Spirit, it is verily and indeed a present Living Teacher: the Truth speaking as an intelligent Person to his person, the Eternal Mind to his mind, the Divine Heart to his heart. [12.]

II. No idea is more fundamental in Christian Theology than that of Mediation; and none so obviously depends for a right conception upon its relation to the one and indivisible Person of Christ. With reference to our present purpose the term may be viewed under three aspects. In the union of His Divine and human natures, our Lord is in the highest sense of the word, and in virtue of His twofold nature, a Mediator; but this only on the ground of a mediatorial reconciliation of two parties through His sacrifice as a Third between the Two; and, combining these, His incarnate Person is the Mediator of the Christian covenant in all His acts. Hence our doctrine may be referred to the Incarnation, the Atonement, and the Redeeming Ministry of Christ, in their order.

1. In Jesus, God incarnate, mediation has its highest and fullest meaning. Human nature is actually brought into fellowship with the Divine in the Person of a Being "who hath made both one." Too much stress cannot be laid upon this, provided only we remember that the eternal pledge of reconciliation was given to man only on the presupposal of an atonement which in human nature Christ should offer for our race.

The birth of Jesus was a sign from heaven that mankind was restored to God. Immanuel was the incarnate "Peace on earth:" not only as the prophecy of a future harmony which the angels sang, but as an accomplished and blessed reality. Nor was it only the announcement of a fact that then began: though the incarnation took place "in the end of the world," it must be antedated and carried back in its virtue to the world's beginning. This is an "extension of the incarnation,"—an extension backwards, as well as forwards,—that should never be forgotten. Redemption must follow creation in the order of thought: otherwise the "Second Adam" was really the First. He appeared in the fulness of time to proclaim a secret of eternity, that God had "chosen us in Him before the foundation of the world," had predestinated us to the adoption to Himself (Ephesians i. 4, 5). It is only the one Person of Christ that can sustain the weight of this mystery. The Divine Son joined to an individual member of the fallen race could not have ensured and sealed this catholic reconciliation between the race and God. It is indifferent at what hour in human history the Son of man may be supposed to come, if He bears the verity of our nature with Him; for then "God was and is"—to give St. Paul's word its deep significance—"in Christ reconciling the world unto Himself" (2 Corinthians v. 19). The assumption of our nature goes backward to the beginning, and forward to the end. But, before we proceed, our doctrine must take a watchful and suspicious glance in two directions.

There are some who find deep satisfaction in the thought that the design of the descent of the Son of God into human nature was to crown it with its predestined perfection; and that the ministry of sorrow was only superadded or grafted on that design. There is much that is attractive in this theory, whether as coldly reasoned out by the schoolmen or as embellished by modern mystical theosophy. But, like some other beautiful theories, it is not without danger. The Christ in this hypothesis must needs come—not, however, Christ then—to make permanent our union with God: the manner of His coming was accidental. "The sufferings of Christ and the glory that should follow" (1 Peter i. 11) is a phrase without meaning, or the meaning of which must be inverted. The entire economy of redemption is reconstructed, and can hardly be recognised; something unspeakably precious is gone from the condescension of Christ, and the Father's love has lost its supreme commendation (Romans v. 8). Moreover, we remember that the Lord took not the nature of angels, whether lapsed or steadfast; and must believe that it was in the prevision of our departure from God that the Son of man came, voluntarily and not of necessity, "seeking" that He might "save the lost."

This error, however, does not come near to us: it is, as it were, a false light playing on the distant horizon. There is another which is much more vital, though only a variation of the same: namely, that which in spirit and tendency, if not in words, makes Christ's union with an impersonal nature the essential redemption of the race. In tracing the effects of this error we have to unite two classes of theological teachers who are united in very little else. On the one side are the latitudinarian interpreters of Christ's work, who behold in the indivisible Person "the root of our humanity," one whose abiding contact with our nature as such sends virtue into all its members, virtue which if trusted in will renew and sanctify the soul and make men as gods. The sure result of such a view of Christ's Person is to soften and lower if not to destroy the atonement: to open a way of life in which the Cross is not an object of the soul's self-despairing trust, but a symbol of high devotion; a stimulant to holiness, but not a refuge from sin and wrath. On the other side are the teachers whose exaggerated views of sacramental efficacy tend to make the atonement recede before the incarnation as the point of union where the Person of the Redeemer meets the sinner's soul. It is not that the doctrine of the Expiatory Passion is forgotten, or even neglected: their theology is stamped everywhere, written within and without, with the sign of the Cross. But the sure tendency of their system—the most prevalent in Christendom—is to connect the idea of the mediation which has its highest seal in the union between God and our nature too strictly and exclusively with the Person of Christ as "extending His incarnation" in the souls to whom He sacramentally imparts Himself. To this we shall have to return hereafter. [13.]

2. Mediation is the intervention of a reconciler. In the body of His flesh our Lord—who is God and man, and in His one Person neither God nor man alone—carried with Him the instrument as well as the pledge of our redemption. "In Him dwelt all the fulness of the Godhead," and all the fulness of the manhood also, "bodily." But this is the mystery of His mediating Person, that each nature gives its own virtue to His propitiatory work while that virtue is the result of His intervention as a Third Person. It is Divine in its worth, human in its appropriateness, Divine-human as reconciling God and man.

(1.) The Divinity of Christ's Divine-human Person gives the offering which He presented on the cross unlimited value and acceptance: the blood which purchased the church was His own blood (Acts xx. 28), and the life which in the effusion of that blood was offered up in sacrifice for human sin was the life of that only-begotten Son whom "the Father spared not." It was an "offering and sacrifice to God for a sweet-smelling savour" (Ephesians v. 2)—unspeakably acceptable and propitiatory—because it was presented by Him of whom the Father had said, when He was on His way to the cross, "This is My beloved Son, in whom I am well pleased." Twice we hear this assurance solemnly pronounced over the Son whom He beholds in our nature: first, when He began His way of suffering; and, the second time, when He was transfigured and strengthened for His passion. The third time, when the Father received His spirit, we hear not the words; but it is as if we heard them: we know that the pouring out of His soul unto death was an act of supreme self-sacrifice for the sins of mankind that was precious to the Father in the proportion of the love He bore His eternal Son: that is, in other words, it had a Divine value and infinite merit. This fundamental principle of evangelical doctrine, that the Divinity of the Redeemer gives its value to His ransom-price, can never be argued away from theology. We need not make the most distant approach to the ancient heresy that ascribed suffering to God; but we may boldly say that such is the absolute unity of the two natures in Christ that the suffering of His human soul could not be more truly Divine suffering were the tremendous error found to be truth. It is the blood and passion of God: the atonement stands or falls with this. [14.]

But the Person of Christ is human. He is altogether man. St. Paul's last testimony is, "There is one God, and one Mediator between God and men, the man Christ Jesus," or Jesus Christ Man (1 Timothy ii. 5): not indeed, as a corrupt theology asserts, that in His human nature alone He was a mediator; but, His "ransom" being to follow immediately, the ransom-price is regarded as paid in that fine gold of the sanctuary, His *human life*. Timothy, to whom this testimony was given, had probably heard the counterpart version of the same great truth which St. Paul left with the elders of Ephesus: " Feed the church of God, which He hath purchased with His own blood " (Acts xx. 28). The perfect humanness of His sacrifice makes it ours: all died in Him (2 Corinthians v. 19). Though it is trifling with mere words to say, as is sometimes said, that the multitudes of mankind were summed up in Him, yet it is perfectly true that His Divinity gave His human nature a value available for the whole race. As the God-MAN He paid its penalty for the whole kind of man; as the GOD-man He offered a sacrifice which was accepted before it was offered, which could not but be accepted, which indeed was provided by the wisdom and love of the Triune God, and offered by the Son Incarnate as the servant of the Divine counsel of redemption.

(2.) But we must now more specifically view the relation of the One Person to this great offering, and some important consequences that depend upon its unity.

This makes the offering of Christ, in the highest sense of the term, a *living sacrifice*. It is true, and as essential as true, that the Sacred Sufferer stooped under the weight of the sins of mankind; that He felt Himself for one eternal moment forsaken of God; and gave up His spirit, or, as men say, died, as an expiation of human guilt, a propitiation of Divine wrath against sin, and satisfaction to the claims of inviolable justice. But the law of unity in His Person demands that even in dying He should live. The power of the Godhead still sustained the existence of Him who in the weakness of the manhood was crucified; and our dying Sacrifice was at the very same time our living Redeemer. The original union of such vast antitheses in

His Person brings with it a multitude of other reconciliations of opposites, and this among the rest. The Victim who expiates sin by suffering its penalty is at the same moment the Representative of a delivered mankind and the Deliverer whose ransom-price is the power of a new life. Thus He secures at one and the same moment all the ends of Divine justice, in the salvation of man and the vindication of holy law.

This doctrine effectually silences the objections often and in many forms urged against the vicarious atonement which lies at the foundation of the Christian Faith. The saying of Scripture concerning the blood of bulls and of goats being unable to redeem (Hebrews x. 4), has been turned against the blood of our Saviour's human nature, as if it also "could not take away sin." And the objector would be justified in his challenge were it not for the precious truth which our doctrine sustains, that it is the Saviour's living Self which avails for us whether on the cross or before the throne. The sacrifice offered for us was not simply the blood that was shed; that only carried with it a sacred life. Nor was it simply the life that was poured out; that was to be valued only by the Person who offered it. But it was the living Person of the Christ Himself, who "is the Propitiation for our sins," as St. John's last testimony tells us in the most express and affecting manner. But this will be made more evident if we consider the Indivisible Person in relation to three ideas underlying the atonement,—its vicarious nature, its representative bearing, and its personal realization through union with Christ.

The very soul of the doctrine of atonement is its SUBSTITUTIONARY nature; that taken away, the whole circle of New Testament phraseology—not only in the English translation but in the original—would require to be fundamentally changed: the language of Scripture is adapted to a vicarious intervention, and to no other. But such a doctrine can rest only upon the undivided Person who may be at once a substitute for the race and take the place of the individual sinner. However little we understand the impersonality of the nature assumed by the God-man, we are bound to believe this, that He bore the curse that rested upon the sin of the race. In words that we cannot use too often, provided we use them reverently, He was made "sin for us" (2 Corinthians v. 21). His person was vast enough to be a counterpoise to all mankind, and to offer an atonement that has been accepted for the world—the world of all actual and of all possible sinners. "Behold," said the Baptist, "the Lamb of God, which beareth the sin of the world:" the antitype of the Jewish vicarious lamb, but taking the place of both Jews and Gentiles; a substitute for mankind, but One whose living Person beareth away the sins that are atoned for, and sets free the guilty race. It is not supposed that any human words can lighten much the weight of mystery that is here. But it may be said with confidence that the doctrine is possible only on the assumption that the nature of man is in Christ the Atoning Reconciler. A personal man in union with Christ might save himself, but not another: man's nature in Him may be the substitute of the whole sinning nature of man. And it is the glorious doctrine of Scripture that it has been accepted as such. It has availed in its substitutionary passion for all the world, and for every sinner that rejects it not. St. Paul has left two words which express all this: each is used only once, and wonderful is their force when combined: He " gave Himself a ransom in the stead of all," and He "gave Himself for me." *Himself* is the strength of both (1 Timothy ii. 6, Galatians ii. 20).

But the individual bearing of this suggests at once the REPRESENTATIVE character of the atoning Person: not indeed as displacing the vicarious, but as qualifying it and filling out its meaning, or as being another form of stating it. The very idea of a Divine-human Person is essentially connected with a Representative of the race whom each may claim as a Representative of himself. He did not, apart from us and before we existed, assume our place, and bear our doom, and secure our salvation. To a certain extent all this He did; but the Scripture places another view more steadfastly before us: namely, that He now represents in heaven the race of man, on that account highly favoured notwithstanding the cry of its sins; and that He specially represents the soul and the cause of each. He is the true guardian angel of every one of us in the presence of the Father; and this He is in virtue of the personality which our doctrine gives to Him who bears our nature in heaven. He is not the Substitute of God, but His Representative; and not otherwise our Substitute than as our Representative also.

Still further is the vicarious atonement qualified, and at the same time perfected as a doctrine, by the scriptural teachings which make the Person of Christ and that of the Christian one in a MYSTICAL UNION. Relying upon the acceptance of an offering presented by the Redeemer in his stead, and trusting to a living Representative in heaven, the believer goes still further, and in the very essence of his faith makes Christ his own. United by that faith with the Person of his Lord, the Saviour's sacrifice becomes his. "I am crucified with Christ," sets forth the finished secret of the atonement, without which no theory of it is complete. By remembering that the Person of Christ is not an abstract nature, with which in the nebulous language of much modern theology the Christian is supposed to become impregnated, but a living Person, perfect communion with whom is established by His Spirit, we avoid the perversion of this great truth and receive all its benefit. "We are partakers with Christ," both in His death and in His life, because He is pleased to identify us with Himself, and the Father beholds us accordingly GRACED, as the apostle says, that is, pardoned and accepted in the Beloved (Ephesians i. 6).

Once more, the unity of our Saviour's Person suggests a reflection which may appropriately be considered before we proceed to the Mediatorial Ministry: our redemption was not an experiment that might have failed. On any other theory than that of the one Indivisible Christ, there could be no absolute assurance of this. The Nestorian Redeemer —who reappears in Irvingite and other theories—might in the final possibilities of His probation have yielded to temptation, and failed as the first Adam failed. The Son of God might have been constrained to leave the temple of our humanity desolate as He left the temple of Judaism; or, to adopt the favourite figures of these teachers, might have folded and laid aside the vesture rent under the pressure of unlimited test. Most intimate fellowship between God and a man is known to have been sometimes interrupted and broken; and so might it have been, say these too timid or too daring theorists, in the case of Jesus. Hence they place the Redeemer under a contingent probation; and make our salvation the result of a successful warfare in which either party might have succumbed. All this is required by the current theories of a union between Christ and a representative man. Bound by their error, these men know not what they say, and may be forgiven. But it is the glory of the Saviour's Person that thus it could not be with Him. He came under the Divine necessity of suffering, of redeeming the race, and thus entering His glory (1 Peter i. 2). We feel all this as we read the record of His woes. We cannot suppose ourselves in fear lest He should fail to come back again from the wilderness of temptation; we cannot suppose ourselves trembling lest the three hours' darkness should leave us after all unsaved. We know that He is working out for us a predestined salvation; and that, by virtue of the hypostatic union of the Divine and human in His Person, the conflict for us that redemption demanded could have no other end than victory. As the miraculous conception secured the sinlessness of our nature in Him, so the Hypostatic union ensured the impossibility of His sinning or yielding under temptation. The Lord our God and Saviour is one Lord. [15.]

3. This leads to the third and broader aspect of Mediation which represents Christ's Person as achieving on earth and in heaven the union between God and man. We rise, if such a word may be used, from the incarnation as a pledge of peace, and the atonement as the redemption of that pledge, to the mediatorial ministry of our Lord Himself in which both are united.

(1.) As to His work generally, the process of our Lord's redeeming life can be understood, or be harmonized into perfect consistency, only so long as we steadily keep in view the unity of His Person. He was Man; but how could mortal man, of ever so high a strain, and ever so mightily strengthened from above, accomplish the mission on which our Redeemer entered, and "finish the work given Him to do?" He was more than mortal man: He was God. But how could God give Divine perfection to a work wrought only through a creature? Every act of Deity is performed only by Deity; as all His works are known to God alone from the beginning, so they all are accomplished only by Himself. Our redemption is in its entireness a Divine act, wrought by a man who is God. This leads us once more, and directly in relation to the Saviour's life, to the mystery of His descent into our flesh. "He made Himself of no reputation:" *made Himself*, be it ever remembered; His humiliation into our nature was a Divine act, the link between the Divine omnipotence that created and upholds all things, and the same Divine omnipotence that redeemed the world and purged our sins (Colossians i. 16, 17; Hebrews i. 2). Hence the taking our flesh cannot in strict propriety be termed a humiliation. But, having assumed it, or rather in the act of its assumption, the Divine-human humiliation began. Then was the mystery of the exinanition slowly, awfully, triumphantly unrolled before the eyes of all. But how the incarnate Lord of glory ceased from the display of His glory, from the use or acknowledgment of His inseparable attributes, will be for ever an unfathomable secret. [16.]

But the manner of its exhibition is as plain as the mystery of it is incomprehensible. From the conception of His human nature to the moment of His resurrection, the Incarnate Person is "led of the Spirit," who, proceeding from the Father and the Son, is the ever-blessed Agent common to the Two. Occasionally, and in most memorable words, our Lord still vindicates the interior secret of His Divine independence: "My Father worketh hitherto, and I work," and "I and My Father are one" (John v. 17, x. 30). But generally His language is of another strain. "I came down from heaven, not to do Mine own will, but the will of Him that sent Me" (John vi. 38). Hence His Divine will and His human blend into one Messianic Will that executes the commandment received of the Father (John x. 18, xiv. 31). He surrenders Himself wholly to the Spirit, His Comforter and ours. His incarnation being, as already said, His own act, for "He came in flesh," as well as that of the Holy Ghost, who prepared for Him His body, from that moment onwards the Spirit is the Disposer and Director of His life. By Him He was trained, anointed, led to His temptation, empowered to work miracles, taught of the Father, and appointed His apostles (Luke iv. 18; Matthew iii. 16, iv. 1; Acts i. 4). This was the glorious humiliation of the Mediatorial Person, "in whom dwelt all the fulness of the Godhead bodily," that all He did and suffered upon earth was by the Holy Ghost (Acts i. 8). When all things written of Him had their end He laid aside the garments of His servitude, and, as "Master and Lord," shed forth the Spirit who had been just shed forth on Him, as the "gift" which He had received in His human nature "for men" (Ephesians iv. 8).

(2.) But the twofold Estate of the Christ, His humiliation and His glory, must be viewed in relation to the unity of His Person, and the Righteousness which He accomplished and imparts.

In His humbled condition—and, in this sense, "in the days of His flesh," though in another sense the days of His flesh continue for ever—our Substitute and Representative rendered an obedience, in life and unto death, in which His active and passive righteousness are one. It is of great importance that we should maintain the unity of the one obedience: we must not rend the garments of His righteousness, and give one half to cover our guilt and the other to cover our unholiness. And it is of equal importance that we make it the righteousness of His one undivided Person: it was His, and not ours in any sense; for us indeed, and availing in the economy of mercy for our pardon and sanctification, but still His own obedience, and not another's: offered for the race, but not by the race; for me, the sinner, but not by me in Him. "Though He were a Son, yet learned He obedience by the things which He suffered" (Hebrews v. 8). This states the fact as such, and declares it to be a wonderful fact. It could not be strange that the Incarnate Son should exhibit a full and finished holiness,—*that* He "learned" only as a necessary development of His new human life; but that He should, as the Divine-human Son, learn the obedience of submission through suffering, that He should have learned that obedience which was prescribed in no moral law, written, or unwritten,— was a mystery, solved only by the unity of His Person. In Divine strength, made perfect in human weakness, He exhibited the perfection of holiness, and learned the perfection of sorrow. For man, and in man's nature, He magnified the law, and made it honourable, down to the obedience that died in human integrity. For God, and His righteousness, He endured the holy wrath of love against sin, which entered with infinite subtilty into His spirit from the moment He left the Jordan, and never ceased to pervade, and depress, and rend His soul—save for a few unspeakable moments—down to the time when the great controversy ceased, and perfect expiation cried, "It is finished!" We cannot here too jealously guard the Indivisible Person. Always He is rendering a perfect satisfaction in His holiness, whilst He is rendering perfect satisfaction in atonement. In virtue of His Divine-human Person, He sinks under wrath whilst He is victorious over it. There is no meaning in one half of the New Testament if we do not bear in mind that the Son of God is inseparably the Son of man. Especially is the last scene on any other assumption incomprehensible. We see a total ruin, which yet we know to be a perfect restoration. There seems to be nothing but the cry of utter abandonment; and our representatives can only say, "We trusted that it had been He which should have redeemed Israel!" But on the other side, where the sun is not darkened, we hear the cry of victory that fills the universe. There death receives the living Lord, as John the Baptist once received Him, "Comest Thou to me?" surrendered the keys of Hades, and joined the procession of His triumph. "Truly this man"—once more to quote the Centurion—"was the Son of God."

In His exalted estate the One Person is transferred to heaven, "where He was before." The human nature is assumed into the glory which the Son "had with the Father before the world was" (John xvii. 5), and is itself so glorified as to be capable of sustaining that weight of glory. Thus changed, the Divine-human Person must needs be received by the heavens; earth could no longer have supported His presence. And all His offices above require the doctrine of His unity as God and man. There He presents His sacred Self as being by His very presence our sufficient Friend, and Advocate, and Forerunner. But still He is Man and God, and this is the real "wonder in heaven." Both the voice and the hands of man are assigned to Him with peculiar emphasis. His presence alone is an irresistible plea for every man that lives; but His "intercession" at the right hand of God is added, not as one of the terms that theology has been obliged to invent, but as one of the leading expressions of Scripture itself. And so it is with regard to His government, the peculiar administration of which, as foreshadowed by Daniel in the night visions and described by St. John in the full light of day, is human. That high supremacy to which St. Paul tells us (Philippians ii.) the Lord is now exalted could belong only to the One Person, who is the Son of man, and absolute over the human race, and also the Son of God, whose unbounded authority makes it appropriate that not man only, but all creatures in every part of the universe, should bow before His name.

(3.) The end of our Saviour's mediatorial ministry receives important light from the doctrine of the one Divine-human Person. His last function in the administration of our human affairs, the last act to be recorded in the chronicles of our King, will be the universal judgment. The Father "hath committed all judgment to the Son," "because He is the Son of man" (John v.): judgment over all angels or men, as GOD-man; especially the destiny of all human beings as God-MAN. No severance of the God from the man can be for a moment permitted here. Judgment, universal judgment, penetrating the secrets of all hearts, and following its inquisition by eternal awards, like vengeance, "belongeth unto God:" with reverence be it spoken, no mere man could be appointed to that office (Acts xvii. 31). Yet what heart of man does not instinctively rejoice, apart from every theological consideration, that all judgment is committed to the "Son of Man?"

When the judgment is past, and all enemies are subjected, the Son also shall subject Himself, and God shall be all in all. But it is obvious that He who is one Person, and in whose being there is not a distinct human personality, can never renounce His human nature: not in that sense will "God be all in all." There is no manhood in Christ that can be renounced, even supposing Him—a thing impossible—to be weary of our fellowship, or the Father to demand His Son's relinquishment of us—a thing incredible. His manhood is part of His being: "He cannot deny Himself." The figures that are sometimes used—as if He inhabited a human temple, or was clothed with our nature as with a garment, or was joined to a son of Mary—are all misleading, and should be very cautiously used. Having wrought so marvellous a deliverance in the human panoply we gave Him, He would not ungird Himself at the end, even if He could. But He cannot: we were with Him in His temptations, and He will not forsake us when we rejoice in His kingdom.

The mediatorial authority which will end is that universal and, as it were, sovereign and independent sway which the Incarnate Son exercises in heaven as such. That it is said He will renounce: He will be subject, or subject Himself; preserving His Divine authority still in the act of that subjection, but ceasing to act in His one Person as Lord, because the function of that specific lordship shall expire. The Son will a second time "empty Himself," not of His human nature, but of that special authority which He acquired in our nature, and which was the reward of His Divine-human obedience.

Lastly, the doctrine of our Saviour's everlasting union with our race, as a union which is more like identity than union, explains how "God will be all in all" at the same time that "the Son Himself will be subject" (1 Corinthians xv.). The assumption of our nature was itself a subordination of the Son to the Father; and it may be boldly declared to be impossible that that subordination should cease. But how then is it said that at that time, and not till "then," the Son will be subjected? Because, till then, the high reward that made the name of Jesus the symbol and bond of authority throughout the universe will not have been surrendered; and till then the idea of subjection as belonging to the incarnate estate is lost in the glory of an unlimited dominion. But the hour will come when the dignity of that intervening reward shall cease. That throne "in the midst of which was the Lamb" will be abdicated; and that one among

His "many crowns," perhaps all the many crowns there signified, will be laid aside. The dignity of the Eternal Son in the Holy Trinity will remain: as in the record of His life upon earth, so in that second and unwritten record, there is the silent and implied reservation of His essential Deity. And therefore "God shall be all in all:" the Triune God. The Godhead unchanged and incapable of change will be the sole authority, without the intervention of mediatorial dominion. But the Son—the Son incarnate—will be by the necessity of His early, unrevoked, and irrevocable gift of Himself to us in His One Person, subject for ever. The indivisible unity demands this solution of what is otherwise an insurmountable difficulty. Urged by the keen edge of that difficulty, some adventurous theologians in early times—made heretics unawares by their exaggerated and self-destructive reverence—insisted that the Son in the Holy Trinity would in some sense be absorbed; and God, the Triune God indeed, but without a Father and a Son, be all in all. There is no need of any such artifice of exposition. The economical Trinity is the absolute Trinity. But the Son incarnate is ours: "the same yesterday"—yes, yesterday, for His personal identity is the same—"to-day, and for ever." St. Paul did not say, he could not mean to say—for he knew too well the value of the gift to our nature in Christ, and the truth of the everlasting condescension—that the subordination of the Incarnate Person ceased when He was "highly exalted." That special exaltation we may with strict propriety regard as in itself ending with the day of Christ; and it will then be seen that our Saviour, God-man, being ours to eternity, will not deny Himself, but accept in His one Personality the full consequences of His stupendous act of condescension, and be subject with us for ever.

III. Another very important branch of dogmatic theology

is deeply affected by the doctrine of Christ's indivisible Person: that which treats of His presence, sacramental and otherwise, within the church.

1. According to the doctrine already established, our Lord is at once in heaven and on earth; as touching His Godhead, He is on earth; as touching His manhood, He is not out of heaven; but as touching His One adorable Person, He is either, or both, interchangeably according to the measure and kind of His operation. "Lo, I am with you alway" was spoken to those who were to "see Him no more:" the Lord, who never distinguishes between His Deity and His manhood, does not instruct His disciples to believe that in a higher nature He would be present. At this time of final explanations He would not have left this unspoken had He not purposed to lay emphasis on His One Personality: "I am with you alway!" Yet, "the heavens have received Him until the times of restitution;" and this states another and counterpart aspect, though not an opposite one, of the same truth: here it is not said that the heavens have received His glorified human nature, but, most expressly, that they have received HIM. Between these two decisive utterances the word of the angels, interpreting the ascension and promising the return, mediates: "this same Jesus." Many other instances might be given of the same duplicate style, which has only one solution, the undivided and indivisible personality of the Lord. On the one hand, the veil is rent, and His pervading presence makes of the upper and the lower courts one temple. Our Deliverer, stronger than Samson, not only entered the everlasting doors, He hath lifted them up and carried them away for ever; and now the "house of God remains," but no longer "the gate of heaven." On the other hand, the ascension wove for His manhood another veil behind which our

Forerunner stands, a veil impenetrable as the thick curtains of the sanctuary to sight, but to faith so subtile as to keep no secret hid. Meanwhile, there is, above and below, but one Christ, who rebukes every attempt to separate His Deity from His manhood, for the sake of whatever theory made; who confounds the devices of those who say, " Lo, here is Christ Divine," " Lo, there is the human Christ," by the one steadfast question which I dare put into His lips, " Do not I fill heaven and earth? saith the Lord."

2. This then is the One and only Real Presence. And the question immediately arises, How is that presence glorified, shown, manifested, imparted to the faithful within the church? The very terms here employed suggest at once the answer: By the Holy Ghost, who, though He shares not His other saving titles with the Lord, has this in common, to be another Paraclete. " He shall glorify ME;" "He shall take of MINE," of all the fulness that is in Me, of all the virtue that goeth from Me, of all the merit of My passion, of all the power of My word, of all the inexhaustible grace of My one Person, "and show it unto you." As " he that hath seen Me hath seen the Father," so we hear the unspoken sequel, which however is only a paraphrase of many words that were spoken, "he that receiveth My Spirit receiveth Me also." There is indeed a certain restraint in our Lord's teaching concerning the supremacy of the Holy Ghost as the one Mediator between Him and us: a restraint which before the Pentecost was inevitable, for " His hour was not yet come." But " when He the Spirit of truth is come He shall guide you into all the truth : " as into all truth generally, so also into the full truth concerning Himself in His relations to the Father and the Son in human redemption. Hence we find, and the more carefully we seek the more certainly we find, that in

the epistles the Holy Ghost is ever raising Himself up to the level of the Father and the Son, entering as a Third into that fellowship of the Two, which, for instance, the High-priestly prayer exhibits. It would not be difficult to quote for the Spirit a parallel of every the profoundest word spoken concerning that fellowship, and concerning the fellowship of saints in God and His Christ. But it is enough, with reference to the present object, to refer to such passages as declare that "he that is joined to Christ is one Spirit," that "if any man have not the Spirit of Christ he is none of His:" sayings which represent a large class, all running up into one, "the Lord is that Spirit" (2 Corinthians iii. 17). Whether as speaking to the soul of the believer, or as working within it,—and all His offices may be summed under these two heads—the Holy Ghost is the Representative of the whole and undivided Christ.

All the theories and systems that make union with Christ in the church depend upon an impartation of His glorified Body to the soul, distinct and apart from the indwelling of the Divine Spirit, offend against the dignity and office of "that other Comforter." "If I be a Paraclete," He asks, "where is Mine honour?" Our Lord's own return is in truth sufficient for every need; and Christ gives Himself to us by giving us His Spirit. Nor can it be said that the Holy Ghost exercises His office in forming Christ within the soul, as if He repeated the mystery of the incarnation in every spirit brought to regeneration. There is a sense in which Christ becomes the life as well as the Head of every man; but the indwelling Spirit is the bond of that union, as being Himself within us, "the great power of God," and not as merely ministering to us from without another's life. Seeking to "bring Christ down from above," and to connect

His bodily presence with the sacred elements, these systems cannot avoid disparaging that Sacred Person who, in the unity of the Father and Son, is "the Lord and giver of life." Glorifying Christ, the Holy Ghost is Himself also to be glorified. It cannot be questioned that a fruitful source of much of the corruption of the Christian church, whether in doctrine or practice, has been the dishonour done to the Supreme Administrator of that which is a "dispensation of the Spirit." The charge lies against a number of systems and confessions: including, on the one hand, the carnal Christianity that connects the impartation of Christ with priestly acts; and, on the other, the schemes that introduce a new economy of the Personal Reign to accomplish what the Spirit and all His agencies failed to accomplish. But we have to do only with those which affect the doctrine of the unity of Christ's Person. And these are, of course, the Sacramental theories.

3. The doctrine of Transubstantiation is based upon a theory of the conversion of the Person of the God-man into the sacred symbols of His body and blood, a theory which could not have originated without the aid of Eutychianism. The mystery of the union of the two natures is carried into another region where the Scripture is no longer a guide: the Incarnation, a sealed and determinate and final fact, is "extended" in a manner with which the Holy Ghost has no part. The Romanist doctrine has one element of consistency that is sometimes forgotten when it is compared with variations from it in other communions. Eutychian in its confusion, it does not yield to a Nestorian division of the Divine-human Person: it is the Divinity and the humanity of the whole Christ that is involved in the transubstantiation. For, though the material elements are changed only into the human elements of His person, His one Person

itself requires that the transubstantiated bread should include the body, soul and Divinity of Christ. But at what a tremendous cost is this consistency maintained! It evades indeed the Capernaite objection, "How can this man give us His flesh to eat?" and it avoids the alternative, "How can God give us His flesh to eat?" but it transforms the God-man into human elements of nourishment, and gives Him to man to eat. Our refuge from this error, and its all-pervading effect on Christian theology, is in the truth already insisted on, that Christ becomes ours and we become His only through that Holy Spirit whom He gives us as the common bond of union, and in the reality of whose fellowship we become figuratively "members of His body, of His flesh, and of His bones." Joined to Christ we are one Spirit.

The Lutheran doctrine of Consubstantiation has some vital notes of difference from the former, but also some perilous points of affinity. It does not escape the Eutychian confusion; since its theory of a Divine ubiquity in the sacred flesh, based upon the "communication of properties" between the two natures, borders upon such a composite of the Divine and the human as it requires incomprehensible refinements to protect from the charge. And its notion that Christ's life is imparted to us through the sacramental communication of His glorified corporeity (whatever that may mean), present in, and with, and under the unchanged elements, leads plainly to a Nestorian distinction between the God and the man in the Redeemer. Lutheran divinity may protest against this; but in vain: plead as it may, it still makes man's spiritual life dependent on the infusion of a physical Christ who "giveth us His flesh to eat." Meanwhile, we hold fast our unbending principle that we receive no Christ but the whole Christ; precious as His body and blood are, we open our souls to nothing less than Himself, and all the mystery of His undivided Being. And, whether at His table or elsewhere, we wait for Him only according to the laws of the Third great Revelation of God to man: we wait for the Promise of the Father, which is the Promise of Christ, which is the Holy Ghost. [17.]

The doctrine of the Real Presence held by some modern Anglican divines, not without important deviations from that of their fathers, is only a diluted composite between those already referred to. The formularies to which they attach their dogma, a dogma almost too impalpable to deserve the name, are perfectly consistent with the truth of the One Person of Christ. These formularies we condemn not: they are our own. They do not blend the two natures into one, and give it to the faithful in the consecrated elements. They teach that sacramentally all the benefits of the Lord's passion are imparted to the faithful recipient; and that Christ is verily indeed but spiritually given and received: figurative language being used as to the separate effects of the Lord's body and of His blood which is sanctified by scriptural precedent, and well understood by the true instinct of the believer. But the indefinite dogma now prevalent in many parts of the English Church forsakes the ideas of the ceremonial. It uses the form of sound words; but with a written or unwritten Targum of its own that wavers between the Lateran and the Lutheran doctrines, without the precision of either. Its chief offence, however, as it concerns our present object, is its forgetfulness of the relation between the One Person of Christ, sacramentally brought near in the Eucharistic commemoration, and the Holy Ghost. It speaks indistinctly on other points: for instance, respecting the translation of the Whole Christ into the elements, the actual repetition or extension of the

One Sacrifice, and the impartation of the Sacred Body alone to the faithful. They speak indistinctly—we must think of the men and not of the doctrine, for it is only as yet "a tradition of men"—because on these points they dare not define. But there is no uncertainty about their doctrine of the Holy Ghost. " They limit the Holy One of Christ; " and withdraw Him from His administration of the Redeemer's Person, while they seem to exalt Him in His administration of the Redeemer's kingdom. They maintain that the indwelling of the Divine Paraclete is in the church alone, and that in the individual believer it is only Christ's prerogative to dwell: the Spirit in the body as a great abstraction, Jesus in the man as a personal reality. Thus they separate at once the Lord from His Spirit, and His Spirit from the Christian, in a manner which their sacramental theory may require, but which the Scripture condemns. The eighth chapter of the Romans seems written on purpose to show that there is no Christ in man but by the Holy Ghost's indwelling. The intercessory Spirit within us answers to the interceding Christ above. And " if any man have not the Spirit of Christ he is none of His." Whatever the Real Presence Sacramental may be, it can only be by the Holy Ghost. [18.]

Such a Real Presence there doubtless is. The true doctrine of the Person of Christ lends no sanction to the theory of those who go to the opposite extreme, and make the Eucharistic commemoration only the remembrance of an absent Head. An absent Head He cannot be whose Divine-human Person fills heaven and earth. He presides by His Spirit at His own ordinance, which derives all its dignity and grace from that presence. Our earthly sacrament is only a " shadow of the heavenly things ; " for in heaven our everlasting High Priest presents Himself always as the memorial of His own passion. Above He stands ever at a sacramental Altar diffusing the propitiation of the sacrifice once presented below. Below He presides only at a table, where He keeps the feast with us, whilst we commemorate His life and death; "in remembrance" not only of what He did and suffered, but "of Himself," His whole Incarnate Person and work. And, as we thankfully remember His manifestation in our midst, so we sacramentally partake of the benefits of His redemption: partakers, that is, not of His body and of His blood in any sense whatever, but "of Christ," of all that Christ is by His Spirit to the believing soul. We sacramentally receive Him; the symbols which He consecrated are pledges, then and there exchanged between Him and us, that we have the blessings of acceptance through His blood, and sanctification through His Spirit, sealed to us in the sacred rite. In other words, they are a continual ratification of our union with His Holy Person through the Spirit. And they are tokens and pledges of a bestowment of grace, of all grace, through other than sacramental channels, until His return shall render sacramental ordinances and the whole circle of the means of grace no longer needful.

To sum up what has been said on this subject: the present dispensation is in the hands of the Mediator, as He unites God and man, heaven and earth; but upon earth, and until what is emphatically called "the Coming of Christ," the Third Person of the Holy Trinity, the Spirit of the Father and of His Christ, is supreme. And this is true, not only of the church which is the body of our Lord and informed by His Spirit, but of every rite, ordinance and administration in the church; and it is equally true of the relation of the Redeemer to all the individuals who make up in their gradual accumulation and several increase the complete mystical fellowship.

The New Testament doctrine, like its most eminent expositor, knows not " Christ after the flesh ;" the long-continued corruptions of Christianity have known Him after the flesh, and the reform of those corruptions has kept to too great an extent that one corrupt element; nor will the body be restored to perfect soundness until it cries, with reference to that misunderstood Christ, " Now henceforth know we Him no more."

IV. It is a pleasant transition to the bearing of our doctrine on our individual relation to the Redeemer. "The Head of every man is Christ;" a profound truth, which has no meaning, or at best only a shrivelled meaning, on any other theory than that which has been maintained. As the Saviour, Glorifier and Head of every individual Christian He is not God, nor is He man, but He is the Godman. His indivisible Person itself is the centre of personal religion as it is expounded in the Christian covenant; and the doctrine of that indivisible Person gives its clear explanation to each definition of that religion as it is dwelt upon in the New Testament. As the God-man He claims the allegiance of every soul; He is the express Object of Christian faith; the spiritual life is the result of union with Him through the Spirit; our duty is prescribed by Him as a Divine-human Lawgiver; He presents in His Incarnate Person the example of Christian perfection ; He is the Elect Object of all the affections of the soul, from adoration to human enthusiasm; and, finally, He is the end and crown and exceeding great reward of the soul's probation. This is a large and most important assemblage of truths, which will give a refreshing relief from a strain too didactic and polemic. But, lest the relief itself should prove wearisome, only a very slight review of these can be attempted now.

1. " All power is given unto Me in heaven and in earth :"

this was our Lord's final proclamation of His authority as the Incarnate Redeemer. Since that power was *given* to Him, it was not as God that He spoke; and such absolute and unlimited sway over all human interests, and more than human interests, could not be the prerogative of any mortal man. The Saviour's Me, therefore, is here, as from the beginning, His Divine-human Person. To Him, whom as God they regarded with awful adoration, and before whom as man their loyalty bowed down, that first Christian congregation on the Mountain in Galilee offered the earnest of all Christian homage. To Him "every knee must bow;" and the message of the gospel is as earnest in demanding submission to His authority as it is in urging men to accept His salvation. The Mediator is, as we saw above, God in man, and not merely between God and man: no principle requires more constant enforcement than this in every exhibition of the Redeemer's claims. "Repentance towards God" is no other than repentance towards God in Christ; sin, if not made "more exceeding sinful" by His coming, has derived its keenest aggravation, and more than that its essential definition, from the rejection of God brought near in Christ (John xvi. 9). The Holy Spirit, reproving the world of sin, was to make this His one convicting charge, "that they believe not in Me." In these His last words concerning human sin, we cannot but feel that our Lord is not referring simply to man's rejection of His claims as a Messenger sent from God, but to his rejection of the Supreme Moral Governor in His Person. This was the conviction that pierced the heart of Saul at the gate of Damascus (Acts ix. 4, 5); at the gate of heaven "the chief of sinners" has no other definition of his sin (1 Tim. i. 13); and he is a representative of all transgressors who coming back through Christ to God find God in Christ. The God-man is the revelation at once of our sin and of our forgiveness, of our danger and of our hope, of our wrath and of our peace: "shut up to Christ," even though regarded as wearing the form of man, we are still in the presence of our Judge and of our Saviour. Whether as sinners or as believers, we are in the hands of Jesus alone, of Jesus who is man who is God.

2. As such He is the appropriate Object of the Christian faith that saves. Faith in all its exercises believes a record concerning a Divine Person whom it trusts. Under both these aspects it finds in the Incarnate Jesus its fit object: in its peculiar Christian characteristic supremely in Him. The principle of human trust has in Christ a human person to rely upon: a Man, mighty to deliver and to save, towards whom the heart of mortal feebleness may go out with an instinctive and familiar, and as it were natural, appeal for help. But this fellow of our race to whom our human trust clings is God's Fellow also, is God Himself in the flesh; and man's human trust is justified by the presence of the Great Power of God in Him. All this our Saviour meant when He said, "Ye believe in God, believe also in Me" (John xiv. 1): words the depth of which is too often lost to us in the abundance of the revelations which they serve to introduce. God in the New Testament is not represented as the Object of purely evangelical faith, apart from His Son: His Son, in some aspect of His revelation, and work, and passion, and resurrection, is always at hand to give that faith its Christian character. But Christ as the Object of this faith is always Christ in His Undivided Person: we must not think of reserving for the God in Christ the trust that needs a Divine support, and for the man in Christ the hero-worshipping enthusiasm of human confidence in the "Founder of Christianity." His Person is One; and every

outgoing of trust in His word, and His work, and His presence, meets the sympathy of a heart as human as our own, whilst it brings down to us all the succours of the eternal God.

3. There is no view of personal religion more familiar in the teaching of the Holy Ghost than that which traces its origin, growth, and perfection to union with Christ. "He is our life:" not as God, nor as man, but as the Incarnate Person in whom human nature is sanctified in an unlimited fulness, out of which all we receive (John i. 16). Our jealousy for the honour of the Spirit of Christ and of God, and our anxiety to defend Christian doctrine from the error of supposing our life to consist in an assimilation of Christ's humanity infused into us through His own Divine energy, have by a sad necessity thrown something of restraint over our statements of the direct personal union of the soul with the very Person of Christ. But, having done enough to obviate perversion, we may take our pleasant revenge. There is a union, the description of which almost reaches the language of identification, between Christ Himself and the believer "one Spirit with Him;" and this union we must allow nothing to impair in our estimate of the Christian privilege. To take this away would be to dim the glory of the New Testament; to lower it is to check the tenderest pulsation of New-Testament life. The strength of the new nature is a Divine power within; but it comes to us through our union with that Universal Person whose common Spirit is given to each. "I live, yet not I, Christ liveth in me," is the language of St. Paul the Christian mystic, speaking then as ever the words of truth and soberness.

St. Paul the Christian mystic, I say. The union which he here rejoices in, as the satisfaction of all his desires, is the deep reality of that which mysticism in every age, and almost in every zone of the religious earth, has yearned after as an unattainable ideal. True, there has been a mysticism which, in its despair, has gone out after an abstract, formless, silent, and Pantheistic God: missing the Divine personality at the outset, it has ended in the extinction of the soul's own personality in the vast abyss. But a better and a truer mysticism has set its aspiration on a Form that should bring God near to man, in a Divine Person "bone of our bone and flesh of our flesh," whose mind might have fellowship with our mind, and with whose heart our heart might be brought into harmony and rest. In Jesus we have this Object. The God-man whom mysticism has been ever, consciously or unconsciously, and always ignorantly, worshipping, Him the gospel declares. In the Incarnate Christ the human spirit finds its God, who created it for Himself and out of whom it can never find repose; but that God is "brought nigh to us," so nigh that we can see Him, touch Him, embrace Him, and, as it were, lean upon His bosom.

4. But Christian mysticism is "under the law to Christ." Our Divine-human Lawgiver issues the whole code of His new legislation in His undivided Person. He is God and He is man: like Moses, "He is appointed of God over all His house;" but, unlike Moses, He is the "Son over His own house," who builded it and is therefore God (Hebrews iii. 3, 4). The Christian laws proceed from One who is a human lawgiver, conversant with all our interests, and relations and duties, and whose most blessed enforcement of those laws is His own condescension to obey them. But in uttering them He is armed with Divine authority for the sanction of every ordinance, while a Divine infallibility guards every word of His mouth. To separate the Indivisible Person is most fatal here. If Jesus is ever "left alone" when He speaks, or if He sometimes speaks only as man; if, as some modern

theorists think, He was only by degrees replenished with His Godhead, or, as others, was for a season limited to the exercise of a human intellect: what guarantee have we for the perfection and integrity of His system of doctrine and of ethics? Who will tell us when the human voice spoke fallibly, and when we may implicitly trust the Divine? Whilst we hold fast the human development of our Saviour's human nature, with all processes of growth and final limitation, we must not limit His legislatorial function to that lower nature; we must believe that "He speaketh the words of God," being, on that seat which is higher than Moses', God-man always; and when, although a Son, He is interdicted by His commission from speaking all that we might desire to know—for instance, concerning the day and hour of the judgment—we may be sure that He will not fail to tell us so. It must ever be borne in mind that the mysterious law of our Saviour's restraint in the exercise, or in the possession as it respects His human manifestation, of His Divine perfections, is unknown to us. But not one of His words can fall to the ground; not one be superseded or corrected by higher teaching. He is to us the Divine-human Teacher: a human prophet "like unto Moses," but in all that He speaketh "He speaketh from heaven."

5. The Incarnate Lord, once more, presents to us a supreme pattern of excellence. His redeeming passion as the ground of our hope, and His supreme authority as the rule of our life, are not more clearly set before us in the New Testament than His moral character as the standard of our imitation. And, as we better apprehend both the former when we base them upon the undivided Person, so also the Lord's example is most fully understood when we regard it as presented by the God-man. None but God is good; and no final standard of goodness can be set before the creature

save one that is Divine. But man cannot copy excellence that is not human. As we are bidden to imitate the angels only in qualities which they possess in common with us, or in points which concern the obedience common to them and to us, so also the supreme Divine example must be humanized before it can measure our excellence or direct our pursuit of it. Even in the Old Testament, where the incarnation was as yet unrevealed or disguised, the character of God which was made the model of imitation was brought down into near resemblance to that of man. Whilst nothing was more fearfully forbidden than the presentation of the Divine object of worship under any form that might suggest the creaturely, especially the human, it cannot well be denied that the ethical character of Jehovah was presented under human aspects and with human attributes. And this may be transferred to our adorable Saviour. He presents us by the necessity of His Divine nature, according to His own testimony as confirmed by the Holy Ghost throughout the New Testament, an example of sinless and consummate perfection. All that we can conceive of good in God is the law of His life. The God of the Old Testament, the Jehovah of the law and of the Psalms and of the Prophets, reappears and comes nearer to us in the Lord Christ: the same in all holiness, whether the holiness of severity or of love, whether the holiness that communicates Himself or that which guards His rights. But then in Him this goodness is placed before us in a strictly human presentation. He sanctifies our nature before our eyes, or rather displays its sanctity, from infancy through all stages to the end. What we see is enough to command our faith in that which we see not of His human excellence. Devotion towards God could be carried no farther than it was carried by His days and nights of prayer;

and hyperbole itself fails in describing His charity. It is unbecoming and a theological irreverence to measure His holy career by the standard of the Commandments severally and in order. But that one which unites the Two Tables can hardly fail to suggest itself when we regard His human perfection. The fifth may stand for all the rest: He has made it, not only the first commandment with promise, but in some sense the first in blessing. As the earliest hour of His human responsible obedience showed the loveliness of His filial reverence, and all the more because it seemed to come into collision with a higher law; so His last hour bore witness to the same holy filial love, and all the more because the burden of the whole world was then upon His soul. But it is dangerous to take the first step in this path of meditation. I must leave it, almost thankful to escape from a burden too great, in order to enforce the necessity of remembering here the Indivisible Person of our Example.

His excellence must not be regarded with an exaggerated and too distant reverence, as simply Divine. This carries it out of the region of human imitation altogether; and, though we keep our Saviour, we lose our Pattern. It is possible to make our Lord's excellence a merely Apollinarian beauty of holiness, a Divine and supernatual, or superhuman, display of goodness which seems and only seems to be wrought out in a human life. This is an error which insensibly affects the estimate formed of Christ by vast numbers of His most faithful disciples: their very reverence and loyalty leading them into it. They forget that, while "God is manifest in the flesh" before them, both sides of this wonderful saying must be equally emphasised, its last word not less than its first. The error is, if any error may be, venial: but its consequences are very evil. The beauty of our Lord's grace and submission, and devotion and charity, is infected by a subtile Docetism that makes it little better than a Divine excellence which is not human at all; or, if human in any sense, so altogether unattainable that it must be left for admiration and wonder until it is reflected and toned down in the example of His saints. This mistake robs the most pathetic scenes in the gospel of their deepest meaning, from the wilderness to the expiring cry; and it deprives Christ's humble imitators of what is to them their noblest stimulant, the reality of His human example.

On the other hand, the recoil from this error leads to what is still more dangerous, and much more grievous to our reverence. When our Lord's human moral development is studied too much apart, and unguarded by the unity of His Person, the result is an indecorous familiarity with the elements of His lower nature, and a forgetfulness of the wide distinction, in all things even that are common, between Him and us. It is possible to enter too curiously into the mystery of our Saviour's humiliation, and, under pretence of maintaining the identity between His manhood and ours, to give Him our sinful flesh to combat with. This tendency is very manifest in the present day. In earlier and mediæval times the veritable humanness of our Lord's development was too much forgotten. But, in its eagerness to secure a new found truth, our own age is going to the other extreme. In recent "Lives of Jesus" we see much in this respect that is to be deplored; and not only in them, for many of our most evangelical commentaries seem to think it necessary for the explanation of His human excellence that the Divine Son in Christ should leave Him for a season. They seek to surprise His humanity as it were alone: and think that He can be no example of human virtue who has not attained it in the human way, thus in short making the Lord "a man of like passions with ourselves." Nestorianism, not to say

Humanitarianism, lurks hardly disguised in their pages. Let us be on our guard, and remember certain Divine prerogatives thrown around the flesh of our Lord's humbled estate. So low He never sank as to feel our sin stirring within Him, or to pray for the suppression of any evil in the manhood that He had taken. The Holy Ghost brought our Lord a nature that was as free from sin as Adam's, and to be made by the assumption of the Son more inaccessible to sin than his. There was no germ of evil in Him to which temptation might appeal: "in Him was no sin," and by a Divine necessity no capacity for sin. He "came to destroy the works of the devil," but not in Himself; had it been in Himself, that would have isolated Him from us all; for the destruction of a man's own sin is enough for his own probation. He was "separate from sinners" (Hebrews vii. 26); "and was tempted in all points like as we are," only so far as He could be tempted "without sin" of His own, though the Bearer of others' sin (Hebrews iv. 15). It was not possible that He could fall. Our Redeemer did not first redeem Himself: the Holy Ghost was the only Redeemer of His humanity, which indeed needed no redemption as His. A Divine Person in the flesh raised our nature into Himself that we might rise through Him. Other examples, not His, show us the path of return to virtue, and the secret of the suppression of latent vice: that was no part of our Redeemer's function. His temptation to sin was only the trial that proved His sinlessness; and at those points where His example fails His virtue comes to our help. As much of His Messianic obedience was altogether out of the sphere of our imitation, so much of our obedience as sinners conquering sin finds no pattern in Him. Our doctrine of the Indivisible Person is urgent here; and I follow it where it leads. Nor will I accept the subterfuge that the Divine necessity of His holiness was consistent with His own absolute freedom as man. It is hard to deny this; moral liberty is the glory of man; but when this word is used of Christ, in His Incarnate Person, it must be used with the same abatement and with the same reverent glorification of the word as when we say that God is free. [19.]

6. Once more, the Person of our Lord claims the believer's adoration, worship, homage, and, in a word, perfect love, which is the highest form of worship. The controversy as to the propriety of offering prayer to Jesus, whose human nature might seem to forbid it, has been more or less agitated in every age. It has entered into every controversy concerning the Person of Christ. But it is a very petty controversy. Doubtless, in the economical relations of the Holy Trinity in redemption, prayer is offered to the Father through the Son by the Holy Ghost; and praise as the counterpart of prayer ascends in the same order. But who can approach the Sacred Person in the gospels, the three as well as the fourth, without feeling that He demands such love and such creaturely incense of the heart as God alone can claim? Who can read the epistles without perceiving that there is literally no restriction in the homage which the regenerate soul may offer to the Lord and the Lord will accept? The highest law is the love of God; but the sternest sanction of that law is the anathema on him that loves not Jesus Christ. The Indivisible Person explains all this. Whilst the distinction between the Father and the Incarnate Lord of mediation is carefully maintained, the Scripture never forgets that the Mediator is, in Himself and apart from acts of mediation, God as well as man: it therefore leaves the Christian to the freedom of His loyal effusions, which cannot go astray in their ascent, though they may descend too low. Where there can be no transgression, there is no law. We are not

exhorted to distinguish carefully and separate off the human person, when our souls would worship and call upon the name of Jesus. Nor are we bidden to abstract His Divine majesty when we fix our thought upon His human form— so far as we can do that—and to reserve the pure affections of our human hearts for any Man Christ Jesus. He, in His one Person, is our Lord; and the spirit of the ancient psalm unites all human loyalty and adoration for God in the words of its command and permission, "Worship thou Him!" (Psalm xlv. 11.) As His Person is a mystery absolutely unique, revealed to faith, so it evokes in the heart a perfectly unique sentiment and feeling, as if by the creation of a new Christian sense. It excites through the Holy Ghost a love that is at once perfectly human and perfectly Divine; and it prompts us to offer to Christ a devotion which is, so to speak, His alone: not, however, to be offered to Him in some side sanctuary of lower worship, but in the full glory of the temple of God. Such words as these, however, labour hopelessly to express their meaning. All may be summed in one injunction: Let not the Person of Christ be divided either in our faith or in our devotion. Let not the man be too familiar to us, or we fall into certain Pietistic excesses; let not the God be too overwhelmingly contemplated, lest we forget that Christianity is not Deism, but the revelation of God in man.

7. Lastly, the Divine-human Lord is as such, and as such only, the Disposer of man's destiny and the very End of His being. None but the Creator can decide the fates of His creature. By the Son and for Him, the Son who is Christ, "all things were made" (Colossians i. 16). The fall of man, and his redemption, has not changed the destination of the race: it only interprets to us the meaning of those deep sayings which make Christ the End as well as the

Redeemer of man's life. No doctrine concerning the Incarnate Person other than that which we maintain will bear the weight of this great truth concerning the end of man. If there were any flaw in that doctrine it would be detected here at the last. If the Deity of Christ were less than essential Deity; if the manhood of Christ were in any sense separable from His everlasting Person; if in short He were not to continue the Incarnate Jesus for ever; the "day of the Lord" would declare it. But we learn that when all mediatorial functions are finally discharged, and the redeeming work with all its wonders of justice and grace shall pass into heavenly history, the Lord Christ is to be still the Head of His Church, which will never cease to be " His purchased possession, redeemed and purified to Himself" (Acts xx. 28, Ephesians iv. 30, Titus ii. 14). His saints in their innumerable multitude and distinct individuality, "redeemed to Himself as a purchased possession" (Ephesians i. 14) by His Divine-human power, "given to Him by the Father" (John xvii. 6) as the fruit of His Divine-human obedience, will be His own for ever: beholding His glory in their redeemed spirits, with their bodies fashioned according to His glorious body, they will have their consummation in Him. "They that are Christ's" (1 Corinthians xv. 23) is their description both in time and in eternity. But every point we would establish here—the Divine propriety, the final end, the full disposal, the Divine-human possession of our souls— is summed up in one word of St. Paul to the Ephesians, " that He might PRESENT IT TO HIMSELF a glorious church" (chap. v. 27).

V. This last passage fitly introduces the final aspect of our Doctrine, its relation to the Christian church as the Body of which the Incarnate Christ is the Head. The visible church is the one body constituted of all those who maintain that sound faith of which this doctrine is the centre; the invisible church is the fellowship of all who, in heaven and earth, are united to the Lord's Living Person through the One Spirit; and in everlasting union with Him the visible and the invisible churches will be one.

1. The "Truth as it is in Jesus" means really, in an important sense, the truth as it is concerning Jesus. The doctrine of the one Christ, who unites God and man in the redeeming work, to whom all authority is given in heaven and in earth, whose only name and whose name alone is given for salvation among men, is the most compendious and the sufficient test of evangelical orthodoxy. "Holding the Head" is the scriptural formula; and that Head is the Incarnate Son of God and Son of man. Our Lord's own test in the gospels can never be superseded: "What think ye of Christ?" "Whom say ye that I am?" (Matthew xvi. 15.) He who answers this aright will answer aright every vital question. If "the Name which is above every name" have its true place in Christian theology, all the truths that belong to the common salvation will adjust themselves in their perfection of symmetry, from the Most Holy Trinity down to the "least commandment" that pertains to life. It may safely be affirmed that whatever creed or confession gives the Indivisible Person its rightful place can consistently contain no essential error: perhaps it may be added, no error that shall absolutely invalidate its possession of Christian truth. The charity which asserts that no community holding this faith is altogether outside of the pale of Christendom has the support of Scripture, and therefore of all candid men. And the fidelity which excludes all who maintain not the integrity of our Lord's Person, as God and man, can scarcely be charged with unscriptural severity. It is quite true that many bodies of nominal Christians in East and West, whose

creeds are sound as to the constituents and unity of the One Person of Christ, neutralize their soundness by inconsistent errors and superstitions that go far to render that truth of none effect. The Christ of the Creed may be exhibited in connection with such media as obscure and veil His simple supremacy even more than some of the errors of the heretics who were anciently cast out of the church. On the other hand, many communities, and especially many individuals in those communities, who hold most defective views of the Divine-human Person, even renouncing His Divinity altogether, may nevertheless, through a certain instinctive and irrepressible faith that defies heresy, own Him practically as supreme whom in words they deny. Happy are they, and may we ever be among them, who, making the Scriptures alone their final standard, hold fast the doctrines that were established in the earliest controversies of the Christian church, and formulated in its Councils, without defeating their pure Confession by the traditions of men.

It would be inappropriate here to enter upon a review of the whole Estate of Christendom in relation to this great test of orthodoxy; or even to consider what are the securities and probabilities of a more general consent in the central truths of Christianity. I must content myself with congratulating our own Communion upon its unfeigned faith in the doctrine, and its firm loyalty to the Person of Christ. From the beginning of our existence as a people, there has been no variation, nor any shadow of turning. With all our other unfaithfulness and unworthiness, there has been no unsoundness in this regard. We deserve the rebukes that Simon Peter so often received; but we have never wavered in Simon Peter's good confession (Matthew xvi. 16), nor faltered in Simon Peter's challenge (John xxi. 15). One at least of the doctrinal controversies we have known had reference to the Saviour's Person. His eternal Sonship was for a season disputed by some who, thinking no evil, aimed to conciliate reason, and knew not that they were imperilling faith. Our standards of doctrine repelled their error; it has been habitually disavowed among us; and our teaching has been preserved from its infection. And now, through the blessing of the sole Guardian of our most holy faith upon our fidelity as its guardians under Him, there is not a voice in our ministry which hesitates in the utterance of the three dogmatic Creeds—so far as this doctrine is in them; and not a congregation from the greatest to the least among us that would tolerate for an hour the slightest deflection from the truth concerning the one Christ, both God and man, who suffered for the salvation of the world. We and our people "see the King in His beauty," whatever else we see not; and proclaim the one Christ to mankind, whatever else we are charged with failure to do. And we believe that He who has established this supreme test of a sound faith will, while we are thus faithful to His name, preserve us from every error, pardon and heal our manifold defects, and deliver us from all such minor differences of judgment as might endanger our unity or thwart the purpose of His will concerning us. [19.]

2. The church then with which we have to do, and with which the interests of the world are so vitally bound up, is a visible community, the members of which proclaim in a succession of living witnesses a Confession of faith in Christ against which the gates of hell shall not prevail. But it must not be forgotten that the true, abiding and everlasting church is, under another aspect, the company of those who through union with Christ form part of His mystical body, which also is "growing in wisdom and in stature, in favour with God and with man." We cannot but be familiar with

that law of the Spirit's phraseology concerning the Person of Christ by which the same terms are used interchangeably of His human nature and of His mystical body the church. It might seem as if the new humanity, the new Fellowship of the regenerate, the new order of mankind whose second Head is the Son of man, were regarded as an extension of His own holy manhood, an extension of the incarnation, or, to adopt St. Paul's vast words, "the fulness of Him who filleth all in all" (Ephesians i. 23). It may be said that this is figurative language, and such undoubtedly to some extent it is. But it is the same kind of figure that runs through the whole evangelical covenant: a shadow to which the profound reality of heavenly things corresponds. The Lord's one, common, universal, Divine-human nature is the element of which all are partakers; and, in virtue of that common heritage, they are said to be, in part below and in full above, "partakers of Christ" (Hebrews iii. 14). The result is that transcendent unity of the "perfect stature of the fulness of Christ" which the High-priestly prayer anticipates while it asks, and asks while it anticipates. The completed mystical fellowship of Christ's saints shall be as really one in Him and part of Himself, and the complement of His perfection, as the sacred flesh was in which He wrought our redemption. But in another way. By the energy of the one Spirit this body is formed for Him out of mankind, grows up into Him, and is conformed to His image: not created by any mystical incarnation in His saints, nor fashioned by the assimilation of His sacramental humanity. Rightly understood, this is the grandest and most spirit-stirring application of the doctrine of the Undivided Person. No view of the destiny of the faithful Fellowship can surpass or equal this. Christ shall be one with His body the church in indissoluble fellowship: all to the redeemed made one in Him that His Divinity was to His human nature—its sanctity, its blessedness, and its glorification. Christ in us now the hope of glory will then be in us the glory itself. St. Paul's expatiation on this theme I am afraid to trust myself to quote; and St. Peter follows hard, "We are partakers of a Divine nature." But the Lord Himself uttered all that could be said for wonder, for adoration, and for hope, when He cried, in words which never yet have had their meaning told, "I am come that they" His flock the church "might have life, and have it more abundantly"—and have it MORE, περίσσον : more than Adam lost, more than unfallen man could have known, more than eternity itself can limit. For He spoke of the life that He should give His body the church for which He waits in heaven.

3. The analogy between our Lord's incarnate Person and His union with His body the church will suggest the closing observations on this subject. Even with regard to the incarnate Christ Himself, we have to speak of a natural and of a spiritual body: first that which was natural, afterwards that which was spiritual. All that connected Him with earthly conditions, and partook of physical humiliation, the Redeemer left behind when the heavens received Him. Yet He remained the same Jesus, unchanged in His transformation. So also will it be with the natural and spiritual, the visible and the mystical, body of the church. As the Lord permits us to say that His manhood underwent dissolution, though it knew not corruption, in the separation of spirit and body—"Destroy this body" is His own language —and that He was changed into another form after His resurrection and in His ascension, so also the visible church will be dissolved without corruption, will be transfigured, and glorified into the spiritual perfection of the body that shall never know increase or diminution, infirmity or decay, that shall not again be separated either from the love of

Christ or from Christ Himself for ever. Every member not meet for the Master's use will perish with the world that never received His life. Then at length, and after the long process of ages and dispensations, the visible church will be exactly one with the church invisible; and "Immanuel, God with us," will have its second glorious accomplishment. Not, as was said before, by a second incarnation; for the union between Christ and that outer body will not be hypostatical, but wrought by the bringing of many sons, each in his personal integrity, to glory, and so conforming them to the Incarnate both in body and in soul, that He and His shall form one everlasting and indivisible Object, in a unity of which the Lord Himself has given us the only parallel and explanation: "that they all may be one, as Thou, Father, art in Me, and I in Thee, that they also may be one in Us" (John xvii. 21).

And here I take farewell of this "Good Matter," this *Verbum Bonum*, this λόγον ἀγαθόν (Psalm xlv. 1, Vulg., Sept.). We have examined the testimony of Scripture to the constituent elements of our Saviour's Person, and shown it to be One in the indivisible unity of the God-man. We have seen the manifold bearings of this truth on the fundamental doctrines of theology, upon which its seal is everywhere impressed. We have paid regard to the laws which regulate the theological phraseology of the subject, not without some side references to the controversies that have disturbed the Christian church. Withal it has been shown that the full understanding of the mystery of "the Christ of God" is not possible to man in this life, perhaps not possible for ever; but that our faith in that which may be known of it is essential to our Christian completeness, whether of belief or of practice.

Let us now rise from the doctrine to HIMSELF; and confirm to our hearts what has been said by one common act of reverent contemplation. Let the epistle to the Hebrews, to which we have been so largely indebted, furnish us an example and a guide. After the first chapter has proved that Christ is truly Divine, and the second has exhausted the evidence that He is perfectly man, the sacred writer, leaving the incarnation an unexpressed secret behind the veil, proceeds to dilate upon the wonders of His redeeming work. But, before he does so, he reverently lifts the veil and summons His readers to "consider" the Wonderful Person Himself. To that consideration—that fervent, concentrated, absorbing, never-weary study—the Holy Ghost invites us all: not only us, who are appointed to be the stewards of Christ's mysteries, but all who are the "holy brethren" of Jesus, and "partakers of the heavenly calling." Let us unite to fix the eye of our faith upon Him now, for He is present in our midst. Let us touch Him with the hand of faith; and we shall find that there was no virtue in the Galilæan plain which is denied to us. And then, under the influence of this evening's consecration, let us devote ourselves afresh to this immortal study, to the pursuit of this knowledge that shall not pass away; until, after having for a season beheld the glory of the Lord as reflected from His word, we, changed into the same image by His Spirit, may reach the Beatific Vision, and see Him as He is, to Whom, in the unity of His Sacred Person, and in the unity of the Father and the Holy Ghost, be ascribed might, majesty and dominion now and for ever. AMEN.

THE DOCTRINE OF CHRIST'S PERSON AS DEVELOPED IN SCRIPTURE.

THE SCRIPTURAL DEVELOPMENT OF THE DOCTRINE OF CHRIST'S PERSON.

The revelation of the doctrine of Christ's Person is governed by the same law of development which regulates the gradual disclosure of every truth of the Christian faith. The Redeemer was manifested in the flesh and made perfect as the Incarnate Son only after a long succession of ages; and the disclosure of the mysteries of His Person kept pace, being slowly imparted through a variety of instrumentalities, whose several contributions were overruled by the Holy Ghost for the presentation of the perfect image of the Mediator in the theology of the Scripture. Having the whole Bible in our hands, we may study it as the historical development of this one doctrine; even as all revelation has been only the historical development of Him concerning whom the doctrine speaks. The gradual formation of the complete image may be traced according to many principles of arrangement. That which I adopt will take the Old Testament first; then proceed to the testimony of Christ Himself; then proceed to the several Apostolical types.

I.

The Old Testament was more than once referred to by our Lord as being in its entire fabric a testimony to Himself. And a large proportion of the individual quotations which He made were such as brought into prominent relief His own form in the Psalms and the Prophets. "Search the Scriptures; for in them ye think ye have eternal life; and they are they which testify of Me" (John v. 39). Christ is the Life of the world; the ancient Scriptures testified concerning Him, not His work only, but His Person also, and in such a way that the testimony must be searched for, being not always obvious and on the surface. That His Person as well as His work—in this case His Person rather than His work—was referred to, is evident from the impressive allusion to Eternal Life, which the New Testament everywhere connects with Christ Himself: "In Him was life; and the life was the light of men" (John i. 4). When, after the resurrection, Jesus illustrated His own precept, and searched the Scriptures for His disciples, and with them, it is said that He expounded to them the things "concerning Himself." Remembering that He found these things in Moses and all the prophets, we must, of course, understand that the mysteries of the atoning economy and government were the main subject of His discourse; but not to the exclusion of His Person, for the things concerned "Himself." Finally, it must not be forgotten that our Lord's testing questions—the questions by which He tried the scriptural knowledge both of His enemies and of His disciples—had reference to His personal relation to the Father. "Whom say ye that I am?" was a question which He doubtless often asked of the latter; and "Whose Son is He?" one which doubtless often in various forms convicted the former. In short, a careful collation and pondering of the Saviour's appeals to the Old Testament will produce the impression that He regarded, and would have us to regard, the Old Testament as containing the beginnings and germs of all revelation concerning the mystery of His incarnate Person.

But there is one preliminary consideration of great importance, referring to the distinction between development in the Old Testament and development in the New. As to the latter, it may be confidently affirmed that with the very "beginning of the gospel" the doctrine of Christ's Person is in a certain sense complete. The earliest announcement of the heralds of the incarnation presents the mysterious union of God and man in one incarnate Saviour. All subsequent witness and teaching only contemplates more and more closely that glorious Object: marking and describing with ever-increasing clearness the lineaments of its perfection, over which suffering only throws a veil for a season, which glorification removes for ever. Development, properly speaking, has ceased when the word Immanuel is spoken. The fully revealed Person of the God-man has only to be studied or considered (Hebrews iii. 1) in all its absolute and relative meaning. But with the germs of truth in the Old Testament it is otherwise. No revelation is perfect there: a proposition this which has almost universal application. Of each preparatory disclosure it might be said, "the day shall declare it:" that is, the earlier Day of Christ. No flower in the ancient garden of the Lord was fully unfolded; no fruit was fully mature. For as yet the Sun had not risen upon the earth. Hence it follows that the hints and preintimations of truth concerning the Person of Christ must not be studied apart from the perfected revelation of the New Testament. We must not too curiously ask what the early symbols and prophecies conveyed to those who received them: certainly we must not limit ourselves to any interpretation which they may seem to bear apart from the light thrown back upon them from the manifested Sun of righteousness, who has risen not only with healing but with revelation also in His wings. When our Lord sent the Jews to the Scriptures to find Him there, His meaning was that they should search them through and through with the key and the light which His personal presentation of His claims put into their hands. In their Scripture they thought they had eternal life: this our Lord acknowledged and approved. But they must now search again under better auspices, and think also that that Eternal Life was He Himself "which was with the Father and was manifested unto us" (1 John i. 2). He never condemns the unbelief of His enemies, nor His disciples' slowness of heart, because they had not come from the Old-Testament school fully expecting His Divine-human appearance; but because, after He had come and spoken to them, His presence and His words failed to explain to them the mysteries of the older revelation. In accordance with this principle we must take the great and leading characteristics of that Being who "was to come" in the Old Testament and search them under the full light of the Gospel morning, and the Pentecostal midday of the New-Testament teaching. So doing we shall find, with regard to our present doctrine, that all its fundamental elements were foreannounced, and that the older and later Scriptures blend into one harmonious and perfect image of Him who is the Son of God and the Son of man, in the unity of His Incarnate personality.

To the eye of faith, thus enlightened, there appears throughout the Old Testament a Holy Form, as of One who should come in the future, man and yet more than man, God and yet in the mystery of His essence distinct from God, or rather distinct in God, and, in the unity of His Person as Incarnate, the Agent of the Divine will in redemption, first as a servant and then as the glorified Lord. For our present purpose it will be necessary and sufficient to trace the broad outlines of these three truths of the earlier revelation. An exposition in detail of this portion of Old-

Testament Christology would be inconsistent with our limits, and would derange the proportion which must be preserved between the introductory hints of prophecy and the perfection of fulfilment.

The earliest form that the prediction of Christ's Person assumes is that which announces Him as the future SEED, first of the Woman, then of Abraham, and finally of David. In all these His manhood, the verity of His human nature, is declared, without any reference to His Divinity, though that, as will be seen, is another revelation keeping pace with the former, and in some respects interwoven with it.

The first proclamation of Hope to the human race—which the devotion of the church has agreed to call the Protevangelium—promised to mankind that the Seed of the Woman should bruise the head of the serpent. Interpreted in the New Testament this "beginning of the Gospel" signified no less than that a Person who should be divinely born of woman, not after the manner of other men, and yet so as to be a perfect member of the race, should, in virtue of His Divine strength, Himself destroy the works of the Devil and abolish the sin of man, but only at the expense of the sacrificial suffering of which His purely human nature should render Him capable. This infinite meaning lay folded in that earliest revelation to fallen man. But the words themselves pay their tribute only to the manhood of Christ, the future Deliverer. We know that no mortal man could contend with the sin of mankind or the higher principalities of evil; but the secret of the more than human strength of One who was human was not yet disclosed. The Bible thus begins with the foreannouncement of the human nature of our Lord. Of this Seed we hear no more until the time of Abraham, when the voice of prophecy, uttered, as we shall see, by the Redeemer Himself concerning Himself, and at the second great crisis of human hope, declared that "in thy seed shall all the nations of the earth be blessed" (Genesis xxii. 18). From that time Abraham saw the day of Christ and was glad. He joyed in God, receiving the atonement: though only "in a figure," and not knowing the mystery of His future Seed. But we know it. The New Testament has shown us how to lay the emphasis on "the Seed, as of One," as of One solitary among mankind, representing all nations and capable of blessing all nations as the Son and Servant of God raised up in human nature and sent to bless us in turning us away from our iniquities (Acts iii. 26). Silence concerning this future Seed is once more kept until the times of David, when there is a third limitation. The Seed of the woman, belonging to the human race; the Seed of Abraham, the representative of all believers, whether Jew or Gentile, is promised as the Seed of David: "I will set up thy Seed after thee . . . and I will establish His kingdom. He shall build an house for My name, and I will establish the throne of His kingdom for ever" (2 Samuel vii. 12, 13). David knew not fully, at least as yet, the true dignity of his future Seed. We may possibly read more meaning into his words than they bore to him, when he said, "Thou hast spoken of Thy servant's house for a great while to come." But David's Son has told us that He was David's Lord. Though no further explanation was then given to him, we know what the kingdom of the Messiah is, and what the House He builds for God to dwell in. It is still only His human nature that is foreannounced; but it is with the glorious Future present to us that we read the words of David, type of the Father: "and is this the manner of men, O Lord God?" In due time it will be seen to be not after the manner of men; but for the present the Seed is David's lineal descendant only. This great foreannouncement recurs in the Psalms. But it will be enough to have traced the threefold process of the prediction of Christ's Person in the verity of His human nature.

Concurrently with this prediction, however, there is a parallel series, not of prophecies proper, but of manifestations which the New Testament shows to belong to the same Person who is the promised Seed. A Being who, to borrow a later prophetic word, is Jehovah's Fellow, appears in the patriarchal times as the ANGEL JEHOVAH, and in such a manner as to be inexplicable except on the principles of New-Testament interpretation. Now this mysterious manifestation of a Divine Person is perfectly distinct from the promised Seed; yet it is remarkable that the earliest records of it are connected with the prediction of that Seed. The first mention in the Bible of an appearance of God to man is in Genesis xii. 7: "And the Lord appeared unto Abram, and said, Unto thy seed will I give this land." The ancient Jews had a presentiment of the truth that God could not manifest Himself save by a Being, not distinct from Himself, and yet only a visible expression of His invisible essence. They therefore referred it to the Shekinah, the Metatron, the Memra, or Logos, or Word of God. The New Testament tells us that "no man hath seen God at any time; the only begotten Son, which is in the bosom of the Father, He hath declared Him" (John i. 18). After that first intimation of an appearance of God, made to Abraham His friend, we find the Angel Jehovah appearing to him a second time when the promised Seed was more expressly promised. This Angel is God the Lord Jehovah: "By Myself have I sworn ... in thy Seed shall all nations of the earth be blessed." But, wonderful as it may seem, the Lord Jehovah who utters the promise is promising the future gift of Himself. Though no other than God, the Angel is mysteriously distinguished from God by the very name, even as the Son is afterwards distinguished from the Father: that name of Angel, however, does not indicate inferiority of essence; it simply predicts the subordination of the Second Person in the Trinity in the likeness not of angels but of men. The human form, however, is not altogether wanting. In Genesis xxxii. 24—32, "Jacob was left alone; and there wrestled a Man with him until the breaking of the day." The faith of the Christian church has always regarded this as an anticipation of the appearance of the Angel Jehovah in the flesh. To Jacob himself this Man was an object of profound curiosity: as he wrestled with His person so he wrestled with His secret. "Tell me, I pray Thee, Thy name." His request was not granted, but he was blessed instead; the blessing told him with whom he had contended: "I have seen God face to face." But the face of God no mortal hath seen nor can see save in the face of Jesus Christ. Shedding the rays of the New Testament back upon that wonderful night, the day breaks in another sense, and we may say "It is the Lord," and, though this was not the meaning of the words, we may give them another application: "As a prince hast thou power with God and with Man, and hast prevailed:" with Him who is God and man. Elsewhere this Angel is sent: which is the Old-Testament method of stating the New-Testament truth: "The Father sent His Son." Thus in Exodus xxiii. 20, it is said: "Behold, I send an Angel before thee, to keep thee in the way, and to bring thee into the place which I have prepared." "My Name is in Him" (Exodus xxiii. 21). This Angel appeared to Joshua, chap. v. 14, "the Prince of the Host of the Lord," and to Manoah who vainly asked His name, again in a human form: in the latter instance again declaring that His name was not yet to be revealed: "Why askest thou thus after My name, seeing it is secret?" (Judges xiii. 18). Those appearances finally ceased, having served their purpose. But in the prophets their remembrance is preserved. In Isaiah lxiii. 9, He is called "The Angel of the face of Jehovah," the Saviour of Israel and the Redeemer of Jacob. The prophet Hosea (chap. xii. 5), that Angel with whom Jacob wrestled is "Jehovah, God of Hosts." And in Malachi the whole long series is terminated by the express announcement that the Lord who should suddenly come to His temple was Jehovah "the Angel of the Covenant." Looking back again from the last prophet to Isaiah we rise to the grand revelation that the Jehovah of the Old Testament, as the manifested God, is no other than the Second Person of the Trinity. The glory of the Lord which the prophet saw in the mystical temple was the glory of Christ (John xii. 41); and thus the Divine nature of the Incarnate is found to be set forth as distinctly as the Human. But, so far as we have yet seen, they are kept entirely distinct.

Proceeding forward into the clearer dawn we find that in the later Old Testament the Person whose human and Divine natures have thus been announced distinctly and apart, becomes the Object of prophecies which unite these natures in One, with the further revelation of a progression from humiliation to glory in Him whose Incarnate appearance was to accomplish the Divine will and redeem the world. The prominent passages will alone be referred to: those, namely, which deal with the Indivisible Person as the Mediator between God and man. Those passages, if eliminated from the great mass that include the work of the future Redeemer, will be found to be few, though amply sufficient to establish what we now seek to establish.

Precedence must be given to the Psalms: not so much because of the order of their composition, but because the Saviour Himself sought His own Person—distinctively considered as such—almost entirely in them. The offices of the future Messiah are almost everywhere extolled in these sacred songs; nor are there many of them from which He is altogether excluded. But there are gradations of reference. In some the allusions are like flashes of prophetic inspiration lighting up a strain that does not expressly point to Him: so the twenty-second Psalm, which prepared for the Redeemer the saddest words He ever uttered, but cannot be throughout regarded as Messianic. In others the Saviour seems to divide the hymn with His typical representative: as in Psalm xvi., where He suddenly appears in the middle and continues to the end, though the beginning cannot be His. In others again He is the main subject; but, as in Psalm lxxii., it is not His Person, but His kingdom and its blessings, which the Psalmist dilates upon. But there are three Psalms which are altogether His: that is to say, whatever historical substratum there may be, His Person in its form and dignity covers the whole, and gives the whole its meaning. These are the second, the forty-fifth, and the hundred and tenth Psalms. In each of these He has Divine names, while in each His perfect human nature is exhibited most fully. They are quoted largely in the New Testament; and there ascribed to David, which renders it needless that we should digress into any side-discussion as to their date and authorship.

The second Psalm, anciently the first, begins the strain of Old-Testament tributes to the Incarnate Person of the Redeemer. As a Hebrew hymn, and as understood by those who sang it first, it has not so large a meaning. It speaks of a Messiah, or Anointed One; that this Messiah should be a Son begotten at some future time; and that He should by an irreversible decree be set in authority over all mankind. Beyond this it does not go. But the New Testament rejoices greatly over this Psalm; directly or indirectly it is quoted more than any other save one; every individual verse has its echo. Expressly is the central decree "Thou art My Son, this day have I begotten Thee," made prominent. It is applied to the incarnation of the Redeemer as it was perfected in His risen Person (Acts. xiii. 33): not that in His resurrection Christ became the Son of God, but that He was then finally and perfectly begotten in our nature as the Divine-human Son, "declared to be the Son of God with power, according to the Spirit of holiness"—that is, in virtue of His Divine nature—"by the resurrection from the dead." By a collation of Hebrews i. 3, ver. 5, and Acts xiii. 34, it will be seen that the passage is also referred to the three several offices of the Christ who was begotten or raised up in our nature to be the Teacher, Priest, and King of mankind. But, behind this generation in time, there is the eternal generation; for the First-begotten brought into the world was the Brightness of the Divine glory, the express Image of His Person, whom the angels were commanded to worship (Hebrews i.). A fragment of this great saying, changed accordingly, as if it were a suspended quotation, is heard at the Baptism and the Transfiguration of our Lord: "This is my beloved Son:" as from eternity Only-begotten, so begotten anew in human nature.

The hundred and tenth Psalm is pitched to the same note. It begins with the passage which, as will be seen hereafter, our Lord used for the conviction of the unbelief of the Jews: "The Lord said unto my Lord." The former "Lord" is Jehovah, and the latter Adonai; but the latter as well as the former belongs to God alone. Elsewhere the coming Messiah is Elohim and Jehovah by abundant testimonies;

here He is Adonai, to complete the ascription to Him of Divine names. The "right hand" of this Psalm has given the New-Testament term for the mediatorial supremacy of Christ in heaven : a supremacy which the Epistle to the Hebrews exalts far above what angelic or created nature generally could by possibility attain (Hebrews i. 13). The "for ever" of His priesthood is also interpreted in that epistle (chap. vii. 17) as based upon "the power of an endless life," or the essential eternity of the Mediator. "Adonai at the right hand of Jehovah," is the theme of the Psalm ; and, granted that He is the Man Jesus, must He not also be God ? The Epistle to the Hebrews once more answers by a quotation from the Psalm to which we now pass : " Thy throne, O God, is for ever and ever."

It is the forty-fifth Psalm which most emphatically and affectingly presents an Old-Testament image of the Incarnate Person. Whatever else it was or is, it sings the song of rejoicing over the union of Christ and His church and " the children princes in all the earth." " Thou art fairer than the children of men : grace is poured into thy lips : therefore God hath blessed thee for ever : " let the first Sermon in Nazareth, and the complacency of the Father at the Transfiguration, and the Prologue of St. John, illustrate this tribute to the perfect Manhood of the Messiah. And let His entire history explain that commingling of tenderness and severity in His government which the Psalm depicts. " Thy throne, O God, is for ever and ever :" though a dominion to which He has been raised, it is an eternal dominion in virtue of the eternal Divinity of Him who sustains it. " God, Thy God, hath anointed Thee with the oil of gladness above Thy fellows," completes the delineation of the Incarnate Mediator : who, whether in the Old Testament or the New, whether He Himself speaks for His

Apostles, is, as Incarnate, subordinate to the Father, His God and our God.

The Prophets carry forward into another sphere the preparatory revelation of the Incarnate. Some allusion to the Divine-human dignity of Christ the Coming One is found in every prophetical book that bears on the subject. But, in searching for them—or rather in marking them, for they need no search—we must limit ourselves to those which refer solely to the Person of our Lord.

Isaiah is the Old-Testament expositor of the redeeming work of Christ. He was favoured also with a vision of His Person more glorious than any save that given to Daniel. In his sixth chapter he is prepared by a manifestation of the Three-One Jehovah in His temple: which, however, whether the prophet knew it or not, was, as St. John tells us (chap. xii. 41), the glory of Christ; the Jehovah of both Testaments in the unity of the Father and the Holy Ghost. Thus prepared, he announces in the next chapter the glorious truth of the coming incarnation: " Behold, a virgin shall conceive, and bear a Son, and shall call His name Immanuel" (Isaiah vii. 14): a prediction which takes the lead of all others in the New Testament, and is then heard no more. In chapter ix. 6, the Incarnate One is invested with His dignity and many names, every one of which carries with it a Divine-human dignity. " For unto us a Child is born, unto us a Son is given: and the government shall be upon His shoulder: and His name shall be called Wonderful, Counsellor, the Mighty God, the Everlasting Father, the Prince of Peace." The Child BORN in human nature is the Son of God GIVEN. His is that Wonderful or Secret name which was at an earlier time suppressed by the Divine Angel (Judges xiii. 18, *margin*, Wonderful). He is God supreme; yet a manifestation of the everlasting Father (" I and my

Father are one") and the Procurer, the Dispenser and the Lord of the great reconciliation. It is remarkable that the Septuagint, for some reason unknown, has interpolated a clause which connects this sublime description of the Messiah with the Angel of Jehovah, heading the name with μεγάλης βουλῆς Ἄγγελος, "the Angel of Mighty Counsel." With Isaiah, Micah is naturally connected. He also is a prophet of the Incarnation. "But thou, Bethlehem Ephratah, though thou be little among the thousands of Judah, yet out of thee shall He come forth unto me that is to be ruler in Israel; whose goings forth have been from of old, from everlasting.... And this *Man* shall be the Peace" (chap. v. 2, 5). The evangelical narrative claims this as a testimony to the descent of Jesus "of the seed of David" (John vii. 42; Matthew ii. 6), and subsequent teaching instructs us how to understand the everlasting goings forth of the Eternal Son.

The prophecies of Jeremiah range for the most part wide of the Messiah's kingdom. But they contain some most emphatic allusions to the redeeming work and the new covenant. And one passage is almost unequalled for the condensed fulness of its reference to the Person of Christ. "Behold, the days come, saith the Lord, that I will raise unto David a righteous Branch, and a king shall reign and prosper, and shall execute judgment and justice in the earth. In His days Judah shall be saved and Israel shall dwell safely: and this is His name whereby He shall be called, The Lord our Righteousness." Here is His human lineage, and He is raised up to David; His Divinity also, for He is JEHOVAH; and His atoning work is added to complete His name: the Jehovah who in the mystery of the Triune Redemption is the Author and Finisher of our justification. It is no disparagement to this glorious name that it is in chapter xxxiii. 16 given to Jerusalem: the name of Jesus our righteousness is called upon His saved people, who are "the righteousness of God in Him."

The pathetic close of the prophet Zechariah adds a striking contribution to the Old-Testament description. The "goodly price" at which the good Shepherd was estimated has its compensation in the high dignity put upon Him by His Father: put upon Him at the very time when He is represented as smitten: "Awake, O sword, against My Shepherd, and against the Man that is My Fellow, saith the Lord of Hosts: smite the Shepherd, and the sheep of the flock shall be scattered" (chap. xiii. 7). In what sense He is the Fellow of God appears from chapter xii. 9, 10: "And it shall come to pass in that day"—that day, which is the day of Christ—"I will pour upon the house of David, and upon the inhabitants of Jerusalem, the Spirit of grace and of supplications: and they shall look upon ME whom they have pierced." These prophecies were among the last in the Redeemer's thoughts before His death. And the wailing of those who pierced Jehovah Incarnate is heard again and again in the New Testament down to the book of Revelation, which leaves no doubt as to the smitten Christ being the Jehovah of the Old Testament. "Behold, He cometh with clouds; and every eye shall see Him, and they also which pierced Him" (Revelation i. 7).

Daniel, highly honoured of Christ in His quotation, whose predictions are more comprehensive and at the same time more minute than those of any other prophet, makes this solitary advance upon his predecessors, that he terms Messiah "The Son of Man," or rather "One like the Son of Man." Neither the expression "Son of God" nor "Son of Man," as such, had occurred before; nor is it possible now to trace the human origin of the term Daniel uses. Looking at the passage as isolated, or as connected with a subsequent passage, verse 27, where the same dominion is said to be given " to the people of the saints of the Most High," some have supposed " a Son of Man " to be a symbol of sanctified manhood generally. But the entire prophecy pays homage to a Person exalted to supreme authority who bears in His form all the signs of man. And the New Testament brings out into perfect day the "night visions" of Daniel: not only does our Lord select this denomination for Himself during His estate of humiliation, but both the Gospels and the Apocalypse expressly cite the prediction. In fact the final testimony of our Saviour before the bar of unjust judgment is a literal quotation from this passage, adapted to His purpose: " Hereafter shall ye see the Son of Man sitting on the right hand of power, and coming in the clouds of heaven" (Matthew xxvi. 64).

Malachi closes the prophetic testimony which Isaiah began. He looks forward into the same Holy Week which Isaiah and Daniel saw. But in his perspective there is not the Man of sorrows approaching His sacrificial death. Malachi's prophetic eye is fixed upon the temple of the Jewish economy, and He sees Jehovah, the Lord, suddenly "coming to His temple" (chap. iii. 1): coming however Himself in the Person of the Angel or Messenger of the Covenant. This designation of the future Messiah, " Jesus the Mediator of the New Covenant," is by no means a mere echo of " the Messenger " sent to prepare His way. It is a remembrancer of that ancient Angel who revealed Jehovah, and was Jehovah, to the Patriarchs, and it is at the same time a final interpretation of the term. The " Angel," that is, has no relation to essence or nature: it is the designation of His office as sent to the human race, " the Apostle and High Priest of our Profession " (Hebrews iii. 1). Hence it fitly closes the Old-Testament foreannouncement: the silence of ages reigns until the Messenger, travelling slowly in the greatness of His way, appears suddenly in our nature, and "the Father sent the Son to be the Saviour of the world" (1 John iv. 14).

Such is the broad outline of the form and fashion of "Him who was to come" as presented in the Scriptures which testified of Him. But that outline would not be complete without some further reference to the two estates of humble subordination and delegated authority which make up the history of the Mediator as sketched beforehand in the Old Testament, and have their final expression in the "Messenger" of Malachi.

The same Wonderful Being whose unity, or rather identity with Jehovah, and whose lower origin in the human race, are separately and together exhibited in the manner already described, is represented as occupying a place of subordination to God in the accomplishment of redemption. He is generally the Lord's Anointed, or the Messiah: but anointed in so peculiar and transcendent a sense as to leave His anointed types immeasurably below. In the fulfilment of His functions as the Christ He is exhibited as the Servant of God. This term was first used by the Prophet Isaiah; and with such precision of reference to the future Person of the Messiah that all attempts to give his words another reference are vain. "Behold My Servant, whom I uphold; Mine Elect, in whom My soul delighteth; I have put My Spirit upon Him: He shall bring forth judgment to the Gentiles" (Isaiah xlii. 1). This strikes the keynote of a long series of predictions concerning the Divine-human Minister of redemption who "came not to be ministered unto, but to minister, and to give His life a ransom for many" (Matthew xx. 28). "Behold, My Servant shall deal prudently, He shall be exalted and extolled, and be very high" (Isaiah lii. 13). This is the first of a long series of allusions to the ascended dignity of the Redeeming Person: a Servant still, but in humiliation no longer. These two combined, and collated with the Angel of Jehovah, the Angel of the Covenant, and the ministering Wisdom of the Proverbs, contain the Old-Testament foreannouncements of a truth concerning the Person of Christ which essentially belongs to the doctrine that as Incarnate " He emptied Himself and took upon Him the form of a servant " (Philippians ii. 7).

In the Book of Proverbs there is an altogether new presentation of this wonderful Person. The "Angel of mighty counsel," the "Word of the Lord" of Samuel's days, is the eternal Wisdom of God. In Proverbs viii. 22 seq., Wisdom is introduced as speaking in a personality distinct from God, and yet essentially God Himself. "The Lord possessed Me in the beginning of His way, before His works of old. I was set up from everlasting, from the beginning, or ever the earth was," " and My delights were with the sons of men," among whom " Wisdom hath builded her house." When we remember that the attributes of this Wisdom are described in almost the same terms used by Isaiah concerning the Servant of God ; that our Lord Himself appropriated this name of Wisdom (Luke vii. 35); that St. Paul terms Him "the Wisdom of God" (1 Corinthians i. 24); and that St. John makes the Word the medium or instrument of all those "works of old ; " there can be no doubt that here also we have an Old-Testament revelation of the Eternal Word or Wisdom who became among the sons of men a Son of man, and ministered to the accomplishment of the Divine designs and counsels in a sense in which Solomon with all his wisdom reached not to understand.

It remains to ask in conclusion what was, after all, the

amount of knowledge as to the future Incarnation, or the amount of preparation for knowledge, attained by the ancient Jewish church under the teaching of its Pentateuch, Hagiographa and Prophets. The answer to this question must be that to the possessors of the ancient oracles that union of the Divine and the Human which is the foundation and the glory of Christianity, was a mystery profoundly veiled from the mass of the people, dimly anticipated only by a chosen few, and clearly apprehended by none. For the evidence of this we may look at the internal character of the preintimations themselves, to the religious literature of the Judaism of the Interval, and to the testimony of the New Testament.

We must be cautious in speaking of the ancient law of the revelation of "the Spirit of Christ." But it may be said without hesitation that He did not will His foreannouncements of the Redeemer to carry to those who received them the irresistible conviction of a Future Saviour in whose one Person the Divine and human should be united. These foreannouncements were given at long intervals, generally veiled in most mysterious language, and so connected with a lower primary and obvious fulfilment as to satisfy the common mass of the students of prophecy with that first fulfilment. It is impossible to apply this statement in detail to the several leading predictions. But it will strike every reader that precisely those predictions which are now most luminous to us in their sole and supreme application were those which were most effectually hedged about with historical circumstances that concealed their eternal meaning even from those most interested and most prepared to meditate upon it. In fact, there are many references to the future Messiah which the New Testament claims for Him in which the readers of the Old could not have discerned His Person. For instance, Psalm cii. has no direct Messianic allusion; but the Epistle to the Hebrews (chap. i. 11) by a single flash, and the insertion of the word Lord, makes the everlasting Jehovah of that psalm our Lord Himself.

Finally, we may appeal to the evidence of the later Jewish church, the abundant theological writings of which decisively show that the incarnation of the Son of God was a mystery of godliness that had not entered into the imagination of their best and holiest writers. Neither the Palestinian nor the Alexandrian Jews anticipated this great truth of the Gospel. Not that they were blind to the evidences that some great mystery was in store. The apocryphal book of Wisdom carries the idea of a personification of Eternal Wisdom almost as far as the Proverbs carry it; but with some perversions which mar its meaning. Semi-philosophical speculations as to Adam Kadmon, or other intermediaries between God and the world, anticipated the Gnosticism and Arianism of later times. Philo's Logos, almost contemporary with the Word Himself, carried the human gloss in the Old-Testament revelation to its highest point. But that point is far as the poles are sundered from the Logos doctrine as given in the sublime correction of the Apostle John. We have not, however, in this Essay to do with extra-Biblical development.

The evidence of the New Testament is decisive on this point. Instead of a long series of proofs it may suffice to allude to the fact that the Christ, the Incarnate Christ, is termed by St. Paul the "mystery of God" (Colossians ii. 2), precisely as the universality of the Gospel, and the annihilation of the distinction between Jew and Gentile, is called "the mystery of the economy of the fulness of time" (Ephesians i. 9, 10). Concerning both the term mystery must retain its full meaning: a mystery is something that has been "kept hid;" not hidden merely because of its unfathomable character, but specially reserved for a future revelation. St. Paul says as it respects the two mysteries united that "in other ages" it "was not made known unto the sons of men" (Ephesians iii. 4, 5). And the "mystery of Christ" was not known. It was not the will of God that it should be known. It was the glorious secret, the Wonderful Name, that was, like the Triune Name itself, reserved for the revelation of Him who bore it. And to His revelation we now turn. [20.]

II.

It is customary to merge our Lord's witness to Himself in the testimony of the Gospel records: namely, that of the three Synoptists and that of St. John. But this is obviously wrong. Whatever differences exist between the accounts of the Three and the Fourth evangelist, they all four give the Lord's own words spoken during the same term of years, mainly to the same kind of audiences, and, as He Himself said, for an open testimony to His generation. We have a perfect right, we are under absolute obligation, to collect the sayings of our Lord Himself in the Gospels, in the Acts, and in the Apocalypse, as one body of simultaneous testimony on earth, with its Supplement from heaven.

Notwithstanding this, there is undoubtedly a certain justification of the distinction made between the Three Synoptists, whose records are framed on the basis of one synopsis or sketch of the Lord's history, and the fourth Gospel. In due time we must briefly consider this, as it is connected with the development of doctrine in the New Testament, and in the first instruction of the church. But assuredly the Lord's testimony to Himself must have precedence: not only because it is His own supreme testimony, but also because it was given before the Gospels were written.

Our Lord's testimony to Himself—that is, to His Divine-human Person—may be said to pervade His discourses. It will simplify the question if we first eliminate from it all those testimonies which only in an indirect manner affect His Person. For instance, we need not include His claims to be the Messiah or the Prophet preeminently, which, though involving His Divinity, do not expressly assert it; nor His assertions of His sinlessness, which, though ensured by His Divine nature, does not necessarily declare it; nor His constant assumption of an unlimited authority in the affairs of men, which, though based on His equality with God, does not strictly speaking proclaim it. All these are excluded, it must be remembered, not because they are essentially unconnected with His Incarnate dignity, but because they refer rather to His Work than His Person.

It is important to take notice of the variety of ways in which our Lord asserts the supreme dignity of His Person. First, we have His testimony on earth. There are those utterances, whether of discourse to man or of communion with God, in which He directly announces His relations to Divinity and humanity: giving so to speak His spontaneous witness to Himself. There are also those in which He evokes, receives, and seals with His approval the confessions of His disciples. Then there is a large portion of His testimonies delivered in conflict with the unbelief of the Jews; in these our Lord appeals to His works and to the testimonies of Scripture. Further, the confession which He Himself witnessed—to use St. Paul's words—before His judges, confirmed and perfected the testimony of His whole life. Secondly, to these we may add the manifestations of Himself from heaven after His ascension, especially that final Apocalypse which it was given to St. John to record.

The testimony on earth may be summed up in the Names which He assigns to His one indivisible Person: the Son of God, the Son of man, and the Son absolutely. Of these the first points rather to His eternal consubstantiality with the Father, the second to His realization and representation of pure humanity, while the third will be found on a careful consideration to combine the two former in the One Person common to both natures. We shall confine ourselves to these names, the study of which renders needless any further reference to the preceding classification. They include all the elements of the question, as it involves the Divine Personality of the Incarnate Son, His veritable Manhood, and the indivisible unity of His Person.

It is to be observed with regard to the title, Son of God, that our Lord did not usually appropriate it to Himself. He accepted it as the confession of His disciples and as the matter of charge brought against Him by His enemies; but He used either the term Son of Man, or Son absolutely, when speaking of His own Person, and very often expressed His supreme Sonship by referring to God absolutely as His Father. It may seem scarcely fitting to seek in the utterance of the Child Jesus the first illustration of our Lord's permanent practice. But, if we bear in mind the significance of the crisis which marked His transition from youth to maturity, we shall not hesitate to receive His solitary word in the temple as the first accents of His Filial relation: "Wist ye not that I must be in the house or business of My FATHER?" (Luke ii. 49). From that hour through all the histories down to the final words of the Apocalypse our Lord's most profound reference to the mystery of His Person was veiled under this Filial word: MY FATHER. But the Youth in the temple teaches us already that God was His Father in a preeminent and unparalleled sense. He was answering a question that referred to His father according to human repute; and, in the full and peculiar sense which the Jews long afterwards attached to His words, "said that God was His Father." The response to the Holy Child was given at His Baptism: "This is My beloved Son" (Matthew iii. 17).

There are two questions which here arise. Taking literally many of the expressions used by our Lord and His evangelists, we might suppose that the incarnation was the production of a new Man by the direct influence of the Divine Spirit, and that this offspring of a new order of paternity was therefore called the Son of God, and therefore called God peculiarly His Father. This has been the thought of very many at intervals from the beginning: it is now an opinion largely current. For its sufficient refutation we have only to show that, as the Son, the Saviour ascribes to Himself preexistence. Secondly, the preexistence being granted, it has occurred to many, influenced by a groundless jealousy for Monotheism, to assume that the Son was begotten of the Father before all worlds, but yet in time; and that, as St. Luke's genealogy says of Adam, "which was the son of God," so another leap would add for the other and Divine-Human Adam, completing on the Divine side what the genealogical table had begun at the human, and in the same sense, "which was the Son of God." As the effectual safeguard against this Arian sentiment the passages may be quoted in which our Lord expressly claims for His Sonship the Divine Glory of light, and life, and love, equality with the Father, and the honour that belongs to God alone. Only the leading proofs need to be given: around them many others will arrange themselves in the mind of every thoughtful reader.

It may be said with confidence that there is nothing in the New Testament, nothing in the Gospels, more plain and more variously revealed than the preexistence of Him whom we honour as our Redeemer. But we are limited to the preexistence as Son, and as testified by Christ Himself, whose testimonies on this subject pervade the Gospels. Three instances strike our attention at once. The first is that comprehensive epitome of His historical manifestation given to Nicodemus: "And no man hath ascended up to heaven, but He that came down from heaven, even the Son of man which is in heaven" (John iii. 13). He came from heaven; He is even in heaven; He ascended to heaven. This saying has but one interpretation. It contains our doctrine in its entireness; nor have we at least to cry, "We cannot tell what He saith." It has its strict parallel in the words to the disciples (John xvi. 28): "I came forth from the Father, and am come into the world: again, I leave the world, and go to the Father." The second is the word to the Jews in that most memorable of all His contests with them when He declared Himself to be the Light of the world, and extorted from them that almost judicial question, "Who art Thou?" Impressed as they had never been before by His appeals to the Father that sent Him, by His assertion of His sinlessness, and by His condemnation of them as the children of Satan, they took refuge in the reprisal of blasphemy and charged Him with having a devil. When He declared that faith in Himself would save from death, His enemies charged Him with raising Himself above the father of them all, Abraham. "Whom makest thou thyself?" was their half petulant, half awestruck question. Then came the greatest of all the Redeemer's testimonies: "Before

Abraham was, 1 AM!" (John viii. 58) in which His eternity is asserted in the loftiest language of Scripture. The third is in the High-priestly prayer, when He no longer speaks to His disciples or to His foes, but holds communion with the Father Himself: " Glorify Thou Me with the glory which I had with Thee before the world was " (John xvii. 3). As the Son, and approaching the cross, He refreshes His soul by the remembrance of the Divine glory which He had voluntarily surrendered, and claims its restoration as the reward of the Father's complacency in His sacrifice. Words could not more plainly express His preexistent Divine fellowship with the Father's eternal dignity.

That His preexistence was in the highest and only sense Divine, that as the Son He was consubstantial and coeternal with the Father, is placed beyond doubt by our Lord in a striking variety of ways.

First, He never fails to draw a broad and clear distinction between His own Filial relation and that of mankind generally, or that of His regenerate people in particular. This needs no special proof: it is a distinction inwrought into His language from the first " Our Father," which is the Lord's Prayer not as being used by Him but as given to us, down to the last, " I ascend to My Father, and your Father; and to My God, and your God." Though He also prayed and watched and submitted His will and made His Father's will His law in all things as our Pattern, He always distinguished His devotion and consecration and obedience from ours. This is rendered more remarkable by the fact that both He Himself and His apostles after Him lay so much stress on His perfect identification with the nature of man. " Both He that sanctifieth and they who are sanctified are all of one: for which cause He is not ashamed to call them brethren" (Hebrews ii. 11). But though He calls His disciples

"My brethren," He never joins them with Himself in "Our Father." This does not itself, and necessarily, declare His eternal consubstantiality with Him who is "His own Father;" but it sends us on the track of the reason and the proof, and prepares us for it when we find it.

Only on very few occasions did our Lord voluntarily assert His Divinity, even in the presence of His disciples. The reason lay in the subordination of His mediatorial commission. "Though He was rich, yet for our sakes He became poor:" poor in spirit and humble in language. But there were times when it became Him to assert His dignity, and He spake plainly both of the Father and of Himself: precisely as we find it in the apostolical epistles generally, where the uniform tenour of subordination is sometimes broken by the unusual declaration of the Lord's Divinity.

The solemn demand of His disciples' confession at Cæsarea Philippi, as recorded by St. Matthew (chap. xvi.), was one of these occasions. Before finally setting out on the way of His lowest humiliation our Lord received a glorious manifestation of His Father's eternal love on the mount; and this was preceded by a tribute of devotion, almost equally dear, from His disciples below. His testing question was· "Whom do men say I, the Son of Man, am?" that is to say, "What are the current opinions about Me, the Messiah?" This was asked in order to found upon it another: "But whom say *ye* that I am?" that is, "Whom say ye that I, the Son of Man, am?" A heavenly illumination fell upon Simon Peter as he answered, "Thou art the Christ, the Son of man; the Son of the living God!" the eternal Son of Him who is the eternally Living God! That Simon Peter, under that Divine revelation, did not simply reply that the Son of man was the Christ, is obvious from the tenour of the Lord's question, the peculiarity of His own answer, and the Saviour's gracious and very strong acknowledgment and benediction. But some light is thrown upon the scene by comparing it with another somewhat similar, where not the Lord's disciples but His foes were catechized. After a series of captious assaults, our Lord, on one occasion, took the aggressive, and said to the Jews who had been seeking to entangle Him, " What think ye of Christ? whose Son is He?" as if recalling the very words of Simon Peter. When they replied, as He knew they would reply, " The Son of David," He alluded to Psalm cx., and a question that had no meaning, and could not have produced the embarrassment it did produce, if it did not intimate a Sonship of Divine dignity which constituted David's Son, the Messiah, something essentially higher, even David's Lord and God. " If David then call Him Lord, how is He his Son?" (Matthew xxii. 41—46.)

Though Jesus did not count His Divinity the object of solicitous self-assertion, it is observable that He never refused the highest ascriptions from friend or foe. It is hard to say whether the demons are to be classed among the latter. Certainly their tributes to the Lord range over some of the most lofty titles He ever received. Now, though He sometimes repressed their tumultuous cries, and even forbade them to speak of Himself, He never rebuked either Satan or his agents for doing Him too much honour. The worship of His disciples He never declined: He never diverted their thoughts to God as the only object of reverence : " Worship God." He did not instruct them to distinguish between Divine homage and that which they might yield Him as the Messiah, the commissioned Agent of His Father's will. Before His ascension, and before He had said, " All power is given unto Me in heaven and in earth," He saw Thomas, the type of all devotion " made perfect through suffering," fall at His feet, and heard him cry, "My Lord and my God!" without any sign of disapproval. He did indeed pronounce His prospective benediction—the last of His benedictions—on those who see not and yet believe; but He did not refuse to allow His servant to go on from the customary "Lord" to the "God" which supplements and consummates all devotion to Himself.

This leads, however, to a necessary consideration of those many passages in which the Redeemer asserts His equality and consubstantiality with the Father. These are to be sought first in His colloquies with the Jews, and secondly in His final discourses to His disciples. In each case there will be found some seeming qualification or deduction from the strength of the testimony, which is such, however, only in appearance.

Already reference has been made to that wonderful self-revelation in which Jesus declares at once His preexistence and His eternity: "Before Abraham was, I am." But there is an earlier testimony in the fifth chapter of St. John's Gospel, which, thoroughly pondered, yields the same weight of meaning. The Jews rightly interpreted His words "My Father worketh hitherto, and I work," as saying that "God was His Father, making Himself equal with God." The Lord's discourse on that occasion does not begin by disclaiming that equality, or the assertion of it. On the contrary, while stating at large in what sense His work of judgment was committed to Him "because He is the Son of man," He declares in one of the very few passages in which He calls Himself "the Son of God," that "as the Father hath life in Himself; so hath He given to the Son to have life in Himself," to that Son of God, namely, whose voice the dead hear and live. "Life in Himself" is the supreme definition of the Divine self-existence: and the Son in His eternal generation hath "life in Himself," "that all men should honour the Son, even as they honour the Father."

A subsequent controversy carries this evidence, if possible, further. When, in John x., the Jews demanded assurance concerning His Messiahship, our Lord went beyond their demand, and declared, "I and My Father are One:" not one in purpose, not one in Person, but one in a mysterious unity that the language is expressly chosen to assert. This declaration they accounted blasphemy; and the charge is answered in two ways. First, in the spirit of accommodation our Lord pleads that they had no right to refuse Him, "sanctified and sent into the world," the title of God, which had been given to some to whom only "the word of God came." Secondly, He goes on to make that great declaration, which, once made, often recurs, "that ye may know and believe that the Father is in Me, and I in Him." Were it only "the Father is in Me" we might hesitate to give these words the full weight we assign to them; but when it is added "and I in Him," and when it is remembered that they follow "I and the Father are One," testimony can go no farther.

The words spoken to the Jews are amplified in the farewell discourses to the apostles. They assert throughout such an intercommunion and oneness between the Father and the Son as transcends any possibilities of creature relationship. There are two ways in which this is expressed. "He that hath seen Me hath seen the Father," "Believest thou not that I am in the Father and the Father in Me?" (John xiv. 9, 10.) Let this be compared with the many passages in which the seeing of the Father Himself is denied to every creature; especially with John vi. 46: "Not that any man hath seen the Father, save He which is of God, He hath seen the Father." Then the eternal Son is the intermediary between the Invisible God and His worshippers. He seeth the Father eternally; and all who see Him by faith see in Him the Father. Further, the inhabitation of the Father is the inhabitation of the Son: "We will come unto him, and make Our abode with him" (John xiv. 23). That this unity of the Father and the Son involves the unity also of the Holy Ghost appears throughout these discourses, as also in the first epistle of St. John, and in all the passages which speak of the indwelling Spirit. But we have now only to do with the Saviour's testimony to the fundamental truth of revelation, that the Only-begotten Son in the bosom of the Father is in every attribute and glory of Divinity for ever one with the Father. This is the Saviour's witness to His Divine nature as the SON OF GOD. [21.]

None among the many names of our Lord is more precious and at the same time more sacred to the Christian than that of "the Son of Man." It was the name by which He elected to speak of Himself, and which His Spirit suffered no other to use with reference to His Person, at least as an ordinary appellation. Both the use by Himself, and the absence of the use by His apostles, suggest a peculiarity which invites speculation. But, before we inquire into this, or rather instead of inquiring where there is really no help to our inquiry, let us consider what the name itself imparted. It was first the Messianic name of the Redeemer, and secondly it declared in the most absolute manner His essential Manhood.

We have seen that Daniel the prophet gave this word from the Old Testament to the New. He used it of the same future Governor of the people and of the nations who as the Messiah was cut off for sin. The title "Son of Man" was in Daniel a new name revealed by the Spirit of Christ in the prophets; and it was given as it were for the Redeemer's future use: coordinate with Messiah, but distinguished from it nevertheless. Into the later perversions of the word, as first used by Daniel, it is needless to enter. Suffice that, though not current among the Jews as the name of their Messiah, it was understood by them when the Lord used it. "We have heard out of the law that Christ abideth for ever: and how sayest Thou, The Son of man must be lifted up? who is this Son of man?" (John xii. 34.) We may ask why our Lord left in comparative neglect the ancient and popular term, which has been for ever sanctified afresh in Christianity and in the name of Christians, and adhered almost exclusively to the term "Son of man." Nor is the answer far to seek. The term Messiah, even when taken out of the Hebrew into the more universal Greek, nevertheless had a limited significance: at least in the case of those who surrounded our Lord. But the "Lamb of God was to take away the sins of the world." Hence the preference of the term which implied an unlimited relation to mankind. Save in quotation from Scripture, and in argument with the Jews, Jesus never assumed the title Christ. On one ever-memorable occasion, indeed, He called Himself Jesus Christ: when He finally turned away from man and addressed His Father in the High-priestly prayer, He set the seal of His last distinction on the sacred word, and sanctified it anew for ever: "Jesus Christ, whom Thou hast sent" (John xvii. 3). Generally, not in the Synoptists only but in St. John also, His name for Himself as the Christ was the "Son of Man." He used it in all His relations, and in all His discourses down to the last. And thus He declared that the Christ belonged to the whole family of man, and that all His functions and offices were for the race. [22.]

This leads to the significance of the term as belonging more particularly to the Person of Christ, and therefore to our present subject. He was the Son of man among men, as He was the Son of God in the Holy Trinity. Not the Son of a man, but the Son of mankind: the ideal, the realized, the new, the representative, the perfect, Man. His relation to human nature is universal; as universal as that of Adam, and in some respects more so. Though no writer in the New Testament uses the term in the treatment of the Messianic work, the idea involved in it is common to them all. St. Paul never uses it, but he speaks of the "last Adam." Whenever we read that the Son of God was made flesh, or partaker of flesh and blood, we have the apostolical version of the name that the Saviour reserved for Himself.

When our Lord did not call Himself "the Son of man," His ordinary substitute was "the Son" absolutely. It is a bold affirmation, but one that may be substantiated, that this word on His lips was not used of His Divine Sonship alone, not of His human Sonship, but of the One Person who bore both Sonships in Himself. Not that we can accurately distinguish the occasion of His use of this and the other terms: the attempt would show that the discovery of any peculiar law is impossible. It may be said, however, that our Lord never called Himself the Son without some more or less direct reference to His incarnation, as super-adding a new nature to His original essence in the bosom of the Father. The word assigns His personality to His Divine Sonship, but always as a personality revealed in human relations. "Neither knoweth any man the Father, save the Son, and he to whomsoever the Son will reveal Him" (Matthew xi. 27): the eternal personality and the twofold nature are both here. So throughout down to the baptismal formula: baptism is into the "Son," not only as the Eternal Son, but as revealed in the "name of Jesus," which therefore in the Acts is sometimes the compendium of that formula.

Here then we may consider the Saviour's testimony to Himself as One undivided and indivisible Person. And this assumes three aspects. We may view it as a personality which knows no distinction of the two natures; as a personality which is nevertheless always Divine in its origin and ground; and, lastly, as a personality which is throughout subordinated to the Father in the work of redemption.

To establish the first would be to quote the entire series of the passages in which the Lord speaks of Himself. The evidence is first a negative one. He never distinguishes between a higher and lower I or Me. On the supposition that He lived a lower life consciously separate from, however dependent upon, the higher, there were many occasions on which this fact would have been betrayed in His words. But there is no necessity for dwelling on an absence which no one dares to contradict. It is also positive. Our Lord does, like His apostles after Him, distinguish between His two natures, though never in such express terms as they were instructed to adopt. In His heavenly decorum He leaves the plain statement to His evangelists and apostles. But He adopted the language of a sole and supreme personality of which attributes may be used taken from either nature interchangeably. The proofs cannot be given in full: they can be only indicated. They are to be found in such passages as imply the consciousness of Divinity and Manhood coexisting in Himself, the attributes of both being indiscriminately His own. For instance, He terms Himself the Son of man when speaking to Nicodemus, and shows the verity of His human nature by reckoning Himself among the teachers in Israel, speaking "what we know;" while at the same time that Son of man "came down from heaven" and "is in heaven." His Person is Divine-human; but His personality, as that of one unchanging agent, is Divine. This is one of many passages of which it is both the example and the key. Similarly to the little company of His disciples, and to Simon their spokesman : " Whom do men say that I, the Son of man, am?" The I is the Divine personality in the Person of Him who is the Son of Man, and something beyond, even what Simon Peter avows, " The Son of the living God;" and this complementary truth of His being He expressly declared to have been revealed to the apostle, not by flesh and blood, but by the Father. It is obvious that the entire strain of the language must have been modified if two distinct beings or personalities addressed the apostles that day. This is a second standard and exemplary text. A third is that of the final prayer : "Glorify thou Me"—the Me of the marred and crucified Form—" with the glory which I had with Thee before the world was." Not " glorify My human nature," but " glorify Thou ME " (John xvii. 5).

But the origin and ground of this twofold personality is in our Lord's testimony Divine. He speaks not of having assumed a new personality which is human, but as continuing in time and in the world a personality which was with the Father from eternity. In all His words His eternal I has the preeminence. He never once alludes to a human personality : on the contrary, He takes every opportunity to speak in such a manner as to shut out its possibility. It may be said that the habitual use of the term " Son of man " implies the consciousness of a human origin. But it is not so. At the very outset, when He began to use the term, He foreclosed for ever such a thought, by declaring that the Son of man, speaking to Nicodemus, is while He speaks " in heaven," whence He " came down." Such language is inconceivable on any Unitarian or Arian hypothesis. On the former it were impossible that a man could be on earth and in heaven at once, save in the mystical sense which the express words concerning the ascension to a local heaven forbids. Similarly no created Son of God sent down into the world could remain in heaven while on His mission below. There is another passage which closely approaches the very expression of the truth here insisted on. It is that, already alluded to, in which the Saviour claims honour equal with that paid to the Father: because as the Son it was given to Him to have "life in Himself," and therefore the unqualified power to quicken dead souls and bestow, what God alone bestows, life upon whom He would. It was then added that all judgment was put into His hands—that is, the administration of the mediatorial kingdom,—" because He is the Son of man." (John v. 26, 27.) When our Lord declares "Ye know not whence I am, but I know whence I am," He uses words that can have no other meaning than that no mortal but Himself knows the mystery of His eternal personality. That personality was not interrupted, changed, suspended, or lowered by His incarnation. "I came forth from the Father, and am come into the world: again, I leave the world, and go to the Father" (John xvi. 28).

The last, the most difficult, and theologically the most important, element of our Lord's testimony, and that which gave the law to all His apostles, is the subordination which He, though One with the Father in essence, always assumes and declares. Subordination in relation to the Redeemer is a word that has two theological applications: the one, Divine, is the ground of the other, Mediatorial.

There is a subordination—the word being most carefully reduced to its true meaning—which is sometimes predicated of the Son's eternal relation. "For as the Father hath life in Himself, so hath He given to the Son to have life in Himself." This subordination involves no inferiority of essence, no beginning of being: hence it is a term which, required by the mission of the Son, as similarly of the Spirit, belongs to that "mystery of the Father and of Christ" which passeth knowledge. It is not a Scriptural term; and the Scripture is not responsible for either the use or the perversion of it. But it suggests rather than utters an eternal truth on which the redemptional mission of the Son is based.

The distinction which we are obliged to make between the eternal generation of the Son given "to have life in Himself," and the descent of His mediatorial person below the Father, is not made by our Lord. He does not explain or even allude to, the mysterious exinanition by which He "made Himself of no reputation." But this must be always and carefully borne in mind, that He never allows us to suppose that it was other than a voluntary abnegation of what He might have retained. In this His servants, and especially St. Paul, are careful to observe and reproduce His spirit. They never speak of His original humiliation save as voluntary: He "became poor," "made Himself of no reputation." Our Lord submitted to what fell upon Him after His incarnation, and bore His preparatory cross through life unto the cross of redemption. But the primary act of condescension is not called by Him, nor by the apostles, a humiliation. It was the voluntary descent into the relation of subordination which the assumption of our nature rendered possible and necessary, but does not explain.

Remembering that it is a voluntary subjection, and bearing in mind the many passages in which our Lord reserves, as we have seen, His equality with the Father, we may boldly assert that the current of His testimonies to Himself bears the stamp of a personal subordination to God His Father and ours: that is, of His condescension to a position in which the Divine limits itself to a human manifestation and utterance. Only the restraint of space prevents the collocation of Scriptural texts that support the following exhibition of this truth: that is, of the mediatorial submission of Him who, conscious of Divinity, makes His human nature the organ and generally the measure of its manifestation.

It is shown in all such passages, for instance, as mark the Saviour's abstinence from the high title which others gave Him, which He demanded of His friends, extorted from His enemies, and did not refuse when offered Him by independent witnesses. It cannot but strike the reader of the Gospels that our Lord Himself is an exception to a general rule. Whilst the Father calls Him His beloved Son absolutely, whilst His disciples honour Him as the Son of the Living God, whilst the demons give him the same title, whilst, in short, heaven and earth and voices from below proclaim Him the Son of God in the highest sense, He Himself is content with one only name, the Son of Man. Occasionally, indeed, He terms Himself the Son of God, and the Son; but the rule of His subordination limits Him when speaking of His Person to the humbler title.

Again, He represents Himself sometimes, and in a very direct manner, as in a certain sense inferior to the Father. Now every such passage must be read in harmony with those which declare Him to be God, and with His own sayings concerning His oneness in essence and dignity with the Father. Thus read, they are to be explained only by reference to that voluntary, mysterious, and incomprehensible subordination in which He speaks through His human nature. Of these passages we may select a few, which have always been the stumblingblock of the doubting spirit, but the test of loyal faith.

The first is that in which our Lord seems to repudiate the

ascription of that absolute goodness which belongs only to God. "Why callest thou Me good? there is none good but one, that is God" (Matthew xix. 17). Another reading is, "Why speakest thou concerning the good? none is good, save one, that is God." This, however, does not affect the question before us; especially as the other evangelists have "Why callest thou Me good?" Here it is obvious that the Saviour accommodates Himself to the sentiment and feeling of the young man; and, in fact, condemns him for giving the title of "good" to one whom he did not know to be God. Jesus does not assert that He Himself was not good, and therefore not God: on the contrary, His assertion of His sinlessness is constant, and therefore the present affirmation tacitly implies His Divinity. Still, this passage is one of many in which the Teacher of mankind speaks concerning God as of a Being separate from Himself, and therefore it belongs to the sayings of His subordination: spoken not as man simply—for He never spoke from a merely human personality—but as the Divine-human "Apostle" (Hebrews iii. 1) of the will of God, who condescends to reveal the things of God as a human Prophet sent of God. Many of His discourses are so constructed that they might have been delivered by a Divinely instructed human Teacher.

The next is that "hard saying" of St. Mark (xiii. 32), "Neither the Son." Of an absolute ignorance on the part of the Eternal Son, who knoweth the Father as the Father knoweth Himself, "in whom are hid all the treasures of wisdom and knowledge" (Colossians ii. 3), this saying cannot speak. On the other hand, it is not a sound interpretation to say barely that in His human nature He was ignorant, however true that in itself may be; for in His own personality there is no limitation which is not voluntarily submitted to by "the Son." He was ignorant, because

His mediatorial work required Him to be the "Servant of God;" and during His voluntary self-abasement there was a certain incomprehensible sense in which even He on one subject speaks as a Servant, who "knoweth not what His Lord doeth." He condescended to have His sacrificial career opened before Him by the Father; to enter His hour when He "knew that it was come;" and to "wait" for the end until all enemies were subjected to Him. He speaks in His Divine-human subordination: "Neither the Son."

Another testing word is that of St. John (chap. xiv. 28) in which the Saviour gives a plain declaration of the truth which the previous testimonies gave in a veiled form: "My Father is greater than I." Not that the Father is greater than the Only-begotten—"I and the Father are One"—but that "the Father is greater than I," than the I of the mediatorial and subordinate Person. With this may be compared those passages in which the Redeemer calls His Father His God: the rarity of these appeals and their deep solemnity bespeak their peculiar character. Once, on the cross, He cried: "My God! My God!" where the mediatorial subordination reached its lowest point. Once, after the resurrection, "I ascend to My God, and your God," where, however, the distinction between Himself and His disciples in relation to God is maintained. And, after the ascension, He still retains the subordination, though in the glory of heaven, and promises "I will write upon him the name of My God" (Revelation iii. 12).

Finally, the Lord's own Prayer addresses the "only true God, and Jesus Christ whom Thou hast sent" (John xvii. 3). Remembering all that has gone before, and all that follows, we hear in these words a testimony that the Son had revealed the only God, even the Divine Trinity, and Himself the Christ through whom alone that God is known.

The subordination of our Lord's Person is further exhibited in the long series of passages, found chiefly though not only in St. John, which declare Him to be sent under a commission from the Father, the duties and obligations and rewards of which He is gradually taught. These do not admit of quotation or analysis: they are the staple of doctrine concerning Himself. It is as if the Lord speaks the secret of a new consciousness, not Divine, not human, but Divine-human: the consciousness of a new Self which is not another, but simply the mystery of the mediatorial Will apprehended humanly by a Divine Person. The mystery: for we cannot fathom what nevertheless we must accept. Jesus in the temple in His twelfth year began to utter it: "I must be about My Father's business" (Luke ii. 49): in My Father's School and in My Father's Work. The same Eternal Son, who, ever "in the bosom of the Father," hath "declared Him" (John i. 18), is gradually taught the whole substance of His commission, or the commandment He received. What the Holy Child said is confirmed by the Man: "My meat is to do the will of Him that sent Me, and to finish His work" (John iv. 34). And it is sealed at the foot of the cross: "I have finished the work which Thou gavest Me to do" (John xvii. 4).

Once more, that subordination for the redemption of man is proclaimed throughout the whole course of the mediatorial discipline to which, "though a Son," He is subjected in His humbled estate. He who might have acted as the Son in His independent supremacy over His human nature yields Himself to the Spirit, through whom His manhood is replenished with infinite and all-sufficient graces; He is led to be tempted, and undergoes the assault of Satan in every faculty of His humanity; He fortifies His soul with prayer and meditation; He submits to the suffering of death, and all that led to death; and for us men, that He might bring us to God, suffered the awful desolation of the Divine abandonment. In all this, however, we have still the voluntary submission of One who has a mediatorial commandment unshared by man, holds communion with God into which none are admitted with Him, and undergoes His passion with the perfect Divine consciousness that He came to His hour that He might be saved in it, and in it save us also.

Lastly, this mysterious truth is exhibited in the affecting series of declarations which dwell rather on the human side of His mediatorial relationship than on the Divine. To illustrate the meaning of this, let us consider some classes of His sayings in their difference. There are some few, very few, in which He seems to look down upon men as from an infinite elevation: speaking of them and to them as their God. "He that hath seen Me hath seen the Father." "There am I in the midst." "Neither knoweth any man the Father, save the Son, and he to whomsoever the Son will reveal Him." "If ye being evil." "I am from above." There are some again in which He seems to pay an equal tribute to the two sides of His mediatorial relation. "I ascend unto My Father, and your Father; and to My God, and your God." "I in them, and Thou in Me." But there are many more which seem almost to forget, or hold in abeyance, the Divine side of His mediatorial being, and cling with tender singleness of purpose and tenacity to the human side. These need not be quoted: they take a great variety of forms. He is the Vine of the new humanity; the elder Brother of His brethren; and as such identifies Himself with us in all things. But here, also, as in every other illustration we have given, the truth is protected from perversion. His union with His people is declared to be the indwelling of Himself and the Father through the Holy Spirit.

It has been again and again observed that the Saviour never explains the mystery of this subordination, which is not that of the Son absolutely, nor that of the human nature, but of the Incarnate Person. Suffice that He prevents misunderstanding by many indisputable declarations of His existence as God unaffected by the possibility of change. In His incarnation and on His way to the cross, in His ascension and in His waiting for the end, He condescends to make His human nature the organ of His revelation; and in His Divine-human Person the human, raised to a perfection which only union with the Divinity could explain, gives the law to His utterances. But it must be once more declared—it cannot be too constantly enforced—that every single exhibition of His mediatorial submission is connected, to the eye and ear of disciplined faith, with such reservations and saving clauses as show that there is a voluntary surrender of the use and manifestation of Divine attributes. He prays; but does not kneel with His disciples, who stand apart. He delivers the doctrine which is not His, "but the Father's who sent Him," yet "all things that the Father doeth the Son doeth also." We cannot explain the Exinanition of the Mediator, nor the "new name" (Revelation ii. 17) which it gives Him. It will hereafter be seen that Historical Theology has made the attempt; but in vain. We are limited to our Lord's testimony in Scripture; and He teaches us that until God is "all in all" the Mediator is the revelation of God IN MAN.

Before leaving the Saviour's testimony to Himself we must ascend with Him into the place "where He was before" and hear Him speak "from heaven." As we have only to do with His Person, and not with His work, there is little to be added here; but that little is of supreme importance. The heavenly testimony is confined to the Acts and the Apocalypse. In the former, the mediatorial subordination is still prominent, though not to the exclusion of His Divine dignity; in the latter, while that subordination still remains, of necessity, it is so blended with the absolute Godhead of the Redeemer as to set the final seal of Scripture on the two fundamental truths of the Saviour's Person: His eternal oneness and consubstantiality with the Father, and His everlasting subordination as the Divine-human Head of mankind.

The unseen Redeemer, exalted to the throne of universal dominion, sends down His Holy Spirit to be the Paraclete in the church as He Himself is the Paraclete within the veil. He does not reveal Himself directly; and His testimonies therefore are few. But the occasions of His manifestation are full of instruction as to His Person. Before the Pentecost He proves Himself to be the hearer of prayer, when the waiting company left to Him, as "knowing the hearts of all men," the choice of the successor of Judas. The words of Simon Peter sprang fresh from his remembrance of the scene in which his own heart had been searched, and he evidently ascribed to the Lord a Divine knowledge of the human spirit. It is scarcely possible to doubt that the intercourse of the disciples with Christ had taught them to regard Him as One who read their souls as God only could read them. In fact, we have evidences throughout the gospels of the impression produced by this manifestation of knowledge. From the effect of it on Nathanael through a series of illustrations down to Thomas and Peter—a series which literally begins and ends the evangelical narrative—we see that Christ thus impressed His Divinity on those with whom He had to do. Between the Ascension and Pentecost the prayer of the Church finally expresses this faith; and our

Lord's answer is His own testimony to His Divine knowledge. The same may be said of the prayer of Stephen, who saw the Son of Man standing before him in the opened heavens, and called upon Him and cried, " Lord Jesus, receive my spirit." Stephen in his death gave stronger evidence to the glory of Jesus than even in his life; and, when at such a time such a prayer was permitted to him, we find in this abundant evidence of the Deity of our Lord. But generally the testimony in the Acts is that of the Mediator in the exercise of His authority; and, allowance being made for the difference between the humbled estate of our Lord on the sorrowful side of His cross and His glorified estate when His sorrows were over, the Jesus of the Acts is the " same Jesus " who ever speaks of His Father as the Fountain of the authority which He Himself exercises. While believers are " baptized in the name of the Lord Jesus " (Acts viii. 16)—Jesus Jehovah-Adonai, LORD in the highest sense and Lord in the lower—and men " call on His name " (Acts ix. 14), He is " Lord of all " (Acts x. 36), as exalted to the mediatorial jurisdiction of the universe. But here we are forsaking our subject: the Lord's testimony to Himself.

We return to it in the Apocalypse, the preface of which, though a vision of St. John, is really a manifestation of Christ; and, in fact, His final testimony to His own Person before the glorious unveiling of it at the end of the days. The " Revelation of Jesus Christ " is not only the disclosure of the future of His kingdom which " God gave Him " in His mediatorial relation, but the revelation of Himself: the perfect and final unveiling of His Person. The mystery of Christ theologically made manifest in the epistles of St. Paul and in St. John's other writings is here sealed by an appearance of the Lord which excels every other in glory: in which He assumes the incommunicable attributes of the Godhead, but in the form of one like unto "the Son of man," and asserts His supremacy in the church and over the world as the Incarnate glorified Son of God. He whom John beheld, before whose majesty he fell as dead, reveals Himself as "Alpha and Omega, the Beginning and the Ending, saith the Lord, which is, and which was, and which is to come, the Almighty" (Revelation i. 8). In this last exhibition of Himself to His most favoured disciple, and through him to His church, the last vestige of the veil is gone: Ecce Homo! becomes Ecce Deus! "Behold the Man!" is one with "Behold the God!" "I am He that liveth, and was dead; and, behold, I am alive for evermore" (chap. i. 8—18): the God of eternal life, the Mediator who died and liveth to be the Lord of the dead and living. No artifice of exposition can avail to invalidate the force of this final testimony of Jesus. In it the Sun "shineth in its strength." The glory of God is "given to another" unless Christ is God Himself, and not another, the Eternal and the Almighty. Hence His servant John bare record of the Logos of God, and of the testimony of Jesus as the WORD of God, and then of all things that he saw (chap. i. 2).

Like the Prologue of the gospel, this introductory manifestation must govern and explain all that follows: the other sayings of Christ concerning Himself must be interpreted in the light of this introductory testimony. After uttering it as the sublime protection of His own glory He afterwards throughout the visions descends, if it be a descent, to His mediatorial subjection. He speaks to the church of Philadelphia of the temple and the name and the city of "His God" (Revelation iii. 12), where we have the third and last instance of His mediatorial acknowledgment of God as His God: His God as His eternal Father, His God as He is God-man. He applies to Himself many titles, new and old, which hover around His " new name." For instance, He is "the Amen, the Faithful and True Witness, the Beginning of the creation of God" (chap. iii. 14): words which St. Paul has taught us how to understand as making the Eternal Son the author of the creation, "begotten before every creature," " by whom all things consist," who is the medium of the revelation of God through the creature and in the creature. He is the Lamb, who is " Lord of lords and King of kings ;" and with God the light of the eternal temple, and the temple itself (chap. xxi. 23). But, when the end approaches, and the last accents of prophetic revelation fall from His lips, He reverts to the first and the Divine self-assertion. The angel, the angel of Christ, shrinks from John's adoration as one of the servants of Jesus; and the Lord Himself afterwards proclaims, without angel mediation, His own essential glory. " It is done. I am Alpha and Omega, the Beginning and the End" (chap. xxi. 6). Again the angel ministry is used; and for the same reason again withdrawn. For the last time the Redeemer speaks : " I am Alpha and Omega, the Beginning and the End, the First and the Last " (chap. xxii. 13). And that testimony to His supreme Divinity the Redeemer leaves lingering in the ears, and in the hearts, and in the minds of His people for ever.

Two observations may be made, or rather repeated, in conclusion. First, our Lord's testimony to Himself is always under a reserve while He speaks upon earth, being left to the fuller glorification of the Holy Ghost. And, secondly, all the germs of subsequent development on the subject are to be found in His own words. They are in error who make the utterances of the Word, spoken before the cross from behind a veil, the rigid standard by which the later sayings of Scripture are to be interpreted. " Ye cannot bear them now," He said with regard to the mysteries of

His Person; and promised that after His departure His disciples should understand how He was in the Father and the Father in Him. Hence they who record the Lord's words, and expand them according to the teaching of the Spirit, in some points surpass their Master Himself; as they did "greater works," so they spoke "greater words." This may be said of St. John and St. Paul especially; but is true of all. On the other hand, the Saviour's own testimony must needs govern all other. Whatever we shall hear spoken of His Divinity finds its original type in His own doctrine; and also whatever we shall hear spoken of the verity of His human nature. And the subordination of His Divine-human Person as the Son—of God or Man, of God and man—is strictly and perfectly the same in the Saviour's own words, and in those of His apostles. With these preliminary reflections we may turn to the testimonies of the witnesses of the Faithful Witness.

III.

The testimony of the Evangelists takes precedence in the third branch of the subject: not only because they contain the earliest authoritative history of our Lord's life given to the church, but because they are the Holy Spirit's explanation of that history furnished as the basis for all subequent theology, whether inspired or uninspired. But the method we have adopted renders it needless to examine them at length, or to observe the current distinction between the Synoptists and St. John. We have only to regard them in the residuum after the Saviour's own testimony is extracted. And of that residue we omit St. John's, which must be reserved for the crown of the apostolical testimony. There remain the three Synoptists; and it will be enough to make a few remarks on their real agreement with St. John, and on their distinct historical contributions to the doctrine of our Lord's incarnate Person.

Beginning with the latter, it is to be noted that the one peculiar element of the Christology of the Three Synoptists is that of the Conception of the human nature of our Lord, recorded in St. Matthew and St. Luke. These two alone in the New Testament narrate historically the mystery of the Incarnation: the former as the evangelist of Judaism and the Old Testament; the latter as the evangelist of the world and the New Dispensation. Nor is there any portion of the gospels better authenticated externally and internally than this.

St. Matthew's first chapter gives, as it were in epitome, the development of our doctrine. First, there is the genealogical derivation of our Lord according to the flesh, so presented as to be a basis for subsequent teaching and a key to much subsequent Scripture. In the gospels the emphasis is laid on the Messianic dignity of "the Son of David;" in the epistles He is the "Seed of Abraham;" and both are set before us in the first sentence of the New Testament, which thus connects itself directly with the Old. Then follows, with unconscious art, the clear and indubitable account of our Lord's Divine nature: the Descendant of David and Abraham comes from them only through the line of His mother, and the fruit of the Virgin is "of the Holy Ghost." Yet not as if this were all. A new member of the human race, introduced after a miraculous manner, might have been only a Second Adam into whom, not formed of dust but in the Virgin's womb, the Spirit breathed the breath of life. But the Son of God unites Himself with this new Man before any distinct personality could be predicated of it; and His name is Emmanuel, God with us: it remains for the sequel to show that this name was not merely symbolical, but the very expression of the Lord's mediatorial relation, which is the third element in our Christology. As the Seed of Abraham, and also the Son of God, His name, Two-One, is Jesus. Thirty years afterwards, when the first of the several stages of our Lord towards perfection, viz., the perfection of His mature humanity, was reached, the Voice from heaven added the Name that had been wanting: This is My Beloved Son!

St. Luke's account of the incarnation is in many respects the counterpart of St. Matthew's. It also begins where the Old Testament begins, with the "Seed of the Woman;" and traces the human descent of our Lord up to Adam, "the Son of God." It also shows that the wonderful Offspring of Mary was the "Son of God" in a higher sense: to wit, that the holy thing conceived in her should bear that name as being a new representative of mankind among whom appears the Son of God, "the fulness of the Godhead bodily." What was not fully revealed to the Virgin in St. Luke, nor to Joseph in St. Matthew, St. Paul was afterwards commissioned to declare, that "God sent forth His Son, made of a woman:" not therefore His Son, so called because His human nature was conceived by the Holy Ghost in the Virgin, but His Son Eternal, who took to Himself, being sent from heaven, this new thing prepared for Him, this Body of flesh, to inform it and make it His own for ever.

St. Mark goes not up to the beginning of Christ, but chronicles rather "the beginning of the Gospel." St. John, writing long afterwards and to the church which already possessed, as he himself possessed, the earlier evangelists, takes as his starting-point a third beginning, which is no beginning, but the eternal Origin of "God Only-begotten," "the Same yesterday, to-day, and for ever," in the bosom of the Father.

In many respects the Synoptists and St. John differ: presenting diverse but consistent aspects of the Saviour's preparatory ministry upon earth. As to His one Incarnate Person also they more or less vary; but not nearly so much as it is the habit of some divines to assert. It is not true that the Three exhibit the Man, and St. John the God: nothing can be more plain to the reader than that the most minute and affecting instances of our Saviour's Manhood are in St. John; as also that his three predecessors exhibit the Divinity of the Son, though not as yet in fully announced and perfect formula. St. John, writing the Gospel supplement, leaves not the faintest shadow of doubt over the supreme Deity of the Son; whilst the Synoptists, though their words are not so express, declare the same truth by the record of the Saviour's deeds generally, and on a few occasions by words which seem various readings or slightly modified echoes of St. John's highest teaching. The close of St. Matthew's eleventh chapter is unsurpassed as a Synoptical exhibition of the Eternal unity of the Father and the Son, combined with the delegated authority of the Son Incarnate:—this, however, has been already considered, as part of our Lord's own testimony. Without referring to the many passages which prove our assertion, we may say that in all respects, so far as the essentials and salient points of the Lord's Person and work are concerned, there is perfect unity between the Four. Let us mark this with regard to the beginning, middle, and end of the Redeeming ministry. St. John's Prologue announces that Jesus is the Only-begotten Son of God, Himself God Only-begotten. The Synoptists record the same truth only less clearly in the history of the incarnation; St. John exhibits throughout the course of our Lord's ministry a Son who, though a Son, learns obedience and executes His Father's will. The

Synoptists set forth the same truth, in an unlimited variety of terms, of which one word will be a hint and remembrancer: "They will reverence My Son." And at the close, St. John is scarcely more emphatic than the Synoptists in depicting the Saviour's perfect consciousness of "the end" to which all things "concerning Him" converged, and of the certain issue of the passion that awaited Him in resurrection, dominion, and glory.

The apostolic testimony proper comes last, as being the complete exhibition through the Holy Ghost of the mystery—revealed and yet unrevealed—of the Person of Christ. "He shall glorify Me: for He shall receive of Mine, and shall show it unto you" (John xvi. 14). Hence the apostles only continue the self-revelation of our Lord. The testimony of Jesus is the Spirit, not of prophecy only, but also of apostolic teaching. It will tend to simplification, and reduce the subject within easy limits, if we briefly indicate the points in which all apostolic testimonies agree as to the Person of Christ and His claims, before we consider the characteristics of each.

There is common to all the ascription of that special "Lordship" to Christ which is the dignity conferred upon Him as the mediatorial representative of the Trinity; but which is in all their writings so qualified and described as to demand the Jehovah Lordship as its basis. If required to give the one most universal designation—loved of all and common to all—we naturally think of "Our Lord Jesus Christ." Always used in relation to God preceding and the church following, this title combines all that belongs to the Divine-human dignity of our Lord; but as belonging to Him in His subordinate mediatorial dominion. Not, however, that the name sprang from delegated authority, or was prepared to be its expression. Nothing is more certain to one who pursues the name Jehovah through the Scriptures—

from the "Angel of Jehovah" downwards—than that it resides in Jesus, "the same yesterday, and to-day, and for ever;" and that it is the eternal foundation which bears up the pillars of the doctrine of the Person of Christ. Both St. James and St. Paul call Him "the Lord of Glory" (1 Corinthians ii. 8, James ii. 1): a title which no reverent contemplation of the glory of God will ever find it possible to ascribe to a creature.

On this foundation we may raise a goodly superstructure. Without referring to individual passages—for it is the happy necessity of our subject that the entire range of the epistles renders it needless—we have only to refer to the uniform habit of the apostles to unite Christ with God and the Father as the source of all blessing and grace; to make the indwelling of Christ by His Spirit the life of the soul; to regard union with Christ as union with God; to claim for the name of Jesus the Divine honour of invocation and prayer, and to ascribe to it glory and dominion; to demand for Jesus an absolutely unlimited love and devotion. In all these respects there reigns the common consent of "one faith" in the Divine-human Person of Christ. As in the gospels no language of humiliation can hide from us the glory of a Divine Person who is one with God, and which constrains us to "honour the Son even as we honour the Father," waiting for the fuller revelation promised as to the mystery that "He is in the Father and the Father in Him;" so throughout the apostolical epistles we feel ourselves always in the presence of a "Son of God" who is humbled to fellowship with us, but retains all that can claim reverence, worship, obedience, love and hope in God Himself. We feel, in short, that there is no other solution of the mystery than this: that, in the unity of the Divine Trinity, One Person, who is Man as He is God, represents the whole fulness of the Godhead bodily to man.

The doctrine of the Trinity has scarcely been introduced into this Essay. But it is impossible to separate the Person of Christ from its relation to the Triune revelation of God in the economy of redemption. The exhibition of the Trinity in the New Testament seems—if such words may be used—to be conformed to the incarnation and bound up with it. The Lamb is "in the midst of the throne," according to the profound disclosure of the Apocalypse (Revelation v. 6). The Second Person is in the Trinity no longer alone in His Divinity, but Divine-Human. The Baptismal Formula prepared the way for this: the people of God are consecrated into the one Name of the Father and the Son and the Holy Ghost; where the Son is not the name of the Only-begotten only, but, according to the invariable usage of our Lord, the Incarnate Son. Hence baptism into the name of Jesus is the epitomised expression of the full formula. Now, it is not too much to say that throughout the epistles we have a Trinity which includes the Form of the Son of Man, and in fact we have in express teaching no other Trinity. Concerning the Father, or God absolutely, the Son or Jesus Christ, and the Holy Spirit, respectively, language is constantly used which implies Divinity. But the Trinity is always the Mediatorial Trinity: this is a rule without exception. Through Christ we have access to the Father by One Spirit. The Spirit of Christ is the Spirit of God; He is everywhere the Revealer of the Father and the Son. The indwelling of God, of Christ, and of the Spirit in believers is one and the same indwelling. Life, eternal life, is the gift and energy of each Person interchangeably. The apostolical epistles are under the law of this Redemptional Trinity, and into that Trinity the Son Incarnate is exalted: the Son Incarnate is in the Father and the Father in Him; and both are revealed in the believing spirit by the Holy Ghost.

Before passing to the several types of Apostolical doctrine we must further observe that the Apostles write independently, but not without perfect knowledge of each other's writings, and under the influence of the one common revealing Spirit. The four Gospels were only partially current when St. Paul began his epistolary teaching; but the general basis of the Gospel narratives was before him, and in St. Luke's gospel particularly his hand is seen, even as St. Peter's hand is seen in St. Mark's. St. Peter knew St. Paul's epistles; and St. Paul knew St. Peter's preaching and oral testimony. All the Apostles "agree in one;" but each has his distinct charisma or gift, and St. Paul and St. John especially, in relation to the exhibition of our present doctrine. Perfect independence and perfect unity reign throughout. Nor has it ever been alleged that there is any essential discord among the Apostolical testimonies to the general Form of the Son of God made man.

St. Peter must have the preeminence as a witness to the Person of Christ, were it only in remembrance of the great confession he bore at Cæsarea Philippi. It is true that his written doctrine comes late: late in his own life, and late as compared with some of St. Paul's. But his testimony as a preacher is preserved in the Acts; and that, as compared with the testimony in the epistles, yields matter of some importance to our general subject.

It is manifest, first, that there is a certain difference between the tone of the discourses and pleadings of this Apostle immediately after Pentecost, and that of his own final letters and the Epistles generally: a difference which cannot but be marked, and demands to be accounted for. In the Acts the Apostle is preaching the simple historical facts of the redeeming work, repeating in the ears of the Jews the narrative of the Passion especially, and confining himself to the Divine purpose wrought out through that Passion. Moreover, the multitudes who first heard him were gathered from all parts of the world, and many of them were strangers to the doctrines taught by Jesus and the works wrought by Him. Hence the Apostle laid the foundation by speaking simply of his Master as "a Man approved of God among you by miracles and wonders and signs, which God did by Him in the midst of you" (chap. ii. 22). He afterwards gives the Redeemer some of His most august names: "the Just One," "the Holy One," "the Prince and the Saviour," "the Prince of Life," "the Son or Servant, or Servant-Son," "raised up" in our human nature. But at this the outset of the missionary ministry the Apostle does not make prominent His Divinity: there is the same reserve which is marked in our Lord's own testimony to His enemies, whom He would win, in the Gospels. That the Holy Spirit, speaking through St. Peter, had a reason of Divine wisdom for this, is obvious. For the Apostle under the fuller and richer teaching of that Spirit could not have receded below His early sublime testimony that "the Son of Man" was "the Son of the living God."

But, marked as this difference is, it is lost in the evidences of perfect identity as to the substratum of the two testimonies. In both, St. Peter is the apostle of the circumcision, proclaiming the accomplishment of the promises made to the fathers through Jesus Christ. Hence he took up and continued our Saviour's testimony, just as our Saviour took up the Baptist's, concerning the redeeming work. And, as to the Redeemer Himself, St. Peter adheres generally, both in preaching and writing, to the prophetic Messiah as come and perfected in the last days of the Gospel dispensation. In his first epistle he remembers the Lord's testimony to the Eleven: "I ascend unto My Father, and your Father; and to

My God, and your God;" and opens with a benediction of "the God and Father of our Lord Jesus Christ." And in chapter iii. 18, he gives us his only specimen of the manner in which he viewed the union of the two natures in Christ: "being put to death in the flesh, but quickened by the Spirit." The Spirit is obviously the counterpart of the flesh: as in the regenerate, but in a different and higher sense. It was in His Divine nature that our Lord preexisted in the days of Noah. St. Paul gave him the example of this distinction between the "Eternal Spirit" of Christ's Godhead and His human flesh. In the second epistle, which has every internal mark of genuineness, the Divine-human Person of our Lord shines out most clearly. It pervades the document. The one Gospel righteousness is "the righteousness of God and our Saviour Jesus Christ;" it is "Jesus our Lord, according as His Divine power hath given unto us all things that pertain unto life and godliness," whose "Divine nature" we partake: Christ's Divine power and Divine nature are indisputably asserted here (chap. i. 1—4). The "majesty" of Christ, of which the Apostles were eyewitnesses when "He received from God the Father honour and glory," was not the gift of God at the Transfiguration, but the Father's acknowledgment of a preexistent glory: "This is My beloved Son" (chap. i. 17). "The Lord" of the third chapter is Christ, and with Him "a thousand years are as one day" (chap. iii. 8). We haste "unto the day of God" (chap. iii. 12). And, as the crowning testimony of His Divine dignity, we read: "But grow in grace, and in the knowledge of our Lord and Saviour Jesus Christ. To Him be glory both now and for ever. Amen" (chap. iii. 18).

St. James occupies a distinct place in his mediatorial theology, and in reference to Christ's Person. But that Person in his epistle is Divine. He is one with St. Paul in the designation "Jesus Christ, the Lord of glory," which St. James, writing as it were between the Old Testament and the New, could not understand in any sense lower than the highest; nor is the force of the word diminished, it is rather increased, by the omission of the second Lord: "Our Lord Jesus Christ, of glory." And no student of the Old Testament can doubt St. James's estimate of Christ his God, when he says: "Do not they blaspheme that worthy name by the which ye are called?" (Chap. ii. 1, 7 ; comp. 1 Corinthians ii. 8.)

St. Jude in his short epistle unites the "denying the only Lord God and our Lord Jesus Christ," in one condemnation, in such a way as to make the Redeemer the foundation of the one faith. And, in his final Trinitarian exhortation and doxology, Christ is Divine. His mercy is the passport to eternal life. And "to the only wise God our Saviour" he ascribes "glory and majesty, dominion and power, both now and ever." It may be said that this ascription is not to Christ alone. But it is obvious that Christ cannot be excluded. The salvation of man has been connected with the love of God, the mercy of Christ, and the communion of the Spirit of all devotion. The doxology goes up to that one common God in His triune grace (vers. 4, 25).

St. Paul's testimony to the Person of Christ is the most abundant, the most comprehensive, and, it may be said, the most complete of all the Apostolical testimonies. The history of his conversion might lead us to expect this. His first experience of Christianity was a revelation of the Divine-human glory of the Saviour, who "appeared unto him." He became a Christian by the revelation of that Saviour within him: "it pleased God . . . to reveal His Son in me" (Galatians i. 15, 16). And his whole life was a medium of the revelation of that Saviour to the world: "Thou shalt be His witness unto all men of what thou hast seen and heard"

(Acts xxii. 15). There are evident proofs in his writings that the "knowledge of Christ Jesus" was communicated to him directly by the Spirit of Christ: it was this which gave his apprehensions of Jesus their distinctness and freshness; and it was this which insured their perfect harmony with those of the other Apostles who were under the Lord's immediate teaching. That knowledge was also communicated at once. Though subsequent revelations, and subsequent study of the Old Testament under the light of the Spirit, gave him an ever-deepening insight into the connections and relations of the fact of the incarnation, the fact itself and the doctrine of Christ's Person based on it was the very earliest acquirement of His faith. Who art Thou, Lord? was his first question. And the answer was the revelation of the Son of God within him. But, in regard to this as to every other subject, St. Paul's references and allusions were governed by circumstances. This doctrine was at once the foundation, the sun, and the canopy of all truth; but it was not necessary that it should be perpetually proved to be such. Accordingly, there are some epistles which contain no distinct reference to it. We shall select a few salient points in the leading Christological epistles in their order; and then make some general remarks that will apply to all the rest as well as to them. The classical passages are to be found in the epistles of the Imprisonment at Rome. But very important elements of doctrine are found in the epistles to the Romans and Corinthians preceding them, and in the Pastoral epistles which closed the series.

In the great mediatorial epistle we might expect the Person of the Mediator to be exhibited at least in its relation to the distinction and unity of His natures. That is precisely what we find; and we find it in his epistle more expressly set forth than anywhere else. Of all the proof texts and effectual supports of the doctrine there are none more precious to the theologian than those which expressly combine the two natures of our Lord in one statement. These do not often occur: in fact, their number is few. The truth is everywhere assumed, but only seldom does reverence permit the writers to discuss the secrets of the mystery.

In the epistle to the Romans there are three such passages: the first makes the "Spirit of holiness" the Divine nature as distinguished from the "Son of David after the flesh;" the second presents "His own Son" as the counterpart of "the likeness of sinful flesh;" and in the third "God, blessed for ever" is the opposite of "the Flesh" of Christ simply. These are the chief instances in St. Paul's writings of the express juxtaposition of the two natures. "God was manifest in the flesh" or the Mystery "Who was manifest in the flesh, and justified in the Spirit" (1 Timothy iii. 16), that is, in His Divine nature, must be classed with the first of the three above named; and the passage in Galatians iv. 4, concerning the "Son sent forth, made of a woman," with the second. Three more important passages than these cannot be found. They expressly set one nature of our Lord over against the other; and it is obvious that the force of these declarations must be increased when they are thus collated and compared. Taking the central one first, we have an expression never elsewhere used, by which the Apostle stamps with the utmost emphasis the Divine Sonship of Him who was sent " in the likeness of sinful flesh " (chap. viii. 3). He was the "own Son" of God, the Son of God Himself: an expression that signifies the very utmost that St. John's " Only-begotten " and St. Paul's " beloved " elsewhere signify. The words cannot bear either a Humanitarian or an Arian sense: the Son was sent only "in the likeness of sinful flesh," and therefore was not mere man; and the Son of the Divine Being Himself could not be a creature of His power. Now, let this central text throw its light backwards and forwards on the two others: it will relieve both of some of their difficulties. The first (chap. i. 4) has been encumbered by an interpretation which makes "the Spirit of holiness" the Holy Ghost. But the Holy Ghost, with caution be it written, belonged rather to the human than to the Divine nature of our Lord. The Lord Himself is Spirit. And the Spirit of holiness is the Divine essence, the necessary prerogative of which is not to be capable of death, and to continue in endless life the Person of Him whose flesh was crucified through weakness. Our Lord was "defined" to be the Son of God in the resurrection; for, while it is true that in the economy of redemption the Mediator is said to be raised from the dead by the Father, it is the teaching of Scripture that through the power of His own Godhead He "could not be holden" of death. Here then we have the first of a series of texts in which we find, what we might have expected to find, the Divine nature of our Lord expressly termed "Spirit." "God is Spirit;" and each of the three Persons bears equally that designation, though One in the economy of redemption more particularly appropriates it. The last text, in chap. ix. 5, is robbed altogether of its symmetry and force, unless it is interpreted in harmony with the other two. The Apostle had just spoken of God's "own Son," using a second time a unique expression: as in the former it was τὸν ἑαυτοῦ Υἱὸν, here it is τοῦ ἰδίου Υἱοῦ (chap. viii. 32). And then, in enumerating the privileges of the Israelites, he sums up all by declaring "Of whom as concerning the flesh Christ came, who is over all, God blessed for ever. Amen." Those who would refer this doxology to God as independent of Christ are forced to admit that grammar and the usage of Scripture are against them. Let the three texts—which are the glory of the Christology of the Romans—be taken now in their order. Our Lord Jesus Christ, the Son of God (chap. i. 3), has come in the flesh in all of them. First, His Divine Sonship is defined as that of the Spirit of Holiness; then it is the peculiar and unshared Sonship of God's only Son; and, lastly, it is that of the ever-blessed God Himself, in the unity of the Father and the Holy Ghost. [23.]

The force of the passages which bring the two natures of our Lord into union, with their distinction in unity, is much augmented in this epistle by the fact that in it St. Paul more plainly than anywhere else calls Jesus Christ Man: approaches, indeed, most nearly the Saviour's "Son of Man." "The gift by grace, which is by one man, Jesus Christ, hath abounded unto many" (chap. v. 15). The parallel is with another "One Man;" and, that reference is made to the Divine-human Person, but under the aspect of His relation to mankind, is obvious to those who consider the force of the texts already considered which surround it.

The Corinthian epistles throw several important sidelights upon the Apostle's doctrine. The only instances in which they refer to the preexistence of Christ are three. First, in chap. ii. 8 of the first epistle, where the mystery of God is the "Lord of Glory" whom the princes of the world crucified: His glory here is His eternal glory, for the glory of His mediatorial dignity did not invest Him when He was crucified. And then in chap. viii. 9 of the second epistle: "Ye know the grace of our Lord Jesus Christ, that, though He was rich, yet for your sakes He became poor, that ye through His poverty might be rich." This passage interpreted by its expansion in the Philippians can refer only to the preexistent riches of Christ. And, thirdly, in chap. xv.

47, where the Second Man is expressly distinguished from the first man as being "the Lord from heaven." The parallel would be lost if this referred to the future coming of Christ. In fact, we have here one of the evidences, which are frequent in these and some others of the epistles of St. Paul, of a remarkable freshness and variety in the denominations of Christ in relation to His two natures. As in the Romans, He is, in His higher nature, "the Spirit of holiness," so He is here the "Lord from heaven," and, in the beginning of the epistle, "the Lord of glory." It is idle to oppose the evidence of St. Paul's unique expressions because they are unique.

But they contain the most explicit of all St. Paul's direct assertions of the mediatorial subjection of the Son. In fact, they formulate it in the most express terms, and under its twofold aspect: first, generally, in reference to the present mediatorial work and authority of Christ; and, secondly, in reference to the future resignation of that authority. These passages give a quite peculiar cast to the Corinthian epistles, where some of them occur as absolutely unique.

But not all. In regard to the mediatorial relation of Christ to the Father, as the Servant and Agent of His will, we find the usual reference to the Saviour as the channel through whom alone all blessings come to us. But, if possible, this is more vigorously expressed in these epistles than elsewhere. For instance, "God was in Christ, reconciling the world unto Himself" (2 Corinthians v. 19), with its context, expresses to the prepared ear, the ear of faith, at once the verity of the union of God and man in Christ, and the soleness of Christ's mediation. The same may be said of the sublime close of the first chapter of the first epistle. In verse 29, no flesh may glory in the presence of God; in verse 31 all who believe shall glory in the Lord Christ; and between these the reason is given:

"Of Him are we in Christ Jesus, who of God is made unto us wisdom, and righteousness, and sanctification, and redemption." Here it may be observed, once for all, that, according to the tenour of the entire series of the Apostolical epistles, Christ is capable of being thus the channel of all the virtue of God flowing forth to man, because "God is in Christ." This is confirmed to us in 1 Corinthians ii. 16: "Who hath known the mind of the Lord, that he may instruct Him? But we have the mind of Christ." Let this be connected with the preceding part of the paragraph, and it will be seen that the "mind of Christ" is the "mind of the Lord;" and both include the "things of the Spirit of God," which are the "things of God" known to no man. Our Lord, therefore, is not a human revealer of the things of God.

Another class of Corinthian passages descends, without descending, to the mediatorial subordination. Let us take them in order: the first regards the Saviour as Lord under God the Father; the second, as Lord in the redemptional Trinity. "To us there is but one God, the Father, of whom are all things, and we in Him; and one Lord Jesus Christ, by whom are all things, and we by Him" (1 Corinthians viii. 6). In opposition to idolatry and false gods, the Christian doctrine teaches monotheism: one God. But nothing is here to shut out the Holy Trinity; the Triune God is represented by "the Father;" and, when St. Paul says "One God, the Father," he silently suggests the thought of His Son. "And one Lord Jesus Christ" is his testimony that the power and jurisdiction of God over His creatures is committed to the Son, during the Christian dispensation. The distinction between the Father and the Lord is only this: that here, as everywhere, "all things"—not merely all Christian truths and privileges, but all things that are not

God—are of the Father, and by the Son. Could it be said of any creature that all things were by him? It is in the light of this great fundamental assertion that we are to understand those two very remarkable and peculiar passages: "Ye are Christ's, and Christ is God's" (1 Corinthians iii. 23), and "the head of Christ is God" (1 Corinthians xi. 3). In both these cases the seemingly incidental way in which so great a word is introduced, and the striking novelty of the expression itself, arrest attention. It is manifest that the fundamental Christian idea of the mediatorial character of Christ, as essentially in His mediatorial relation subordinate, is perfectly familiar to St. Paul and his readers, and "known of all men." In the other passage the Mediatorial Christ is in the Trinity (1 Corinthians xii. 3—6): "No man can say that Jesus is the Lord, but by the Holy Ghost:" the Lordship of Jesus belongs to the Trinity, and is revealed by the Father through the Spirit. "Now there are diversities of gifts, but the same Spirit. And there are differences of administrations, but the same Lord. And there are diversities of operations, but it is the same God which worketh all in all." The same God worketh all in all. All in the several Persons of the Trinity: for gifts, administrations, and operations are essentially one; no creature could accomplish for Him the acts of God. All among us: for the Father, and the Son, and the Holy Ghost are one God variously manifested in the church. The Lord in that Holy Trinity is God with the name held in abeyance for a season, and merged in that "new name" which belongs to the Mediatorial God made man, which we shall know hereafter better than we know now, for it will fill eternity.

This leads to the other unique presentation of our doctrine: the final abdication of the authority of the Incarnate Son. Much might be said on this subject, if the redeeming work were in question; but as an illustration of the Pauline doctrine of the Incarnate Person it simply presents two elements: first, that the subordination of the Son, who is essentially the "quickening Spirit," or eternal Divinity, and "the Lord from heaven" (1 Corinthians xv. 45—47), continues in heaven until the last day; and, secondly, that when the present supremacy over the universe is no longer exercised by the Incarnate Son, He will voluntarily—"the Son shall subject Himself"—continue in His union with the human race His mediatorial position without mediatorial functions: for "God shall be all in all:" the Triune God, with the Second Person in that Trinity the Incarnate Son. But this and every other Corinthian revelation concerning Christ is glorified and sealed by the great Trinitarian doxology at the end of the second epistle.

The epistles written during St. Paul's captivity in Rome are undoubtedly the crown of that part of the Apostle's Christological doctrine which has to do with the Saviour's Incarnate Person. In this Triad he makes Christ's Person his express subject. As in other epistles, every reference is introduced in relation to the mediatorial work, and as it were incidentally: but there is more fulness and directness in the treatment. In these epistles he dwells and dilates—this word alone suits the amplitude of each epistle—upon the preexistence, Divinity, and incarnation of the Only-begotten, and upon His union with His body the church, as it were in a secondary incarnation. In them he uses an order of expressions not found in his other writings. And such is the glory of his exhibition of his Master's Person in these letters in his Roman captivity, that we cannot help silently applying while we read those words of wider meaning: "As thou hast testified of Me in Jerusalem, so must thou bear witness also at Rome" (Acts xxiii. 11). These observations apply to the

Ephesian, Colossian, and Philippian epistles; but especially to the two latter: the former dwelling mainly on the Eternal Divinity of the Only-begotten; the latter on the mystery of His descent to human nature; while both give ample evidence and clear illustration of the indivisibility of the Person who unites the two natures. The Ephesian epistle connects the Person of Christ with the Holy Trinity more distinctly than any other; and so identifies Him with His body the church as to prove that the Fulness of the Godhead dwells bodily in the church through His indwelling in it. In the Colossians the preexistent Son is prominent; in the Philippians the Incarnate in His humiliation; in the Ephesians the same Incarnate Person glorified in His church and filling it with His Divine glory.

In the epistle to the Colossians, who were troubled by the aggressions of a vain philosophy, St. Paul writes, so to speak, as a Christian philosopher: it contains his sublimest and his simplest teaching combined. The Redemptional Trinity is most marked at the outset: God is the Father of our Lord Jesus Christ, the revealer of "the grace of God in truth," and the fruit of the Colossians' faith in Christ was their "love in the Spirit." The peculiarity of this last expression stamps the Trinitarian character of the whole. Soon does the Apostle rise to a new contemplation of the ever-present object of his adoration, the Person of Christ, who is "the Son of the Father's love," of His eternal love; "the Image of the invisible God," and therefore coeternal with that God who cannot be made visible by any fleshly representation, even that of Christ; the firstborn of every creature," that is, before every creature, as the term $\pi\rho\omega\tau\acute{o}\tau o\kappa o\varsigma$ signifies, and as the following words prove. Those words must be quoted in full; for they rise above every subordinate thought, and ascribe to our Lord what is elsewhere generally ascribed to the Father, reminding us of the supreme words, " I and the Father are one." " For by Him were all things created, that are in heaven, and that are in earth, visible and invisible, whether they be thrones, or dominions, or principalities, or powers: all things were created BY HIM, AND FOR HIM: AND HE IS BEFORE ALL THINGS, AND BY HIM ALL THINGS CONSIST " (chap. i. 16, 17). These words are on a level with the prologue of St. John, and go up to the eternity of the Son, " God Only-begotten." Then the Apostle glides into the revelation of Him who is the Christ, " the mystery of God" (chap. ii. 2; i. 26), "the mystery which hath been hid from ages and from generations, but now is made manifest to His saints." Elsewhere the mystery is the universality of the gospel; but here it is the incarnate God of the gospel, " Christ in you, the hope of glory " (chap. i. 27). Three great words are further spoken of this mystery. First, In Him who is "the head of the body, the church: who is the beginning, the firstborn from the dead "—His eternal generation being brought down to His temporal generation in human nature, perfected in the resurrection—" it pleased the Father that all fulness should dwell : " all the fulness of Deity to fill the church with the fulness of God. Secondly, In Him " are hid all the treasures of wisdom and knowledge," so that " the full assurance of understanding " is the " acknowledgment" of this mystery of Christ : there is no knowledge beyond (chap. ii. 3). Thirdly, " In Him dwelleth all the fulness of the Godhead bodily :" where we have a parallel to St. John's " the Word was made flesh;" with this addition, that, in the perfect and absolute, though incomprehensible, intercommunion of the Three Persons, the Son in human nature is the fulness of the essence of God. In other words, the Most Holy Triune God has assumed humanity into an eternal union with Himself in Christ; according to our Saviour's words in the High-priestly Prayer: " that they all may be one; as thou, Father, art in Me, and I in Thee, that they also may be one in Us" (John xvii. 21), and the Apocalyptic symbol of "the Lamb in the midst of the throne" (Revelation v. 6).

This leads immediately to the Ephesian epistle, the epistle which treats of Christ's Person as "extended" in His body the church on the one hand, and as a revelation of the Holy Trinity on the other. These points having been glanced at, there will remain some few other characteristics of the teaching of this epistle.

No document of St. Paul's is so fully pervaded by the doctrine of the Trinity, as revealed in the mediatorial work of Christ. This governs the construction of the epistle; and the Triune glory is so diffused through it, it is so "filled with the fulness of God," that it may be regarded as the Temple-epistle, the counterpart of the epistle to the Hebrews. There are three prominent passages that must be especially referred to: not for the sake of their complete exposition—which does not fall within the scope of the essay—but to indicate the points of St. Paul's doctrine.

"Through Him we both have access by one Spirit unto the Father" (chap. ii. 18—22): here the revelation of the God of the temple is through His Son Jesus Christ, who, one with the Father, and one with the saints, opens the way to the fellowship of God the Triune; through the One Spirit who is the same God drawing the souls of believers to the Mediator. Access to God is entrance into the "household of God," which is the living and "holy temple in the Lord" —in Jesus the Lord—" in whom ye also are builded together for an habitation of God through the Spirit." Now in this passage, which must be taken as a whole, there is a distinction in the Persons: the Father is approached through the Son by the Spirit. But of each Person it is predicated that His Presence contributes to the glory of the Christian temple. The same may be said of the great central Prayer of the epistle, which transfers the temple into the hearts of individual believers. The indwelling of the Father is "the Spirit in the inner man," and that again is Christ "dwelling in the heart by faith," to know whose love, passing knowledge, is to be "filled unto all the fulness of God," the Triune God (chap. iii. 14—21). Almost immediately after this Prayer the unity of the Christian faith is summed up in relation to the Trinity: ascending through the Spirit and the Lord Jesus to the Father once more. "There is one Body and one Spirit." There is "one Lord." There is "one God and Father of all, who is above all, and through all, and in you all" (chap. iv. 4—6). Here there is the full and clear statement of the Trinity of Redemption: the Father in this economy supreme; yet the Redeemer the one Lord, which is such a predicate of absolute authority as cannot be applied to any creature; and the Spirit is the whole Divinity, in another sense than that of the Colossians as spoken of Christ "the fulness of the Godhead," though not "bodily," in the church. Hence afterwards the same "unity of the faith" already referred to is defined and sealed as no other than "the knowledge of the Son of God" (ver. 13), whom to know is to know the Triune God.

Hence we can understand the striking and peculiar expression of the commencement of the epistle: "Blessed be the God and Father of our Lord Jesus Christ" (chap. i. 3). This doxology, in which the two Apostles, St. Peter and St. Paul, unite, (comp. 1 Peter i. 3), pays its tribute to the supremacy of the Father in the economy of redemption. It simply takes the words of the Incarnate Christ Himself and makes of them a formula, which no one who ponders and accepts the mystery of the subjection of the Son in our nature can refuse to accept, or regard as a stumblingblock. The God and Father of our Lord Jesus Christ is the God and Father, not of His Divine essence as the Son simply, not of His human nature simply, but of His Incarnate Person, as the Revealer and Representative of the Godhead, through whom alone we become the children of God.

Before leaving the Ephesian epistle we cannot but advert to the farewell discourse delivered by St. Paul to the elders at Miletus, which contains the same emphatic tribute to the Holy Trinity, and the Divinity of the Person of Christ. There the personality and deity of the Holy Ghost are most clearly announced: " the Holy Ghost witnesseth in every city," as the God of the Apostle's interior guidance; and " the Holy Ghost hath made you overseers," which is a personal act by every token, and the personal act of One who has Divine authority. The injunction to "feed the Church of God which He hath purchased with His own blood" declares, even if " the church of the Lord " is the true reading—of which there is and can be no sufficient proof—that " the kingdom of God " is Christ's church purchased by the blood of Him whose Godhead alone could give His blood its preciousness as the price of the church's redemption (Acts xx. 23—28). Thus St. Paul the missionary and St. Paul the theologian are one and the same in the doctrine of the Mediatorial Trinity as manifested and indwelling in the church through the Divine-human Person of Christ Himself revealed by the Holy Ghost. The church, the kingdom, the body, the temple, are all " filled with the fulness of God " through being the " fulness of Christ who filleth all in all " (Ephesians i. 23).

In the Philippian epistle alone has St. Paul approached

the unsearchable mystery of the eternal act of condescension of the Son of God as made manifest temporally in His incarnation. The second chapter is the exhibition of the relations of self in the Christian economy: the care of self in personal salvation (ver. 12); the combination of self with the care of others (ver. 4); and the perfect sacrifice of self in devotion to Christ (ver. 21). The supreme example of self-sacrifice that Christianity sets before the believer is the devotion of the Son of God to the salvation of the world. And this gives the Apostle occasion to make those comments on the Redeemer's self-renunciation which have been the wonder and the study of Christian divines from the beginning (vers. 5—8).

The Person who manifests this self-sacrificing devotion is "Christ Jesus:" the subject of every predicate, whether Divine or human or Divine-human. It is needless to ask whether St. Paul referred to the condescension of the Son of God in eternity (λόγος ἄσαρκος) or of the Son of God in the flesh (λόγος ἔνσαρκος): the indivisible unity of the Person allows no such distinction. As the Divine dignity of Christ stamps all His human acts, so His human nature and His human name goes back to eternity. Christ Jesus is eternal: the same yesterday, and to-day, and for ever. He, "being in the form of God," could never really and essentially change His Divinity for anything else: ὑπάρχων is essential existence; and the μορφὴ θεοῦ, the form of God, could never, as it implies the οὐσία, or essence of God, be surrendered. But He did not count it, and the equality with God which belonged to it, a prerogative or glory which must be seized and held fast tenaciously. He took the form of a servant; and, in the likeness of men, laid aside, so far as concerned humanity and the work of redemption, the exercise of His Divine authority, the "equality with God" that He might have assumed. Though His glory was "manifested forth" in some of His miracles, declared by the Father in His transfiguration, and on many occasions was asserted by Himself, yet all this, as demonstrative of His equality with God, was exceptional, and not the tenour and general character of His life and work. His reputation in the world was that of a servant of God; and, though He was conscious of Divine perfections, He did not use them. "He emptied Himself:" His humiliation was His own will and act, before and in His incarnation, and after His incarnation down to the last sorrow of His active-passive obedience. It was the proof of His Divinity that He could renounce the Divine; and make Himself in the flesh the Subject or Person of a human consciousness apart from the Divine. And His exaltation is to the Lordship of the universe, corresponding to the subjection of the humbled estate. When the end shall come this special reward of the obedience will cease, and the "Form of God" will in humanity be seen for ever.

The Philippian epistle yields another demonstration of the Saviour's Divinity in the mystery of His incarnate Person: the place St. Paul gives Him as the object of reverence and love. His Lord is the sphere of all spiritual existence; and in such a way that He must be God. That glorious truth concerning God that "in Him we live, and move, and have our being"—and nothing is more absolutely the prerogative of God than to be the ground and sphere of creaturely life—is literally transferred to Christ. "In Christ," "in the Lord," are phrases which return with perpetual iteration, and in reference to every circumstance of life. Let any devout reader ponder the third chapter, and see how entirely the Apostle fills his future eternity with the thought of the prize which he should find in Christ for ever won, and he must be convinced that the Being who inspires this emotion, and rewards it with Himself, must be more than human, more than creaturely, not less than Divine. This argument is strengthened when we remember the counterpart in the epistle to the Corinthians, where St. Paul consigns to anathema the Christian who, knowing Christ, does not love Him.

The epistle to the Hebrews, if not written by St. Paul, was written under his influence: he is present in spirit at least if not in his own hand. It contains every element of the doctrine of Christ's Person, or nearly every element, that has been collected from the other apostolical writings.

It is the epistle of the Christian temple rather than of the mediatorial court, or the Father's house. And "the Lord is in His holy temple: " the Lord Christ, the Son who is over the house, and who built it as God : " One greater than the temple." The first chapter is simply and purely an induction of Scriptural evidences that Christ is God: a reproduction, first, of New-Testament testimonies, and, secondly, of Old-Testament testimonies which support them. Of the " Son " who is the " Brightness of the Father's glory, and the express Image of His Person," St. Paul had taught and St. John will further teach; and His " upholding all things by the word of His power," as the Divine creator and sustainer of all things, has been declared in the epistle to the Colossians. Our present epistle confirms this from the Old Testament in citations which have been already referred to. The whole of the first chapter is one irrefragable demonstration that the Son Incarnate is very God. Echoes of this statement of Christ's Divinity recur : " By the Eternal Spirit " Christ offered Himself: that is, the virtue of His Divine essence,—" God is Spirit,"—gave His oblation its value: not the Holy Ghost, who belongs rather to the manhood of Christ, as the medium of its perfect consecration, but the Divine nature of the Son Himself:

"Christ, who through the Eternal Spirit offered HIMSELF" (chap. ix. 14). And the last words of the first chapter, which assign to Christ the Divine attribute of abiding existence in the midst of all changing phenomena, return again at the close of the epistle: "Jesus Christ, the same yesterday, and to-day, and for ever" (chap. xiii. 8).

The second chapter is mainly devoted to the verity of Christ's human nature: which is more thoroughly and at all points exhibited than in any other portion of the New Testament. Of the Son of the preceding chapter, whom God Himself addresses as God, this chapter says that "He is not ashamed to call us brethren." "Both He that sanctifieth and they that are sanctified are all of one," of one common nature: this, however, not being more expressly declared because of the infinite difference there exists between Christ and His people in conjunction with this identity. "For which cause He is not ashamed to call them brethren:" that is to say, His whole being is made one with them, and His human love to His fellows after the flesh is as perfect as the Divine love with which He had loved His Father from eternity (chap. ii. 11). The verity of His human nature is attested by the express reference to the children's "flesh and blood:" He "took part of the same," (chap. ii. 14), that in the likeness of our sinful human nature, without its sin, He might destroy the works of the devil in human transgression. But it is observable that throughout the chapter the Saviour's assumption of our nature is made His own voluntary act: no point is more carefully guarded everywhere than this; and the remark applies to the entire tenour of New-Testament references to the union of the two natures in Christ. The comprehensive reference to our Lord's human nature is introduced for no other purpose than to show how it was possible for One equal with God to "make reconciliation for the sins of the people" (chap. ii. 17). Finally, it is remarkable that the angels are introduced in relation to the two natures of our Lord first, and then in relation to His mediatorial authority. In the first chapter the angels are immeasurably below Him as He is their Creator and the object of their worship: a homage continued from adoration in heaven into worship on earth. In the second chapter the Redeemer is made "lower than the angels" as He is man, sharing as such the original inferiority of mankind to the angel world. Then in His Divine-human Person He is once more above the angels, though in another sense than that in which His Deity exalted Him above them. "For unto the angels hath He not put in subjection the world to come, whereof we speak" (chap. ii. 5, 7).

The mediatorial service of the Incarnate Person flows on through the remainder of the epistle: that service being mainly in the temple, and offered by the redeeming Sacrificer, Himself the Offerer, and the Sacrifice, and the Representative of those who need it. Nothing can be more impressive than the transition from the first chapters devoted to the two natures individually, to the One Incarnate Person. Without a word to express the mystery, or any reference to the mystery, the writer summons his readers, as "holy brethren," to "consider" with fervent, prolonged, and never-failing devotion the work of Him who is from God to man the Apostle, and from man to God the High Priest, of human salvation, "the Son over His own house" (chap. iii. 1, 6). In harmony with the rest of Scripture the Son is exhibited as learning a great obedience, both passive and active: in the sinless obedience to the law of redemption, and in the sinless endurance of the penalty of the law broken by man. The teaching of the epistle on the present subject—which necessarily omits the atoning work—is condensed into one of the most pregnant passages in the New Testament, one that demands inexhaustible pondering: " So also Christ glorified not Himself to be made an High Priest; but He that said unto Him, Thou art My Son, to-day have I begotten Thee." Of no human office-bearer in the kingdom of God, nor of any created servant of Jehovah, could it be said that he was glorified in his office. But the Eternal and Only-begotten, begotten again in His human nature in the to-day of His incarnate history, might receive that Divine glory. "Though He were a Son, yet learned He obedience:" no other Son of God, certainly no other human son, could be said to have learned his duty *although* a son. "And being made perfect:" already declared to be sinless, He is now said to be perfected only through the learning of vicarious obedience. "He became the Author of eternal salvation to all them that obey Him:" these words are almost an echo of St. Peter's words in Jerusalem (Acts v. 32); the two passages must illustrate each other; and their combination shows that the Mediator is both God and man, and in the dispensation of human salvation "under authority" to the Father and supremely "over" us (chap. v. 5, 8, 9). Nor must the "order of Melchizedek" be forgotten. This most mysterious of all the ancient types of Christ is left in the New Testament as mysterious as ever: the "things hard to be understood" still remain, as so to speak, a new type of the incomprehensibility of the antitype.

The Pastoral epistles contain the final testimony of St. Paul to the faith generally, and to its individual doctrines: his last and "faithful" sayings. In many of these sayings he is "very bold;" and in all of them there is such evidence of freshness and originality as show how unfailing was the spring of inspiration within him. There is hardly a statement of any fundamental truth which does not present some touch or some feature unknown in all the course of his previous writing: as if he were setting the seal upon the teaching of his life in a final three-one document in which there are no Retractations.

The first epistle to Timothy is, so far as it concerns our present subject, lighted up by two cardinal passages of great importance. The "mystery of godliness" in chap. iii. 16, gives us, according to the present reading, the perfect statement of the revelation of God in the Divine-human Son: "God was manifest in the flesh, justified in the Spirit." Collating this with the related passages in the epistles to the Romans and the Colossians, we are taught that Christ, the mystery of God, was revealed in the flesh and approved as Divine by the " Spirit " of His Divinity. His character, and claims, and work were "justified" by His own higher nature, in virtue of which He was "the Son of God." We retain all this if we accept the more favoured reading: "Who was manifest in the flesh;" and must regard it as the last of St. Paul's statements of the union of the two natures in Christ. It throws its glory back upon the previous saying in chap. ii. 5, where the Mediatorial and subordinate Redeemer is more particularly referred to: " For there is one God, and one Mediator between God and men, the Man Christ Jesus; who gave Himself a ransom for all, to be testified in due time." According to the most obvious canon of interpretation, we must not separate the two passages; uniting them we learn that "Christ Jesus, man"—not "the man Christ Jesus"—was the manifestation in the flesh of a Being who preexisted as God, or the Son of God; that as Mediator He is in the same relation to God as that in which He stands to man, for otherwise there would be no mediation; that, when His ransom is referred to, His human nature, or rather His character as representing manhood, or man absolutely, is made prominent; and lastly that in His Divine-human Person "He gave Himself," which as a "ransom for all" no mere man could in the nature of things do. In fact His Divine nature as "Spirit" is that which "justified" or approved Him as Mediator Man.

Interposing the epistle to Titus, we have what no criticism and no exegesis can take from us as the most convincing evidence of St. Paul's faith in the supreme Godhead of the Divine-human Person. At the outset of the epistle "God our Saviour" is parallel with "Jesus Christ our Saviour:" a community of Saviourship which is characteristic of all the pastoral epistles. Again, in chapter ii. 10, we have "the doctrine of God our Saviour" which teaches the children of that "grace of God that hath appeared" to look for "that blessed hope"—"Jesus Christ our hope," 1 Timothy i. 1—"and the glorious appearing of the great God and our Saviour Jesus Christ," where "I and the Father are One" has its last confirmation by the hand of the Apostle Paul. The usage of the Greek demands that the One Person be regarded as "THE GREAT GOD AND OUR SAVIOUR." And, if it be said that this is not the customary Pauline phraseology, we can only answer that the Apostle is gathering up here his strength for a final, full, and perfect testimony which shall be "without controversy."

In the second epistle to Timothy, St. Paul's last testimony, "Jesus Christ, man," is "the seed of David," as in the epistle to the Romans, and, in His mediatorial capacity, "was raised from the dead" (chap. ii. 8). But this also must be read in harmony with what precedes: we read (chap. i. 10) of the "appearing of our Saviour Jesus Christ, who hath abolished death" by His own Divine power, and "brought life and immortality to light through the gospel."

He is Himself "that eternal life." Approaching now the very last testimony of this "faithful witness," we quote, and need not comment upon, those ever-memorable words: " And the Lord shall deliver me from every evil work, and will preserve me unto His heavenly kingdom: TO WHOM BE GLORY FOR EVER AND EVER. AMEN." St. Paul's last words are a doxology to Christ: let all who accept his witness to his Lord and theirs say, AMEN.

ST. JOHN closes the Scriptural Testimony to the Person of Christ, and crowns it with perfection. His witness has been already to a great extent examined: so far, that is, as it belongs to the Gospel records as such, and as they include the supreme testimony of Christ Himself. But there is a sense in which the last Evangelist sets his own personal seal on the entire revelation concerning the Incarnate. This is to be found in the Prologue and Appendix to his gospel, in his epistles, and in his own portion of the Apocalypse. His contribution to the doctrine is final, not only as having been supplied long after all others, and with the whole compass of the uncompleted Scriptures before him, but also as differing from all others in making the eternal preexistence and Divinity of the Redeemer his uniform point of departure. He does not, indeed, throw any veil over the perfect humanness of our Lord's manhood: the Apostle whom the ancient church termed ἐπιστήθιος, from his lying in the bosom of Jesus, would not be likely to do that. The phrases by which he describes the incarnation, approaching more nearly than any other writer to a definition of the mystery, do the fullest justice to the humble reality of the flesh of the Incarnate. Moreover, his gospel gives the amplest exhibition of the mediatorial subordination of our Lord: being the medium through which our Lord Himself uttered His lowest words of humiliation. But St. John's doctrine, though it is faithful to the humbled estate of the Christ, is not so to speak itself under the law of humiliation. It always and everywhere makes the eternal Divinity of the Son the governing member of its sentences. While the Christology of his predecessors rises from the mediatorial work to the dignity of the Mediator, his almost invariably descends from the dignity of the Mediator to the perfection of His work. This observation requires, however, a repetition of the proviso already laid down, that we are referring to the testimony of the Beloved Apostle, apart from his testimony as one of the four historians of the life of Jesus, that is, apart from his simple and uncommented record of the witness of Christ Himself.

It has already been seen that St. John was not raised up or reserved to add to the previous teaching of Scripture concerning Christ the doctrine of His Divinity. That doctrine was unassailably established in the creed of the churches long before he began his writings. Hence it will be observed that in those parts of his three main documents which contain his individual testimony he does not introduce his statements as containing a new revelation from heaven. He does not write in the style of St. Paul when he introduces doctrine that had been specially revealed to him; he does not preface his communications either in the language or in the spirit of St. Paul, "Behold I show you a mystery." His doctrine is to be sought chiefly in the Prologue to his gospel and the preface of his first epistle; though the sequel of both gospel and epistle contains in each case additional confirmation of a most decisive kind. Both descend from the eternal Sonship to the Incarnation. Both proclaim the incarnation of the Son to be the foundation of the Faith. But both appeal to it as the received doctrine of the church of Christ. St. John does not speak in his own person in any one instance: the supreme manifestation of the Son in the flesh was what he says " We beheld " (John i. 14) : " that which we have seen and heard declare we unto you " (1 John i. 3).

The glory of St. John's testimony is the Prologue of his gospel. This must be regarded as the key to the gospel itself; as his own inspired and authoritative standard for the interpretation of all that follows in the narrative of our Lord's life and the record of His discourses. Those who find in the gospel an Arian Christ—a human Christ merely, it is hard to suppose any finding in it—are wont to invert this order. They insist that the wonderful words of the Prologue must be interpreted by the gospel itself; and as, in the gospel, there is undoubtedly a perpetual strain of the language of subordination, used by Christ in His humbled estate, they seek to lower the high language of the Prologue into harmony with the inferiority of the Son, which they think they find in St. John's subsequent record. To us, indeed, it is matter of indifference which is made the key to the explanation of the other. Both contain the one Divine-human Christ. But it must be maintained that the mind of the Spirit is in favour of our making the lofty exordium of the Gospel the law of our interpretation of all that follows.

In the course of these eighteen verses the incarnation seems never for a moment out of the Apostle's view. But the first, fourteenth, and last are all that we need refer to: in the first, the Divine preexistence is stated; and in the two latter we have, not only the greatest of all the phrases that the New Testament furnishes on the subject, but perhaps the most glorious and perfect sentences of revelation.

First, the eternity of the Incarnate God. The Evangelist's " In the beginning " as much transcends that of Moses as God transcends the created universe. For the Word who was with God was God, the "Only-begotten of the Father." The term Logos, with which the paragraph sets out is lost, as it were, in the superior glory of the Only-begotten Son, which had already become the accepted designation of the Person of Christ as Divine. We know not the precise reason for the choice of the term. It may have been adopted in order to correct those theosophical and false notions current in the East which, tending indeed to hypostatise the Wisdom of Scripture, perverted that wisdom or eternal thought or Word of God into a creaturely emanation: hence when the Evangelist says "The Word was with God" he seems to condense into a short sentence all that is written concerning Wisdom as presiding over the Divine thoughts and works; and when he adds "the Word was God," he, by an emphatic sentence which rebukes a false conception, vindicates the Divinity of the Word as the eternal medium of the Divine temporal outgoing towards the creature. The Logos is introduced no more, save at the close that it may be merged in the supreme and permanent name of Son: just as the similar or related term used by St. Paul, "the Image of the Invisible God," is introduced to convey the precise thought of St. John's Logos, that of the medium of Divine revelation to the creature, and, having been introduced, still depends upon the higher and more personalising name of Son (Colossians i. 13, 15; Hebrews i. 2). Before verse 18 and the words "God Only-begotten, who is in the bosom of the Father,"—the reading which demands to be received as St. John's true expression,—our minds and hearts bow down as containing the last and highest revelation concerning the Divine nature of the Incarnate Person. He is God: that is, indeed, not unique, but paralleled by many passages. But He is the Person in the Divine Essence who alone is begotten; He is eternally subordinate but not inferior to the Father as begotten of Him, that is, eternally and essentially gifted with "life in Himself;" and, lastly, He is that Only-begotten God, through whose Name, and faith in whose Name, we become "sons of God" also (verse 14). Remembering the canon we have insisted upon, that St. John's Prologue is really the introduction of the whole gospel, its text, as it were, and standard of interpretation, let all who falter when they read afterwards the language of the mediatorial subordination, whether as used by St. John or by other writers, go back at once to these awful and once-uttered words, and by contemplating them renew the strength of their faith.

Secondly, unique and striking as is the "Only-begotten God," the incarnation sentence is equally so, "The Word was made flesh." It is obvious that the subject of the affirmation is the Word, as being the term that immediately belongs to the revelation of God in Christ: the very term is an incarnation term; for, as it respects us at least, there is no expression of God which is not from the face and the lips of the Incarnate Christ. The predicate "was made flesh" severely taxes our reason and our faith. "Was made" or "became" has been interpreted in a variety of ways, and each interpretation has given birth to a theory: in fact, most of the strange hypotheses which have been current in later times owe their origin to it. But the Evangelist has given his own protective. When he adds, "and dwelt among us," or "tabernacled among us," as God in His temple, it is evident that he is completing his sentence, and that no interpretation is sound which does not blend the two. The former part, "became flesh," might be made to demand a Eutychian meaning: that which was before the Divine was so blended with flesh, and identified with it, that God was changed into man. The latter, "dwelt among us," might have a Nestorian sense forced upon it: God separable from the Manhood in the Divinity may leave His abode. But both theories, and all their phases and shades, vanish before the full sentence.

This leads, thirdly, to an observation on the indivisible unity of the Person of Christ as here illustrated in the Evangelist's phraseology. The Only-begotten God, who hath declared the Unbegotten Father whom no man hath seen, is Jesus Christ by whom grace and truth came. The glory of the Only-begotten is the glory which was seen irradiating Christ in the flesh. After the two natures are clearly distinguished as the Eternal Sonship and the Flesh or Manhood which He became, there is no further distinction. The revelation is that of the Divine-human Person; the glory resides in that Divine-human Person. Once for all the Evangelist makes the One Person the subject of the two classes of predicates: those belonging to Him as being in the bosom of the Father, and those belonging to Him as made flesh and dwelling among us. Divine and human attributes belong alike to His Person, the new basis of them all.

After the Prologue the testimony of the Evangelist is lost in that of the Person to whom he bears witness. He simply records the wonderful works and the more wonderful words of his Master. There are, however, some few occasional points at which St. John either soliloquises or directs the judgment of his readers; and it is remarkable that in nearly all these instances he takes occasion to point out the superhuman, the Divine, glory of the Redeemer. After the first miracle he says significantly: "This beginning of miracles did Jesus in Cana of Galilee, and manifested forth His glory" (chap. ii. 11), the glory, that is, he being his own interpreter, as of the Only-begotten of the Father. Immediately afterwards, "He spake of the temple of His body" (verse 21) gives us to infer that the resurrection of His human body was the work of Christ's Divinity. Again, "Jesus did not commit Himself unto them, because He knew all men, and needed not that any should testify of man; for He knew what was in man" (chap. ii. 24, 25): this seemingly needless reiteration is the Apostle's own tribute to an attribute that can belong to none but God alone. So that most instructive comment on our Saviour's words concerning the gift of the Holy Spirit dependent on His glorification (chap. vii. 39). Nor must we omit the interpretation of our Lord's silent purpose on the eve of the Passion: "Jesus knowing that the Father had given all things into His hands, and that He was come from God, and went to God" (chap. xiii. 3). Now this affecting scene is the Lord's own symbolical exhibition of the mystery of His incarnation: the laying aside of the garments, and girding Himself with a napkin, explain themselves; it is the Divine-human humiliation which, not renouncing the Divinity, is nevertheless seen only for a season as ministering to man. In His mediatorial and subordinate character nothing is generally seen or heard but the Son of Man who is the organ of the Son of God. The God is present, but speaking as man: as man in humiliation, limitation, and capacity of suffering. St. John seems to make the scene his own testimony, by the manner in which he introduces it. All these profound suggestions of the writer are summed up at the end: "But these are written, that ye might believe that Jesus is the Christ, the Son of God" (chap. xx. 31). The whole record is of One Person, Jesus, the Christ; but that Person was more than the man Jesus; He was and is no less than the Son of the living God, faith in whose name gives life.

This life in Christ is the transition to St. John's other

and formal document. The opening verse of the epistle blends the first and the last sentence of the gospel in one: "The Word of Life." And then follows a striking exhibition of the one personality of that Word as "made flesh." The apostle seems to linger long and reverently on the fact of the reality of the incarnation as bringing the Personal Eternal Life into actual unity with man. The embarrassments which beset the interpretation of the first three verses have their reason in this purpose. They have much perplexed the expositor, who has sometimes been diverted by its grammatical difficulty from the exceeding value of its plain theological teaching. We have in it, first, the eternal dignity of the Son in the essence of the Father; the verity of the human nature, with its most express proofs; and the unity of the Person in the Jesus Christ of the Apostles' fellowship. It will simplify and condense our illustration of St. John's teaching if we make these three the starting points of a brief examination of the rest of the epistle.

The Eternal Sonship has here its amplest evidence: not indeed in express assertion, — "the Eternal Son" does not occur,—but as the obvious result of collation. The Word is "that Eternal Life which was with the Father:" we must not be misled by the neuter pronouns of the clauses into a forgetfulness of the personal character of the Word. It must be borne in mind also that, as in the gospel, the Evangelist soon merges the term "Word" in the "Son;" and, indeed, closes the New Testament by making more prominent than it had ever before been made "the Son of God." There is one passage which gives boundless emphasis and strength to its testimony by what seems to be an enfeebling dilution: "These things have I written unto you that believe on the name of the Son of God; that ye may know that ye have eternal life, and that ye may believe on the name of the Son of God" (chap. v. 13). Here the Scripture ends its long strain of teaching by giving all the honour that belongs to the NAME of God to the Son of God. To deny the Father is to deny the Son (chap. ii. 22), and that, not merely in the logically consistent use of the terms, but in the eternal reality; for "whosoever denieth the Son, the same hath not the Father" (ver. 23).

After this, and remembering the opening words of the gospel, it does not offend us to read, "Hereby perceive we the love OF GOD, because He laid down His life for us" (chap. iii. 16): where the blank which we have filled up is the most eloquent silence of the Bible, and refuses any other pleroma than "God." But the most impressive and satisfying evidence is the last word of the epistle, if read in connection with a vivid remembrance of the first word. "And we know that the Son of God is come, and hath given us an understanding, that we may know Him that is true, and we are in Him that is true, even in His Son Jesus Christ. This is the true God, and Eternal Life" (chap. v. 20). Much controversy has been excited as to the reference of these last words to our Lord; but the controversy is needless. They must refer in one sense to Him, for who else is the "Eternal Life" of the epistle? But they do not refer to Him alone, as if what belonged to Him did not belong to the Father. The only true God is one in the unity of the Father and the Son. What ear, familiar with our Lord's constant identification of Himself with the Father, can fail to understand the force of the paradox, "We are in Him that is true, in His Son Jesus Christ"? "We will come unto him, and make Our abode with him" (John xiv. 23). To him who turns away from this hard saying, and will have either God the Father or Jesus Christ the "only true God" of the text, our Saviour still says, "Believest thou not that

I am in the Father, and the Father in Me?" If another counter-question is asked, "But where is the Holy Ghost in this only true God?" the answer is given in chap. iii. 24, where the Spirit is also the abiding evidence of the Son's indwelling, which is the indwelling of the Father. But the epistle, it must be remembered, is the final answer to Antichrist, and it is the honour of the Son that is supreme in it.

The Apocalypse is in some sense the testimony of St. John to the Mediatorial Person of the Son of God incarnate. But in another and more important sense the Apostle-prophet's testimony is lost in that of Jesus Himself. John is "in the Spirit," and, though retaining his consciousness and never more truly himself than when beholding His Lord and witnessing His visions in Patmos, he is altogether and only the scribe of the Holy Ghost throughout the book. There is not a single element of the record, whether John speaks or the angel of Jesus speaks to him, which is not directly the witness of our Lord Himself. Hence we have already appropriated this final and most glorious "revelation of Jesus Christ" to the great Revealer. Suffice it that the whole tenour of the Apocalypse is in perfect harmony with St. John's own testimony, given not as a prophet but as an apostle, and in harmony also with the rest of the New Testament.

Having now briefly traced the outline of the doctrine of Christ's Person hrough the Scriptures, we may close with a summary review of the whole. Its progress as a gradual revelation within the Bible is twofold: first, the prophetic development consummated in the personal revelation of Christ Himself; secondly, the development of His own testimony in the inspired definitions and statements of the Apostles. Our Lord Himself stands between the two: the interpreter, by His Spirit, of both developments.

The Old Testament exhibits the Person of one who in the fulness of time should come as the Seed of the Woman and of Abraham and of David: the New Adam, the perfect representative of the human race. While uttering this promise it defines that same Person as the Angel of Jehovah who is Jehovah Himself, His Word and His Wisdom hereafter to be incarnate. And its last and highest prophetic voices declare that this Seed of Mankind and Fellow of God should be Emmanuel, God with us, the Servant of God in the ministry of a future redemption. In the New Testament the Lord of Glory announces Himself as that Person: I AM HE. He proclaims Himself the Son: the Son of God and the Son of Man, the Servant-Son of His Heavenly Father; leaving the further disclosure of His threefold relation to the Spirit in the Apostles. Under the guidance of this Spirit these witnesses of the Witness declare the perfect humanity of their Master, His supreme Divinity, and the mysterious subordination of His one and indivisible Person in the work of redemption. So clear, so full, so convincing is their testimony, in its unity and variety, that no further development is needed. All that Christian theology has to do in its dogmatic development from age to age down to the second coming of the Christ is to protect the doctrine from error, and trace its manifold application to the whole round of evangelical truth. To that ecclesiastical development we now turn; but with the silent pledge that we can accept no teaching of man that is not absolutely faithful to the teaching of Him who "searcheth all things, yea, the deep things of God," who alone searcheth that deepest "Mystery of God" which is "manifest in the flesh" (1 Corinthians ii. 10; Colossians ii. 2; 1 Timothy iii. 16).

THE HISTORY OF THE DOCTRINE OF CHRIST'S PERSON.

THE HISTORY OF THE DOCTRINE OF CHRIST'S PERSON.

WHEN we cease to behold the Form of the Incarnate Lord in the New Testament, and begin to trace it as the centre of Historical Theology, we enter upon a series of doctrinal developments that runs on without intermission through the Christian ages to the present day. The dogma of the Divine-human Person has never been absent from the mind of the church: when not itself directly under discussion it silently enters into all other discussions; whilst at certain great epochs it absorbs and entrances the thoughts of the whole Christian world. Meanwhile a deep and strong testimony to the truth may be heard through all the confusions of heresy. To indicate the variations of controversy through which that truth has maintained its steadfastness, and fixed itself firmly in the belief and in the confession of Christian men, is the object of the following sketch.

I.

New-Testament doctrine is continued through the medium of the Apostolical Fathers. They in feebler language teach the same Jesus in His union of the Godhead and the manhood. Clement of Rome, the father of uninspired Christian literature, may represent them all: he speaks of Christ as the preexistent Power of God, who gave His perfect humanity,

"His soul, and flesh, and blood," for our redemption. But these early writers do not, any more than the apostles who taught them, touch upon the formal characteristics of the personal union. Whilst they were writing their simple epistles, heresy had singled out the natures of Jesus for attack. The Ebionites, a scanty remnant of the Judaizers whom St. Paul encountered, denied His Divinity; whilst the Nazarenes, another Jewish remnant, regarded Him as supernaturally conceived of the Holy Ghost. Cerinthus, traditionally connected with St. John, belonged to the former class, though with certain modifications that link him with the Gnostics. Another Gnostic-Ebionite was the unknown author of the homilies that go by the name of Clement. His speculations are remarkable as containing the germ of many wild theories that have since been held concerning the relation of Christ to mankind. He makes Him the original or primal man, who, after appearing in seven other "pillars of the world," Adam, Enoch, Noah, Abraham, Isaac, Jacob, Moses, was finally manifested in Christ. The Spirit of God or of Christ came down upon Him as the last incarnation; filled Him with supernatural knowledge, though not as a spirit separate from His own; and made Him, though not Divine, absolutely sinless. This fantastic speculation has often reappeared among the delusions of mystical Christology.

Gnosticism proper, in the second century, formed its theory of Christ's Person in accordance with its fundamental notions of spirit and matter. Setting out with a dualistic conception of the eternal opposition between God and matter, its idea of redemption was the deliverance of man's spirit from the bonds of sense and the impure material life, and in order to this the release of the people of the true God from the dominion of the imperfect law of the Jewish false God or the demiurgus. Hence the Christ must be a pure Spirit of spirits, one of the highest æons or emanations from the unfathomable abyss of Deity. But, in order to rescue man, He must appear in matter to "condemn sin in the flesh;" yet He must not actually assume the flesh, for that would be to place Himself in bondage. Hence the DOCETIC or fantastic body; a theory which, common to all the Gnostic heresies, assumed a variety of forms in their various systems. In some the æon purged the sin from a true human nature, but destroyed the verity of that nature in the process; in others what Mary bore was an immaterial psychical body that could not suffer; whilst there were some that brought the true Christ down on the man Jesus at the baptism to forsake Him at the cross, thus rendering the Divine alliance with matter an unreality. But all were united in this, that they contradicted St. John's testimony in the gospel, "The word was made flesh;" and inherit that condemnation of "Antichrist" which anticipated their error in his epistle. Thus, while the Ebionites in the second century denied the Deity, the Gnostics denied the manhood, of our Saviour. But both systems agreed in a certain doctrine of the Person of Christ; in all their varieties of combination they made Him different from every other mortal, and in some sense or other intermediate between God and man through the peculiar visitation of a Divine power. A Christ ONLY MAN was unknown till the third century, if indeed then.

Whilst these heresies, composites of Judaism and Heathenism blended with Christianity, were disposing of the human nature of Christ after their own fashion, the representatives of Christian doctrine were intent upon defending both natures, without as yet defining their union. Against the imaginary æon, as fanciful as the Docetic body, was set the Scriptural doctrine of the Son of God; and it may be said that during the entire ante-Nicene age the relation of the Logos to the Divinity was the leading subject in theology. The Greek fathers rejoiced in St. John's great word: whether as expressing the *Ratio*, reason, in God, or the *Oratio*, the word of God to the creature, it stimulated and guided, if it did not altogther satisfy, their deepest speculation. Some of them wavered between an eternal emanation and an eternal personality. Origen may be regarded as their representative. He affirmed an eternal generation, and preferred the term Son, which from his time to a certain extent displaced the term Logos; but he made that generation a process, like creation, eternally going on. Thus he laid the basis of the Nicene formula; but by His insistance on the Son's subordination he paved the way for Arianism. The truth he taught was held fast by the church generally; and the error he interwove with it was already rejected, before the Council of Nicæa, A.D. 325, vindicated both the consubstantiality and the eternal generation of the Son.

Meanwhile, from the end of the second century to the middle of the third, tendencies are observable which resulted in two distinct and permanent forms of error, one affecting the personality of the Lord's Godhead, and the other robbing Him of His Divinity altogether. Praxeas, of Asia Minor (A.D. 160—180), boldly charged the Catholic doctrine with being Tritheistic; yet, anxious to save the Divinity of the Son, and fastening his thought upon one saying of Christ, "I and My Father are one," so intently as to forget all other Scripture, he came to the conclusion that the Father Himself became man, suffered and died in Christ. Noetus of Smyrna, A.D. 200, followed him in this strange device, pleading against his opponents, "What evil have I done, thus glorifying Christ?" This doctrine had the Papal sanction of

Calixtus I., who asserted that the Son was merely a manifestation of the Father in human form, as the Spirit animates the body. Hence this doctrine is known as PATRIPASSIANISM. Sabellius, a convert of this Pope, about A.D. 250, enlarged the theory so as to include the Holy Spirit. His fundamental position was that of the distinction between the Monad and the Triad in the Divine nature: the unity of God unfolds itself in three redemptional forms; and, when redemption is complete, is only a unity for ever, the modes of its revelation ceasing. This error was condemned at a Council, A.D. 262, which, by its precision of language, anticipated Nicæa. But it has never been absent as a latent theory from the speculation of later ages, and reappears in modern times under many forms, but especially in the subtle theology of Schleiermacher. Thus it may be said that Patripassianism began what Sabellianism completed, the Docetic perversion of our Lord's Divinity and the extinction of His personal Sonship.

Precisely at the same time another class of heretics revived the Ebionite error, and made of our Lord man only. It is true they none of them denied His superiority to all other men. Theodotus and Artemon admitted His supernatural birth of a virgin; Paul of Samosata, A.D. 260, even asserted that the Logos dwelt in Him more abundantly than in any former messenger of God, and that Christ won by His moral excellence a Divine dignity. These false teachers, one and all condemned by the church, were thus the ante-Nicene Unitarians; but they differed from the Unitarians of modern times, by admitting a prior dignity of the Logos in Christ as well as a subsequent dignity in His exaltation in heaven. In fact, that Unitarian doctrine which the followers of Socinus have at length reached was not known, in its barest and most repulsive forms, to even the heresy of the ancient church.

As it respects the personal union of the two natures, the early Fathers propounded no clear theory; although we find hints, in their controversies with the Docetics, of the doctrine which was afterwards developed. Irenæus teaches an indissoluble union of Divinity and humanity in Christ; and, like Tertullian, finds the foundation of that union in man's original likeness to the Son, and capacity for union with Him as the true and archetypal idea of mankind. Origen, the source of so much good and so much evil in later theology, came nearest to dogmatic theorising on this great subject. His untameable intellect wrestled with some of the profoundest difficulties of the question. As he originated the two lines of thought which led respectively to Arianism and Athanasianism, so also his speculations were the starting-point of the Nestorian and Eutychian views of later times. For he hesitated much between the human soul of Jesus and His Divine nature, as the seat of the one Personality. His well-known illustration of iron heated by fire, like such illustrations generally, looks both ways. But he extricated himself, and rendered lasting service to theology by the term which his energetic mind was perhaps the first to conceive—that of the God-man.

II.

The decision of the Nicene Council asserted the true Divinity of Christ against Arius, whose restrictions of that Divinity were at every point detected and condemned. In vain he might plead that the creation of the Son was timeless and before all time; and that He was the origin of all other life. The terms of the Creed grant that the Son was begotten, but of the very substance of the Father, and from eternity. As to our Lord's human nature it uses two remarkable expressions, all the more remarkable for the repetition,

"Who was incarnate," and "became man." But, absorbed with Christ's true Godhead, it neglected the precautions which were in the next Council found necessary for the protection of the integrity of the Saviour's manhood. The "Homoousion" was afterwards found to be as needful for the lower as for the higher nature. The direct tendency of the Arian theory was to render a human soul in Jesus needless. It made the Logos in Christ a created nature so similar to the human spirit as to be capable of participating in all the conditions and affections of which man's soul is the subject. In fact, there was no reason why it should not animate the flesh as naturally and perfectly as the spirit of man itself. The finite could not indeed receive the Infinite; but the Created Word or Reason, indefinitely great but not infinite, might coalesce with the protoplasm—to use the modern term—of man's organism, might enter the flesh, and use its head, and heart, and members as an instrument. Now the Nicene formula of "the Son" did really, though silently, preclude such an inhabitation of the flesh by the absolute ὁμοούσιον τῷ πατρί. But its unsuspicious use of the strong expression, now first employed, σαρκωθέντα, "was made flesh," which it might be supposed only an Arian could pervert, did not with the precision of the Third Creed bar the way of over-curious speculation. At any rate, it required to be very carefully watched. Even Athanasius did not, till experience had taught him, discover how perilous was his own manner of treating the incarnation as only "taking flesh." But he and all the Nicene Fathers were soon aroused by the phenomenon of one among themselves laying all the stress upon the one term, "incarnate," and forgetting the other, "was made man."

Apollinaris, Bishop of Laodicæa (A.D. 362), may be said to have been the father of all the strictly Christological controversies, or those which referred solely to the union of the two natures. He was a friend of Athanasius, and a zealous defender of the Nicene theology; but his defence of Christ's Divinity led him to sacrifice the integrity of His manhood by taking from it the human spirit. His doctrine, so far as without the evidence of his own writings it can be understood, had two aspects: one relating to the pre-temporal Christ, the other to the incarnation. "The Lord from heaven" was the watchword of the former; the union between God and man had been eternal in the Logos, who brought the better part of His manhood, the heavenly humanity, with Him from heaven. Hence, in the latter part of his doctrine, the incarnation was only the taking flesh and the animal soul of man. The Divine nature of Christ dispensed with the human spirit; and the resultant was one Person, a composite of God and two parts of the human nature. Apollinaris thought that thus only could the church hold fast the One Christ in the absolute sinlessness of His personal nature and the Divinity of His atonement. But it was triumphantly argued by Athanasius, the two Gregories, and Basil, that Christ never became man if the human spirit was denied Him; that He never redeemed our nature if the noblest part of man, the spirit in which lay the glory of the Divine image and the shame of his sin, was not assumed; and, finally, that there was no such Manichæan necessity of sin in man's triple constitution of spirit, soul, and flesh as should render the assumption of our whole nature impossible to God. The second Œcumenical Council, of Constantinople, A.D. 382, condemned the Apollinarian doctrine; and thus the same Council that finally asserted the integrity of the Trinity, by proclaiming the Divinity of the Holy Spirit, finally asserted also the integrity of our Lord's human nature. But the error thus condemned left the church only "for a season." Within fifty years it revolved in other and much more plausible forms.

We now enter the very heart of the question as to the relation of the two natures in the Nestorian and Eutychian controversies. But these will be better understood if we trace them first to two tendencies of a decidedly opposite character, which had from the beginning stamped their impress upon Christian theology, and were the guiding principles in these Christological contentions. The Alexandrian school of thought was speculative, mystical, and transcendental: to the thinkers of that school the union of God and man in Christ irresistibly presented itself as an unspeakable blending of the Divine and human, in which, of course, the humanity was in danger of being entirely lost. The Antiochian or Syrian school, on the other hand, was sober, reflective, and practical; by the thinkers of that school the union was naturally regarded under the more comprehensible aspect of a moral bond between the Divine Person and a human, or of the inhabitation of the latter by the former. It may be safely affirmed that on these two opposite principles of thought, in their application, hang all the errors which have appeared, and vanished, and reappeared in the history of the doctrine of Christ's Person. And it is equally certain that the truth is to be sought where the wisest theologians have sought it—not indeed in an impossible reconciliation of these opposite views, but in such a doctrine as shall borrow the undeniable elements of soundness in both.

The Antiochian tendency found its full expression in the Nestorian controversy, which lasted from A.D. 428 to A.D. 431, when it was brought to an issue by the condemnation of Nestorius in the third Œcumenical Council of Ephesus, and the assertion of the Unity of the Person of Christ.

Nestorius has given his name to the heresy which divides the Persons. But Theodore of Mopsuestia, his teacher, was really the originator of the doctrine, and of the formulas that tended to sever the Divine from the human person in Christ. Nestorius only declaimed what Theodore taught; but his turbulent latter days and miserable·end were so closely bound up with the heresy and its condemnation that his name has always displaced every other in connection with it. He was a bigoted monk and powerful preacher. When, A.D. 428, he was made Patriarch of Constantinople, he commenced a vigorous persecution of all the heresies save one, Pelagianism, and stimulated that persecution by the vehemence of his pulpit denunciations. There was one thing even among the orthodox that displeased him—the popular habit of calling the Virgin Mary *the mother of God* (θεότοκος). Theodore had taught him to object to this, having maintained that "she only gave birth to a man in whom the union with the Logos had its beginning, but was incomplete until His baptism." Nestorius seemed to have a clear apprehension of the bearing of the question when he proposed to substitute "mother of Christ;" but he neutralised the truth in this by declaring that the union of the two natures in the Redeemer was not personal, but moral, that a perfect man became the instrument of the agency of the Logos, the temple in which He dwelt. Cyril of Alexandria was his chief opponent. The rival patriarchs anathematised each other, worldly power was invoked, and the worst passions inflamed. Nestorius was condemned by the Synod of Ephesus, but in his absence, and in an unworthy manner. His subsequent fate, and the suppression of his doctrine in the Roman empire, and its continuance among the Nestorians of Persia and of India, the present subject does not include.

The condemnation of Nestorius was only negative; nothing positive was added to the Christian doctrine or formula. Soon after the Council of Ephesus a compromise was attempted, and a symbol of union constructed which for a short time satisfied all, but only for a short time. Cyril died A.D. 444; probably just in time to escape the unenviable dignity of a heresiarch. Eutyches, a feeble monk of seventy, who had never been heard of until the Council that condemned Nestorius, became as it were accidentally the father of Monophysite doctrine, in virtue of some terse and emphatic sentences that he published. He declared that after the incarnation he could worship only one nature in Christ, the nature of God become flesh; that all human attributes must be transferred to the one Subject, the humanized Logos, the deified Man; and that thus only could God become capable of suffering and death. Here is the essence of Eutychianism: one nature and one Person in Christ, and no distinction whatever in His acts or our worship. Eutyches was singled out for attack by bitter party spirit, subserving however by the will of God the cause of truth. He was condemned, A.D. 448, at a synod in his own city, Constantinople, which confessed its faith that "Christ, after His incarnation, consisted of two Natures in one hypostasis, and in one Person, one Christ, one Son, one Lord." Both parties were exasperated; but it must be left to ecclesiastical history to record with shame the violence of the "Robber" Council at Ephesus, and the proceedings which led to the summoning of the fourth Œcumenical Council at Chalcedon, A.D. 451. Appeal had been made to Leo, Bishop of Rome, the master spirit of the age. His celebrated *Epistola ad Flavianum* was the result, perhaps the finest theological treatise on the whole subject; and there can be no doubt that it contributed much to the formula which finally, so far as œcumenical decisions go,

o

expressed the full truth of Scripture. In balanced and careful phrases that formula mediated between Nestorius and Eutyches, by condemning both: "Following the holy fathers, we unanimously teach one and the same Son, our Lord Jesus Christ, complete as to His Godhead and complete as to His manhood, truly God and truly man, of a reasonable soul and human flesh subsisting: consubstantial with His Father as to His Godhead, and consubstantial with us as to His manhood; like unto us in all things, yet without sin; as to His Godhead begotten of the Father before all worlds, but as to His manhood, in these last days born, for us men and our salvation, of the Virgin Mary, the mother of God; one and the same Christ; Son, Lord, Only-begotten, known in (of) two natures, without confusion, without conversion, without severance, and without division; the distinction of the natures being in no wise abolished by their union, but the peculiarity of each nature being maintained, and both concurring in one person and hypostasis. We confess not a Son divided and sundered into two persons, but one and the same Son, and Only-begotten, and God-Logos, our Lord Jesus Christ, even as the prophet had before proclaimed concerning Him, and He Himself hath taught us, and the symbol of the Fathers hath handed down to us."

The sentences of this Creed, especially in the original Greek, exhaust at once the definition of error and the defence of the truth. They are as tranquil as the scenes in the midst of which they were composed were turbulent. The Athanasian Creed probably was an Augustinian variation on it, the production of Vigilius Tapsensis, an African bishop: if so, it is not the least of the many obligations which Christian theology owes to the genius and dialectical skill and wonderful command of human language possessed by the African fathers. But that Creed adds little on the Person of Christ; its chief additions have respect to the doctrine of the Trinity, which it for the first time formulated and introduced into the Christian confession as such. One element of novelty it has: an illustration occurs which seems out of harmony with the stately simplicity of a creed, and shows the operation of African rhetoric. "One not at all from confusion of substance, but from unity of person. For, as a rational soul and flesh is one man, so God and man is one Christ." However much propriety there may be in the analogy, it is very faint, and provokes more criticism than it allays. At any rate, it is hardly in keeping with the severity of a confession of faith, which is fact and belief confessed with the mouth to the glory of God. Arguments and anathemas were not introduced till the church had taken many steps on the way of declension.

III.

Here, at Chalcedon, Christology had reached the conclusion of the whole matter. Subsequent controversies and decisions have added but little to the defensive statements to which the Chalcedonian Creed with profound wisdom restricted itself. The mystery of the manner of union of the two natures which it left unexplored, and untouched, has not been solved, and probably will not be solved by theology on earth. But that mystery has never ceased to stimulate a spirit of speculation which does not accept defeat, urging its adventurous pursuit all the more vigorously the more it is baffled. The decisions of the fourth Council cast out the Nestorian and Eutychian heresies from the sanctuary of Christian doctrine; but representatives of both errors soon reappeared: Eutychianism in the long, and wearisome, and disgraceful controversies known as the Monophysite and the Monothelite in the East, and Nestorianism in the obscurer

Adoptianist controversy in the West. To these our attention must be directed; very briefly, and only so far as they affected the doctrine of our Saviour's Person.

The Monophysite heresy, as the name imports, was only a continuation or echo of the Eutychian dogma of a Single Nature in Christ. It disavowed indeed the absorption of the human nature: that evil element perhaps may be said to have passed away for ever from history. But it made our Lord's manhood only an accident of the immutable essence of the God. The Monophysite opponents of the Chalcedonian Creed introduced a liturgical formula to express their sentiment: "Holy God, *Who hast been crucified*, have mercy upon us!" hence their doctrine has been termed Theopaschitism, just as Tertullian gave the name Patripassianism to the error of Praxeas. During a hundred years these sectaries convulsed the Eastern church with their disputes over the body of Jesus. Severus, Patriarch of Antioch, made the first deviation from the orthodox doctrine of our Lord's perfect consubstantiality with our nature. His party believed that the Saviour's body was mortal and corruptible before the resurrection; and hence they were termed Phthartolaters, or adorers of the corruptible. These were opposed by the Aphthartodocetæ, who affirmed that the corporeality of Christ was from the very beginning partaker of the incorruptibility of the Logos: this was a combination of ancient Docetism and Eutychianism. These two leading parties had their subdivisions. One sect receded from the Monophysite principle so far as to deny our Lord's omniscience during His humiliation; and hence were called Agnoetæ. Other sects arose out of the dispute as to the question whether the body of Christ was or was not to be regarded as a creature: these were, on the one hand, the Ktistolatræ, and on the other, the Aktistitæ. Trifling as such distinctions and discussions may seem, they were the natural outgrowth of the Monophysite root. They form one of the most curious subsections of the great doctrine we treat. But in the midst of all these confusions there were not wanting thinkers of a stern Monophysite stamp, who declined every attempt to distinguish between the Divine and the human in Christ : not because the mystery was unfathomable, but because the two had become absolutely one in Him. The historical relations of the Monophysite heresy are irregular. The fifth Œcumenical Council, convoked by Justinian at Constantinople, A.D. 553, anathematised Nestorianism, and to a certain extent gave its sanction to Monophysitism. Yet the sects remained apart from the Greek church; and, like the Nestorians, are found in the East to this day : known as the Jacobites in Syria, the Copts in Egypt, the Abyssinians, the Armenians, and the Maronites.

In the Monothelite controversy the great question at issue assumed a more dignified character. Whilst the Monophysite controversies were confined to the relations of Christ's fleshly body and the soul as the seat of His knowledge, the Monothelite investigation turned upon the unity or duality of His will. The emperor Heraclius proposed a compromise, by which the Monophysites might be won to the catholic church, in the formula which deserves deep attention : μία θεανδρικὴ ἐνεργεία, one Divine-human operation. It was not accepted ; and the question raged furiously until the sixth Œcumenical Council, of Constantinople, A.D. 680, formally condemned the doctrine of One Will. This decision, in which East and West concurred, was arrived at after considerable argumentation. The Monothelites contended simply on the ground that two wills imply two subjects, while all things in redemption proceed from one Divine-human Agent. Their opponents on the catholic side urged that in two natures there must be two wills and two natural operations. And they ended the discussion by teaching the doctrine of two wills harmoniously co-operating, the human will following the Divine. John of Damascus, a generation later, who was in the Greek church what Leo was in the Roman, the most consummate theologian on this subject, presented the whole doctrine of the Council in its fullest form. He defined the relation of the human to the Divine nature in the unity of the Person as enhypostatic or anhypostatic. The manhood of Christ is not hypostatic in itself; yet not without an hypostasis, inasmuch as it exists in the hypostasis of the Logos. It is the human nature only as it is before it has become a personal individual. In other words he taught the doctrine of an impersonal human nature in Christ. But it cannot fail to strike the thoughtful mind that the old formula of Heraclius (or of Dionysius Areopagita from whom it was borrowed)—*one Theandric operation*—was discarded too soon. The term itself, like many others aiming to express the same idea, may be open to objection. But one agency lies at the foundation of the entire history of our Lord. Save in a few passages which speak of His eternal place and relation in the Deity, the New Testament uniformly assigns one character and one operation to the mediatorial Person. Our Lord Himself takes up, if such words may be allowed, His whole being into the past eternity, and "came forth" from the Father, not to do His own will but that of the Father who sent Him. Before He had taken our flesh, He willed and accepted the Triune Will, as already the incarnate Christ. And throughout His manifestation in the flesh His words and deeds and sufferings derive all their significance from their proceeding from one Source, which is the mediatorial

Person. Every attempt to distinguish what is of the Divine from what is of the human invariably fails. Theology is shut up to the theory of the one Theandric operation: of the absolute unity of all the manifold and wonderful developments of the Redeemer's human nature in union with the Divine. Difficulties there are in the conception, no doubt; but that theology will be the soundest which, notwithstanding those difficulties, refuses to separate the two natures for a moment in relation to any part of our Saviour's life.

The Western reaction against the Chalcedonian Creed—and the only one of any importance that ever took place—was that known as Adoptianism, which was Nestorianism with a difference. Two Spanish bishops, Elipandus of Toledo and Felix of Urgella, broached heretical opinions as to the unity of the Son in relation to His two natures. They and their followers urged that in His human nature Christ was not in the same sense the Son of God as in His Divine: in the latter by nature, in the former He was only by adoption, a Son. They contended that Christ as man could not have been begotten of the Essence Divine. They referred to the evidence of Scripture, which, though it does not use the word "adoption" in relation to this, yet defines the thing itself by many cognate terms; as also to traditional and liturgical language which habitually treated the assumption of human nature as being an adoption. In their theological subtilty they supposed Christ as man to have come into the world in the character of a servant; yet the adoption took place at the very moment of the conception, in virtue of His future excellence, while the act of adoption itself took place only at the baptism, and was consummated in His resurrection. Alcuin was one of the chief among the opponents of Adoptianism. He brought to bear upon it the leading arguments with which Nestorianism had been withstood;

and pleaded that, *in adsumtione carnis a Deo persona perit hominis, non natura*, not the nature of man but his personality is lost. And thus Adoptianism, like every modification of the Nestorian heresy, fell before the doctrine of our Saviour's impersonal humanity. It may be observed, before passing from this subject, that there is no affinity between this ancient heresy of a double Sonship and the modern theory that has denied the Eternal Sonship of the pre-existent Lord. The modern doctrine would apply all that is said concerning the Son to the Son as the Eternal Word incarnate.

IV.

To follow the course of Christological doctrine into mediæval times is, in a certain sense, to lose it for some seven hundred years. Not that theology or theological speculation slumbered during those ages; it was never more active, restless, and inquisitive. But there was no appreciable advancement made, either in the resolution of the difficulties of the dogma or in the systematisation of the vast mass of materials of which it had become the centre. The scholastics in their several dialectic and mystical schools spent the strength of their intellect or the fervour of their hearts on the natures and the Person of the Redeemer without adding much to the sum of knowledge. They discussed a thousand subtle topics which earlier decisions had fixed, but without unsettling any of them; and they indulged in a thousand speculations which later philosophy has revived. Hence, full justice will be done to this branch of the subject by considering some of these residuary questions bequeathed by the past, and some of the germs which they deposited for future development.

A few sentences will suffice to dispatch that branch of

mediæval speculation which dealt with subjects which may be held to be interdicted. In the middle of the ninth century the monks of Corbie, Paschasius Radbert and Ratram, carried on a discussion as to whether our Saviour's birth was not as supernatural as His conception. The details of this discussion ought to be left to the obscurity of these ages. But the question involved was very important, as concerning the reality of our Lord's participation in our nature as lying under the curse of transgression. Rather than admit that, one party elaborated incredible theories of a merely docetic birth, which removed the very foundation of the Saviour's true human life. The other party, admitting the naturalness of our Saviour's entrance into life, began to devise methods for removing the sin from the mother in order that the Child might be a "holy thing." In this case, as in almost every other aberration from the truth as to Christ's Person, the Holy Ghost was forgotten. He provided that the Child Jesus should be born amidst the consequences of the curse without inheriting it for His own Person. Edward Irving long afterwards solved the difficulty in another way, by giving our Lord a manhood bearing in it the common taint.

In the same century Scotus Erigena laid the foundation of the Pantheistic conception of Christ's Person, which entered so largely into the mystical theories of the next five hundred years, and has reappeared in modern German Christological philosophy. Christ is here the primal, archetypal Man, man in His nature and essence; and His incarnation is the unity of the finite and the infinite, of the temporal and eternal, which constitutes the idea of man: as consciousness must have in it the element of finitude, so God's own consciousness can be conditioned only by the incarnation of God. Thus personality and limited consciousness seem to be one, and God must be embodied in the Christ to have a personal conscious existence. He who can understand the ancient schoolmen will be at great advantage in studying the modern transcendental Christ of Schelling and Hegel. If he cannot understand it, he will, at least, know whither to trace it.

In the twelfth century Peter Lombard, Master of the Sentences, broached a question which occupied the thoughts of a whole generation, viz., whether, the human nature in Christ being impersonal, the Person of God the Son may be said to have become anything in reality different from the other Persons of the Trinity through the incarnation. The tendency of his inquiries seemed to make the manhood merely a Docetic vesture of God; the union did not make of two natures one Person, because the Son was never conscious of Himself as man. Hence the incarnation ceased to be necessary for atonement, and the Lateran Council of A.D. 1215 condemned the error to which these discussions led, as Nihilianism, a term which itself explains the controversy better than any dissertation could, by establishing its opposite, the profound and eternal reality of the incarnation as not belonging to the entire Divine essence, but to the Eternal Son in Divinity.

The next Christological controversy of the middle ages was perhaps the first which connected the Person of Christ with His work of salvation. It was this, whether Christ must have become incarnate independently of man's sin. When once started, this question had a mighty attraction for the schoolmen, and they carried on a controversy as fruitless as it was ingenious and full of beautiful theorising. Rupert of Deutz was the ablest defender of the thesis that the Son of God was, from eternity, to be the incarnate Head of the creation. Interweaving speculations of his own with the words of St. Paul to the Colossians, he maintained that angels and men, that is, as he supposed, disembodied and embodied intelligences, were created to be the two spheres of Christ's one supremacy, answering to His two natures. He and his followers further asserted that the link between the Creator and the creature must be constituted of One who shall join the two in Himself. They thought that it was derogatory to the dignity of the Son to make the union with mankind dependent upon the accident of man's sin. The scholastic camp was divided. They never, of course, settled the question; it was taken up at the Reformation, and is, to this day, a subject that divides the Lutheran divines, and produces a series of barren, but very interesting, contributions to theological literature.

Thomas Aquinas denied the necessity of the incarnation independently of man's sin. He took his stand on the essential immutability of God: and, regarding human nature as finding its true personality only in the Logos, made the Divine-human Person the medium of the intercommunion of Divine and human attributes. The two wills in Christ he acknowledged as different modes of the same one Divine will, the human will being made an instrument of God. His speculations on our Lord's knowledge, in relation to His two natures, are very instructive: he assigns to the human soul a capacity of knowing all that is or will be, stopping short however at all that might be, as being the prerogative of God alone. Duns Scotus carried his speculations on the union in Christ's Person to much more subtle issues. He held that man's nature is in its deepest essence supernatural, and that there is in the soul a limitless tendency towards God, and an infinite capacity of being filled with the Divine. Hence God and Christ in man may be one in the sense of an indefinite progression of the spirit towards God. It is obvious that in this there lie the elements of almost all heresy on this subject. The theory of Scotus bore its fruit in his doctrines of redemption. He denied the objective importance and necessity of the atonement; which owed all its virtue to the simple will of God that thus, and not by any other method that He might have appointed, man should be saved. Hence he pleaded for the " Immaculate Conception," Christ's predestination being connected in God's foreknowledge with the holiness of His mother. The disciples of Scotus were the founders of Scepticism; and metaphysical inquiry, where not sceptical, became transcendently mystic in its character.

The Christ of pure Mysticism must find its place at this point in our historical sketch. The earlier mystics had been very much independent of Christian doctrine in their speculations; and the later mystics, whether of the old or the new church, lost the Christian doctrine in a formless void of theosophy and transcendentalism. But the scholastic mystics held fast the Christological decisions of the church, however fanciful were their variations on them. They held firmly to the doctrine of the Trinity; but with a Sabellian distinction between the *nature* and the *operation*. According to Tauler, as God brings forth His Son in Himself eternally, and gives Him to man through the virgin birth, so is His Son born in us by a constant incarnation in every devout soul. The mystics make no real difference between the Son incarnate and every Christian united to Him. Believing that Christ was God in the sanctified impersonal nature of man, they thought that the goal of desire must be to enter into Him and lose personality in Him, by sharing His impersonal nature. Christ was to some of them the archetypal Mystic who exhibited not a union between God and a man, but the abased God suffering in the flesh: they not only asserted the capacity of human nature for the Divine, but the capacity of the Divine for human affections. Some of them anticipated the later theories which shrink not from making the power of God in Christ a constricted or lowered potence of God. But none of them added anything to the doctrine of Christ's Person, and therefore we leave them. However rapturous their contemplations of His incomprehensible form, and however intense their yearnings to lose themselves in Him, they never had the incarnate Man of Sorrows clearly before their minds. They would not submit to the letter of the record, and the true and veritable Saviour became one whom they ignorantly worshipped. In common with all mystics of every age they suffered the cross and the atonement to vanish away, lost in the wide expanse of their sublime intuition. In a word, instead of humbly fixing their thought upon that historical Personage who "appeared once in the end of the world to put away sin by the sacrifice of Himself," they lost themselves and almost their Christianity in the contemplation of an incarnation eternally going on in themselves after the pattern of Christ's incarnation. The history of the doctrine of Christ's Person will not need to introduce the mystics of any school again.

V.

The era of the Reformation, which witnessed so great a revolution in the doctrines of grace and in the principles of ecclesiastical authority, wrought but little essential change in Christology, or the doctrine of Christ's Person. What the Reformation did was to bring that Divine-human Person into its central place as the only ground of man's salvation; to remove those accumulations of superstition which had obscured, not so much the doctrine, as the Person Himself; and to bring into prominence the direct individual relation of every believer to that Person. As to the two constituent natures and the union between them, neither Nestorian on the one hand, nor Eutychian on the other, the formularies of the Reformation retained the ancient creeds, and had no contest with the old communities whose fundamental principles on other points they assailed. The incarnate Son of God Himself had never ceased to occupy His rightful place in the creeds of the churches which had dishonoured His work by multitudes of superstitions.

Some points of subordinate, though by no means unimportant, difference among the earlier confessions of Protestantism require a brief consideration. These relate chiefly to the opposite views of the Lutheran and the Reformed communions, and with special reference to their respective doctrines of the Eucharist. Differences as to the mediatorial offices of Christ do not enter into the present subject.

The Lutheran doctrine of the Lord's Supper demanded for its foundation the assumption of the *ubiquitas* or omnipresence of the body of Christ; and this again required a definite theory as to the relation of the two natures in His one Person. The ancient formula, *communicatio idiomatum*, that is, the expression of the fact that, in consequence of the Communion of Natures, the properties of each of the two natures are communicated to the other, and to the whole Person, was found essential to the doctrine of consubstantiation. The Formula Concordiæ sets forth that the Person of Christ was constituted by the Son of God assuming in the Virgin's womb the human nature into His own unity. This act was the decree of the whole Trinity, accomplished by the Logos, who is therefore the Personal Principle. This personal union is entire: not part with part, but the whole Logos with the flesh, and the whole flesh with the whole Logos, so that wherever the Logos is, there He has the flesh most intimately present. This union is not natural, as between body and soul, nor merely verbal, nor mystical, nor internal, nor sacramental, but essential, personal, and abiding. They further analyse thus the doctrine of the communication of properties. There is (1) the *genus idiomaticum*, whereby the properties of one nature are applied or transferred to the whole Person, and here their theology is indisputably sound; (2) the *genus majestaticum*, whereby the one nature gives its property to the other, which however is no communication, because it is only the human that can receive; and (3) the *genus apotelesmaticum*, whereby the redemptional acts of the Person are predicated of one or the other nature, on which also there can be no doubt. It is on the second of these kinds of communication that Lutheranism established the doctrine of an impartation, *at the will of Christ*, of His glorified body and blood, *in*, and *with*, and *under* the unchanged elements, to the communicant.

Consistently with this doctrine the One Person of Christ is seen in Lutheran theology in a state of exinanition and a state of exaltation. The incarnation is a permanent state, and therefore as such is no part of our Lord's self-abasement: it was consummated before the conception, in the assumption of our nature into the Divine. The humbled estate begins with the conception and ends with the burial; the exaltation begins with the descent into hades, and goes on for ever. But the Lutherans were not always at one on the nature of our Lord's humiliation. The Formula Concordiæ taught that "He did not exhibit His majesty always, but when it seemed good to Him, until He laid aside the servant form." In the seventeenth century the theologians of Tübingen decided that "the man Christ taken into God did govern all things as a present King, but *latently:*"

hence theirs was the theory of the κρύψις. The theologians of Giessen denied this, and went so far as to defend a veritable κένωσις, or self-emptying on the part of Christ. The Tübingen school deemed that our Lord already sat on the right hand of God at His conception, and on the cross, and that the exaltation did not impart the reality but the name and appearance of the dignity. They afterwards yielded so far as to admit a renunciation as concerning the priestly office, but no more. The germ of this controversy we shall see hereafter developed.

The Reformed or Calvinistic churches rejected this interpretation of our Saviour's Person, and all the consequences that flow from it. The fundamental principle of their doctrine will best be exhibited by showing its points of difference from the former. They maintained that the Divine perfections could be attributes of the Man to the extent of His human finiteness, and established it as their foundation that *finitum non est capax infiniti*, "the finite cannot be capable of the infinite." Whatever the Lutherans might say as to the Infinite being pleased so to communicate Itself to the finite as to make it one with Itself, to that principle they kept faithful. The Lutherans held that Christ was the God-man before He became man; that the incarnation was the assumption of the human nature into the fellowship of the Trinity in the Person of the Logos; and that the God-man as such must empty Himself of His Divine form before He could assume that of a servant in human existence. His conception being the first voluntary act of the, as it were, pre-existing Divine-human Person, the God-man was a real personality before He descended to a human life. The Reformed denied all this. They held the incarnation to be itself the humiliation, in that the Logos absolute exists as the Logos made man in a developing life and consciousness. They even teach that the human nature is connected in personal unity with the Logos, not immediately, but only by the instrumentality of the Holy Ghost; and in the opposition to the idea of too close an affinity between the finite and the Infinite, they fall into the danger of making Christ's manhood too much like that of other men. When Zwingli would substitute the idea of a mere rhetorical interchange of attributes for the *communicatio idiomatum* he went too far, for any Nestorian would have done the same; and Luther's vigorous epithet had some sense in it, as well as much wrath, when he denounced the Reformed ἀλλοίωσις, or figurative interchange, as a *larva diaboli*.

In an historical review it is not appropriate to enter at any length upon a comparison of these rival systems. Confining ourselves strictly to their treatment of the Person of Christ, we cannot but observe that the Lutheran tendency is as decidedly, though unconsciously, Eutychian, as the Reformed is decidedly, though unconsciously, Nestorian. Hence, as it will be seen, the later speculations of Lutheranism have almost invariably leaned towards the idea of such a union of the God and man in Christ as should abolish the double nature of the Redeemer, while the Reformed churches have found their chief danger to be in such a separation of the God from the man in Christ as concedes everything that Unitarianism asks. This, however, refers to a later time. A reaction of withering Rationalism awaited both, and was not long in coming.

Thus the Reformation era only established more firmly than ever the doctrine of the Incarnate Person, in the perfect but unfathomable union of His two natures, the One Object of faith. Disputes there were on many points connecting the indivisible hypostatic union with the atonement. For instance, the distinction between the active and passive righteousness of the God-man was pressed by many so far as to divide the sacrificial obedience, and make His vicarious holiness as well as passion meritorious for the believer. This error was not, however, confined to the Lutherans; it was bound up with the Calvinistic faith, while only a perversion of the Lutheran. But, apart from this error, it was the glory of the middle of the sixteenth century to unite all the Reformed communions in a glorious confession of the Object of faith, the whole, undivided, and indivisible Person of Jesus Christ, whose work, like Himself, is one, and who is in both the Object of faith to man. The essentials of the ancient creeds were reproduced in the article *De Filio Dei* of the Augsburg Confession, which we quote here, because at the time when it was framed it perhaps expressed on this point the faith of a larger proportion of Christendom than any other article. The same truths, encumbered and disfigured, were found in the creeds of Eastern and Western communions; but these words expressed the truth, and the pure truth, that had descended from antiquity. Socinianism was not as yet known, and the Lutheran, and Reformed, and Anglican Confessions joined in this faith:

"*Item docent, quod Verbum, hoc est Filius Dei, assumpserit humanam naturam in utero beatæ Mariæ Virginis, ut sint duæ naturæ, divina et humana, in unitate personæ inseparabiliter conjunctæ, unus Christus, vere Deus, et vere Homo, natus ex Virgine Mariâ, vere passus, crucifixus, mortuus et sepultus, ut reconciliaret nobis Patrem, et hostia esset non tantum pro culpâ originis, sed etiam pro omnibus actualibus hominum peccatis.*"

The second Article of the Church of England is based upon this, but somewhat strengthens it, especially in the simultaneous original Latin. There we read, "*In utero beatæ Virginis, ex illius substantiâ naturam humanam assumpsit.*" But the English Article, which was the faith of the whole empire at one time on this central doctrine, ought to be familiar to all:

"The Son, which is the Word of the Father, begotten from everlasting of the Father, the very and eternal God, and of one substance with the Father, took man's nature in the womb of the blessed Virgin, of her substance; so that two whole and perfect natures, that is to say the Godhead and manhood, were joined together in one Person never to be divided, whereof is one Christ very God and very man; who truly suffered, was crucified, dead, and buried, to reconcile His Father to us, and to be a sacrifice not only for orginal guilt, but also for all actual sins of men."

Instead of giving extracts from the several confessions that embodied the faith of the Calvinistic branches of the Reformers, the Westminster Confession, of a hundred years later, may be referred to, as expressing almost in the same words the belief of all Calvinistic communities on the Continent, in Great Britain, and in America: "The Son of God, the Second Person in the Trinity, being very and eternal God, of one substance and equal with the Father, did, when the fulness of time was come, take upon Him man's nature with all the essential properties and common infirmities thereof, yet without sin, being conceived by the Holy Ghost in the womb of the Virgin Mary, of her substance: so that two whole, perfect, and distinct natures, the Godhead and the manhood, were inseparably joined together in one Person, without conversion, composition, or confusion. Which Person is very God and very man, yet one Christ, the only Mediator between God and man."

These extracts from the three leading confessions of Protestantism cannot be read and studied, and compared in their minute differences, without profit. Their phraseology should be written on the mind of every one who would understand the doctrine of Christ's Person. But their highest interest is found in the fact that they represent the great result of fifteen centuries of the church's theological history in this central department of the truth. All the creeds contribute to these sentences; and the faith of man need not hope for any clearer definitions to sustain it than these. But now we pass to a less pleasing theme.

VI.

No sooner had the Reformation restored the Saviour's Person, as the one Christ and one Mediator, to the view and the faith of the Christian world, than an Antichrist appeared in the form of what may be called Modern Unitarianism. The early history of the church was as it were re-enacted. The Ebionites, the Gnostics, and Arians, reappeared in the Socinians and Rationalists and mythical theorisers who have been steadily under various forms assailing the catholic truth from that time until now. The spirit of the Reformation was appalled by the beginnings of this deadly evil,—the only essential Antichrist whether of ancient or modern times. By it Luther's soul was stirred within him as it was stirred by nothing else; Calvin joined the Inquisition in striving to suppress it by the stake; states and governments disavowed, proscribed, and punished it. But in vain. Its development was at that time a necessity; it has its place among us still; but it will also have its end.

Passing by Swedenborg's identification of the Trinity with Christ's Person, Socinianism is the first development of Unitarianism in order of time, and the only one that ever formed a confession and a literature. Lælius Socinus was an Italian, who felt the influence of the Reformation in its first advances in Italy; but, becoming infected with doubts, he travelled, and at length settled in Geneva. Under the rebuke of Calvin, and warned by the death of Servetus, he kept in the background, cherishing his opinions, but leaving others to maintain them for him. Faustus Socinus, his bolder and more systematic nephew, took up his abode in Poland, already, as will be hereafter seen, the stronghold of anti-Trinitarianism. There he moulded his heresy, and there the *Racovian Catechism*, the formulary of his tenets, was constructed. In its relation to the Person of Christ the system had some peculiarities not known in antiquity, and since obsolete; but generally it was a revival of ancient Ebionism. It set out with the principle that the Divine and the human natures forbid any such union as the incarnation supposes; that Jesus Christ, born of the Virgin by a supernatural interposition, was a mere man, though free from original sin; that His baptism was the descent on Him of a special Divine efficacy; that He received His commission as prophet, priest, and king, during some mysterious rapture into heaven, probably in the wilderness of temptation; that in His death there was nothing propitiatory, but the highest of all martyrdom for truth; that in His resurrection He received a quasi-Divine but only delegated authority over the universe; and that only as a representative of the power of God is He entitled to reverence and the receiver of prayer. Socinianism was developed in Poland; but it never became naturalized there: in the middle of the seventeenth century it was proscribed and exterminated. During its prevalence it assumed a propagandist character, and sent missionaries to Hungary, where they had no success; to Holland, where they met with more encouragement; and to England, where they were represented by a single congregation which soon died out. The Socinian theory of Christ's Person—and it is with that only we have to do—has not survived. It had so much affinity with Arianism in some of its elements as to be absorbed in many cases into that system. It retained too much of the supernatural, and adhered too closely to the letter of Scripture, to satisfy the growing spirit of pure Rationalism, which gradually discarded it therefore throughout Christendom. Modern Unitarianism has left Socinus far behind; and his theories, while they fill a Polonian library, have ceased to occupy a place in the living process of the historical development of our doctrine.

To modern Arianism a secondary place has been assigned, simply because it has been more sporadic in its character, and has never been able to furnish a creed or a literature to represent its claims. In other respects, and as a power in the history of the Christian church, its importance has been very great. To trace this, however lightly, we must go back to the Nicene Council, and take up the thread again which was designedly left unpursued. A modification of the doctrine of Arius, known by the name of semi-Arianism, and by the formula of *Homoiousion*—of *like* substance with the Father, in opposition to *Homoousion*, of the *same* substance— disappeared from Christian history before the fourth century closed: it was a mere subtle evasion, and was lost again in the spread of the parent doctrine. Arianism proper branched into a variety of denominations, which will not here be referred to, because they refer rather to the doctrine of the Trinity, and introduce nothing new into that of Christ's Person, who, in all of them alike, is a man inhabited by a Being created of the Father. It was for more than three hundred years a formidable rival of the catholic doctrine: prevalent among the Goths, the Vandals in Africa, the Visigoths in France and Spain, the Lombards in Italy, it was not extinct as a public profession until the end of the seventh century. During the middle ages it appears again and again in Italy and elsewhere, secretly held by many who openly professed, with a reservation, the Nicene Creed. At the time of the Reformation one species of the tares that grew up among the wheat was Arianism. Servetus and Gentilis, who died for their errors at Geneva and Berne, held this among other heresies. But it was in Poland that this form of anti-Trinitarianism flourished most: there the Arians formed separate congregations, all of which concurred in maintaining the supremacy of the Father, but differed among themselves as to whether the Son was a god of inferior nature derived from the Deity, or the first created spirit who became incarnate. Some of those who at first believed the latter doctrine descended to the theory of Christ's simple manhood, and were prepared, as we have seen, to receive the teachings, more consistently developed, of Socinus. Driven ultimately from Poland, where alone they had had a corporate existence, it cannot be said that in any part of the world the Arians have ever maintained, or now maintain, their faith as a community. It is only through prejudice or carelessness that the Arminians of Holland are sometimes said to have been infected with Arianism. As a body they certainly were not amenable to this charge; and though some of them, such as Grotius, and Wetstein, and Episcopius himself, spoke very tolerantly as to the condemnation of those who denied the eternal filiation, they were not Arians. Their leanings, so far as they leaned to error, was towards the Racovian school, but they were leanings that betrayed themselves mostly if not solely in inconsiderate language.

Arianism in England has to Englishmen an interesting history, but that history evolves only one doctrinal element that demands attention here. That element is Subordinationism, which only indirectly affects the question of Christ's Person, being really a branch of the Trinitarian controversy.

Dr. Samuel Clarke's *Scripture Doctrine of the Trinity*, published in 1712, opened a series of discussions which brought to light the existence of a strong and definite leaven of Arianism in the English church. His apology to Convocation in 1714 declared his belief that "the Son was eternally begotten by the eternal, incomprehensible power and will of the Father; also that the Holy Spirit was eternally derived from the Father by or through the Son, according to the eternal, incomprehensible power and will of the Father." This is the highest refinement of Arianism, and something very different from the species of subordination doctrine taught by the best English divines, following the early fathers, though using far more cautious language than they. Whatever "eternal" may mean in this definition, it is not possible that it can redeem from Arian imputation the words "by His power and will." This transcendental view of the Godhead of the Son, who is, nevertheless, not consubstantial with the Father, was held by many eminent men, whose names need not be mentioned; it was taught both in and out of the Establishment; but at length, by an easy transition, became that Humanitarianism of which Priestley was the first representative in England, having Lindsey and Belsham as his feeble followers. It strove to interpret the New Testament on the theory that Jesus Christ was only man. With remarkable industry it applied the resources of Biblical criticism to the task, "improved" the version of the New Testament, and succeeded in keeping up and continuing, down to the present century, a Unitarian system of faith and worship based upon the purely humanitarian hypothesis. But this system, which denies the original sin of man, the atonement of Christ's death, the Divinity and influence of the Holy Spirit, and which, denying all these, regards Jesus of Nazareth as a man remarkably endowed of

God, whose claims have been much misunderstood, has no claim to consideration in this Essay. It is an embellished and more complete edition of Deism, and, with Deism, bids fair to disappear before the effect of influences now to be referred to.

With the eighteenth century began, throughout most of the communions of the continental Reformation, a marked indifference to the old formularies. The spirit of subjective philosophy turned away from the objective standards; the supernatural and transcendent was given up in favour of the natural and tangible; and Divine faith was surrendered to the censure and despotism of human reason. The age of Illuminism had come; and upon no object in the sphere of Christian belief was its false light more searchingly shed than upon the ancient doctrine of our Lord's Person. One of its first canons of criticism required that every contradiction be removed from the idea of the historical Redeemer. Then vanished at once the union of God and man, with the *communicatio idiomatum;* and the Lutheran church had its writers who bitterly wrote against this essential of Lutheran theology. Nestorianism was triumphant. Then, with the Homoousion, the true Divinity left the Christ, and an Arian stream of doctrine set in. The Arian Logos became simply a Divine energy, and the descent to Ebionism was made. Soon the touch of Divine power that even Ebionism left in the Redeemer's nativity was renounced; and Jesus was in German theology only man. By degrees, as Illuminism became more luminous, it could criticise the character of our Lord, which was found unable to endure its inquisition. In Germany, as in English Deism, the doctrine of our Lord's Person had thus reached the lowest stage of its abasement, to begin at once to rise again.

VII.

Then commenced what may be termed the modern development, the peculiarly modern philosophical development, of the Ideal Christ.

This had its birthplace in Germany; but has exerted a very strong influence in England and in America—in fact, wherever the Person of Christ is an object of study. It has almost recast Christology, although in itself scarcely worthy to be called a doctrine. The father of this philosophy, Kant—unless indeed Spinoza be the father of it—regarded the Son of God as the representative of mankind, well pleasing to God; as the personification of the principle of all good, the ideal of moral perfection. From that time the idea of the God-man became one of the profoundest and most cherished ideas of philosophy: each giving it, down to Hegel and beyond him, its own specific impress. Kant's system required a redemption from the original evil of our nature, and the human ideal to guide aspiration. But it was matter of indifference whether that ideal became a reality through supernatural generation or otherwise. It sublimely rose above the petty historical Jesus of Nazareth: like the Gnostic æon leaving the man Christ Jesus, after having used Him for its purpose. Indeed, according to Kant, the good principle did not enter the world at any definite crisis, but had invisibly descended into man from the beginning. Schelling's philosophy of identity regarded Jesus as the unity of the finite and the infinite, as the God incarnate in time, who in Christ as the climax of His manifestation ends the world of finiteness, and begins that of the infinite or the supremacy of spirit. The mystery of nature and the incarnation of God were to him intertwined and inseparable. It is an incarnation from eternity. The man Christ forms in

His historical appearance only the crown, or in another sense the beginning, of that incarnation; for, having its noblest form in Him, it was to be so continued in His followers that they should be the body of which He was the Head. But after much that is honourable to the historical Christ, his idealism carries him away again, and he declares that the single incarnation of Christianity is not so rational as the Indian successive visitations of God; and that the narratives concerning Christ are matters of indifference, inasmuch as the great idea depends not on this single phenomenon, but is universal and absolute. Hegel's philosophy has had more influence than any other on our doctrine; but it is exceedingly difficult to extract its fundamental principle, and make it available for our purpose. To take it boldly: God is man, and God is spirit. As spirit distinguishing Himself from Himself the finiteness of consciousness arises: God thinks Himself in man into a finite spirit: not indeed in any individual but in mankind as a whole. God, as the Infinite, has man as the finite for His counterpart, or rather opposite pole. So, to dismiss this incomprehensible travesty of the gospel, what the church attributes to Christ, as His predicates, should be attributed to the great idea of humanity as the veritable God-man. It is obvious that these principles do not of themselves belong to the doctrine of the Person of Christ; nor would they be introduced here save as showing the origin of many influences that conspired to mould the Unitarianism of England and America during the present century, and to throw a haze over much of the theology of those who profess themselves Trinitarian Christians. Some illustrative remarks on this subject will end our sketch of Humanitarianism.

The first noticeable effect of the transcendental philosophy on the doctrine of our Lord's Person was to discredit, in

Germany and everywhere, those theories of infidel Rationalism which founded the historical manifestation of Christ on conscious or unconscious imposture. With those theories, beginning with that of Reimarus the Wolfenbüttel fragmentist, and continuing through a series of cold and irreverent and sometimes blasphemous criticisms of the Holy Life, we need have nothing to do. It is grievous even to be obliged to preserve their names. They were all, both the English Deists who preceded, and the French Encyclopædists who followed them, based on an absolute denial of the supernatural as bound up with the life of Jesus. And the first touch of the transcendental philosophy exploded that error. Whatever else the philosophical patronage of Christianity did, it shielded it and its documents from a purely naturalistic treatment. The Person of Christ was replaced in its position between the two worlds; and men began everywhere to study what was His significance with regard to both.

Schleiermacher marked a new era in modern Christology, inasmuch as he brought the ideal theory into closer connection with theology; Christ, as the normal idea of mankind, into closer relation with the historical Christ. His doctrine of our Lord's Person, however, denies the personal union of the Divine and human natures. His Trinity is not the Christian Trinity, but, so far as it is triune at all, is Sabellian. Jesus was, in his theory, born without sin or the possibility of sin; but, whether by supernatural generation or not, his theory does not ask, and it pays but slight attention to the gospel narratives. God's indwelling in Him simply realizes the idea that human consciousness has of its own possible sinlessness. The impersonality of the human nature in Christ is carried to its extremest point; His humanity passively receives God, or a power of God, and in His historical Person God always, and supremely, acts. He is like all men in independent human volitions and deeds; unlike all men in the everlasting power of His God-consciousness, which is the only idea of the God in Him. Hence Schleiermacher's doctrine of the Saviour's sinlessness, and freedom from error, and absolute perfection, is extremely high, and redeems his Christology in general .to a great extent. Christ is mankind anew created, and His salvation rests upon our entering into His new nature and fellowship, and into a vital union with His representative obedience. His system dismisses altogether the idea of vicarious expiation; but, inasmuch as Christ represents the whole of redeemed mankind, He may be called our Satisfying Substitute. He gives his doctrine of redemption in the form of what to us is a paradox. The redeeming sufferings were vicarious, but without making satisfaction. Christ's obedience makes satisfaction, but not as vicarious. Hence it will be obvious that the entire system of this leader of modern German theology is composed of the most heterogeneous elements, bound together by a mystical and sentimental bond peculiarly his own. He agrees with the transcendental philosophers in making the infinite and finite meet in the ideal Christ; but he differs from them in regarding God, not as *becoming* Himself in Christ, but as *being* in Him as the archetype of a new humanity. He rejects the church doctrines of the personal union, the atoning death, and the supreme importance of the historical facts of Christ's life; but he agrees with the Christian faith in making Jesus man's representative, and in holding something like the New-Testament doctrine of a union with Him by faith. Above all, he nourished in his own soul, and poured into his theology, a deep and tender love to the Person of Christ as he conceived Him, and thus atoned by the affections of his heart for many of the errors of his head. It is impossible to trace here the influence of his teaching on a whole generation of thinkers in all parts of Christendom; nor would it be easy to prove, by individual instances, what, nevertheless, may be safely asserted, that he contributed largely to raise to a higher character the grovelling views of Humanitarianism, above which he himself was greatly elevated.

Whether or not through the influence of German Transcendental Christology, certain it is that the more modern Unitarianism of England, France, and America has undergone a marvellous change—improvement it is not necessary to say. It is not that the doctrine of Christ's simple manhood has risen towards the older Socinianism, or the Ebionism of ancient times. Such a return to their old paths can hardly be predicated of the representatives of modern Unitarianism. They have rather caught the infection of the ideal Christ hovering mysteriously and undefinably in our midst neither God nor man, too low for the one, too high for the other,—concerning whose true character and lineaments they are in hopeless confusion; whom they cannot, like our forefathers, formulate in any creed that words can frame. The works of the most prominent Unitarians of America, Dr. Channing, Theodore Parker, and others, and English writers, of whom Mr. Martineau may be cited as an example, abundantly prove this. They are one and all impatient of the poverty of their creed, and almost every sentence they write concerning Christ is a confession of despair. Not that they make any approach towards a Divine Redeemer. So long as they apply their prerogative of reason to the doctrines of the Trinity and the atonement, and find them incredible, Christ can never be God to them. Their Jesus has ceased to be the Jesus of Priestley and Belsham; He is animated by some higher potence of the Divine than mere human nature can account for. But they have no doctrine, and therefore, as before once and again observed, they have no right to a place in this sketch.

The same might be said of the teaching that proceeds from a considerable section of the clergy of the English church, or, it might be said, of the English churches. The "Essays and Reviews" are not Ebionite or Socinian or Humanitarian, nor Arian, in their presentation of Christ's Person, simply because they have no positive doctrine at all, only a negative abandonment of the faith of the Christian world. "In theology," says one of these Essays, "the less we define the better. Definite statements respecting the relation of Christ either to God or man are only figures of speech; they do not really pierce the clouds which 'round our little life.'" If the writer of these words stood alone, or was a man whose wavering words were soliloquies, like Prospero's in his quotation, there would be no reason to pause for a moment to think of him; he might be passed by like a thousand other representatives of free thought. But he is, in a special sense, a representative, and speaks for great numbers of teachers, as well as to great numbers of hearers. Their doctrine never helps the people to answer the great question, "*Whom say ye that I am?*" The teaching given in the Articles, and Prayers, and Homilies, and the great writers of their church, is discredited, and nothing is substituted that simple minds can grasp. Our Lord is saluted by all His titles, and His Person and work are both often spoken of in the language of conventional theology. But the heart and soul of the old doctrine is gone. When some members of the party, less discreet than the leaders, venture on discussions and definitions, the result is a conglomerate of Mysticism, Pantheism, Transcendentalism, Hegelianism (as some delight to avow), of which the most undisciplined of Schleiermacher's disciples would have been ashamed. Perhaps no thinker has spent the energies of a more powerful mind, or of a more sincere will, upon this great subject that Mr. Maurice. But it is impossible to bring his definitions of Christ's Person and relation to our race into harmony with any creed, formula, or confession that is found either in Scripture or in the church.

Returning again to Germany, it can scarcely be regarded as far-fetched when we trace the influence of the Ideal Philosophy upon the theories of the divines who are now endeavouring, in the Lutheran church especially, to construct a true and philosophical conception of the union between God and our nature in Christ. The effort has reference to the state of humiliation especially: and the self-emptying of which St. Paul speaks when writing to the Philippians is made the object of a scrutiny which even the scholastics scarcely ventured upon, but which the thinkers of Germany consider not only as permitted but as essential to the vindication of the Christian faith. The Logos then is by one class of theories supposed to have limited Himself in the incarnation, undergone a *self-depotentiation* in love, amounting to a surrender of His eternal, self-conscious being; thus to have found Himself in our nature, and in it to have gradually expanded again into one Divine-human existence, unchangeably the same, though proceeding onwards in its development to the ascension: for ever, be it remembered, remaining in the unity of a Divine-human life. The relation of the Holy Ghost is called in to support this wonderful theory, which seems like one of the old Gnostic heresies risen again with its Divine potence in the embryonic nature of man. The gradual restoration of the Logos to Himself, as His human faculties expanded, is supposed to be conducted by the energy of the Holy Ghost, whose peculiar office in regard to our Lord's human nature is thus accounted for. There is a modification of this theory which does not press the depotentiation of the Logos, but prefers the limitation of His self-bestowment on the Man, according to the gradual ability of his faculties to receive the Divine. Thus a Divine-human Person is not the result of the incarnation as such, but the result of the final development of the manhood; the union not being completely accomplished until the human consciousness could grasp it, could appropriate it, and be by it appropriated.

German theologians exceedingly delight in this new stage of the Christological problem. Many of the greatest of them are partisans of the doctrine in some of its forms: Nitzsch, König, Ebrard, Lange, Martensen, Thomasius, Hofmann, Delitzsch, Schmieder, Kahnis, Liebner, Rothe— are names of some of the most laborious and generally orthodox theologians of the Continent; and most of them are teaching among ourselves through translations of their works. It would therefore be inconsiderate to brand as folly the labours of such men, especially as the works in which these theories are evolved are for the most part of great value in other respects. But it is not to be denied that this last phase of Christological dogmatic inquiry is full of the germ of almost all the heresies that have passed in review before us, and of others the composite of these. To get rid of one difficulty, that of the double consciousness of our Lord belonging to one indivisible Person, they bring a thousand equally great into existence. In reading the history of the controversy, and especially in studying the writers themselves, one old heresy after another lifts its horrid semblance to scare us, as it were, from an interdicted part of the garden of theology. In this chapter of speculation it sometimes seems as if almost every form under which the commerce of God and man has been depicted in mythology, heathen and Christian, were reproduced to play its part again, on paper at least, in this nineteenth century. Sometimes the incarnation is spoken of as the entrance into our race of One who must die out of existence in the Trinity before He could live in the flesh; who thus therefore rehearsed as Divine the great wonder of His self-sacrifice on the cross. No marvel that the supplementary question then arises as to what resources there are in Deity for the renewed generation of the Eternal Son. Shocked by such consequences, others nevertheless insist on the suspension of the personal Godhead of the Son, which for a season is either given back to God, or latently existent in the incarnate Christ. All this seems simply heathenism; the same which the Fathers so earnestly condemned under the name of Patripassianism in earlier times and of Theopaschitism at a later date. In some of its defenders it begets Apollinarianism; the potence or power in the Divinity which is called the Son disdains the limits that a human soul would have imposed—such moral and intellectual, and spiritual limitations as are deemed unworthy—but consents to the limitations of the flesh, which are physical only, and give an organ for the experience of human sorrow, and make Him who lives in it capable of death. Convicted of this error, the theorist glides into Sabellianism. The ablest adherent of this many-featured hypothesis, Thomasius, so felt the pressure of this difficulty that he devised the expedient of a difference between the immanent and the œconomical Logos. The essential Son did not undergo depotentiation or self-constriction, but the œconomical Logos, with whom, when once in some undefinable way severed from the essential Logos, theory can disport at pleasure. The œconomical Son may undergo the whole lot of man's infirmity, from the unconsciousness of sleep to the infinite agony of the desertion of God. Other aspects of the theory, which, as in the hands of Hofmann and others, borrow the ideal Christ of Kant and Schleiermacher, might be introduced. They would show, if space and patience allowed of their illustration here, that this system of theorizing on the manifestation of God in Christ is a product of the false philosophy that has for a hundred years, indeed ever since Spinoza, and, to go still further back, since Alexandrian thought infected Christianity, disported with the Person of our Lord as the identity of God and man.

Two lines of error, it has again and again been remarked, have run through Christological thought from the beginning: one that melts the Divine and the human into one form and mode of existence; the other that makes God a close ally and companion of a chosen member of the human family. The doctrine whose history is here sketched oscillates between these two errors, and has its zone of truth between them. The theory that has just been dismissed is the modern form of what used to be termed Apollinarianism, Eutychianism, and Monophysitism. In it everything—philosophy, Scripture, reason, common sense—is sacrificed to the making the Christ mechanically or physically one. Now this error has never been encountered by theology without the concurrent danger of a recoil into the opposite. Hence, the most vigorous opponents of the depotentiation theory, with Dorner at their head, renounce, as it were, with one consent the impersonal manhood of Christ, and are putting forth vigorous efforts to defend their own theory of a unity that shall belong to two persons. Slowly and surely they are constructing hypotheses on the Nestorian side which will rival those of their opponents on the Eutychian side, if not in their unthinkableness, at least in their contrariety to Scripture. A fair beginning is made in the distinction of Dorner between the union of the two natures and the perfection of the unity. The union goes on more and more perfectly, taking possession of the humanity to the end. It is not possible to show in few words what the results of this principle may prove in other and more incautious hands than Dorner's. The union will be, by degrees—indeed, it is already by many apparently sound divines—conceived of as a simply Nestorian union between the Son of God and the man he has " formed for Himself: " a union which becomes more and more strict the more capable the developing faculty of Christ becomes, and which therefore—for the theory must not halt—gradually strengthens the human intellect into unfaltering power, and releases it from the uncertainties of ignorance, and becomes perfect—when? at the passion, or before it, or after? At what point—and no question that man may ask is of more transcendent importance—does God take our nature to Himself in Christ for its infallible guidance into truth, and its perfect atonement for sin?

That region of perfect truth, where the Doctrine, with its mystery, is to be found, lies midway between these. And, while the Chalcedonian formula that we confess defines it well for the theologian, its best, safest, and sufficient expression for all Christians alike is to be found in the "words which the Holy Ghost teacheth."

PRINCIPAL DATES IN CHRISTOLOGY.

70—150. Apostolical Fathers.
150—200. Justin Martyr, Irenæus : Gnosticism, Docetism.
160—180. Praxeas : Patripassianism.
200—250. Clemens Alexandrinus, Tertullian, Origen.
250. Sabellius.
261. Paul of Samosata : Unitarianism (Monarchianism).
325. I. Œcum. Council, Nicæa : (Homoousion).
358. Homoiousion Condemned : Ancyra (Semiarianism).
381. II. Œcum. Council, Constantinople : Apollinaris Condemned (Divinity of Holy Spirit).
431. III. Œcum. Council, Ephesus : Nestorius Condemned.
441—461. Leo Magnus : *Epis. ad Flavianum.*
451. IV. Œcum. Council, Chalcedon : Nestorius and Eutyches Condemned.
482—519. Monophysitism, Theopaschitism.
589. *Filioque* added to Nicæno-Constantinopolitan Creed.
638. Heraclius : *One Will.*
680. The Monothelite Heresy Condemned : VI. Œcum. Council, Constantinople.
730—760. Johannes Damascenus.
794. Adoptionist Controversy ended : Council of Frankfurt.
831—851. Paschasius Radbert.
1050—1100. Anselm, *Cur Deus Homo.*
1160 (circ.) Peter Lombard (Magister Sententiarum), Nihilianist Controversy ; Rupert of Deutz.
1255—1274. Thomas Aquinas.
1300—1400. Duns Scotus, Tauler, Suso, Rusbröck.
1489. John Wessel.
1522—1586. Chemnitz and Lutheran Doctrine.
1525. Sacramental Controversy.
1530. Augsburg Confession.
1580. Formula Concordiæ.
1539—1604. F. Socinus.
1619. Kenosis Controversy.
1689—1772. Swedenborg.
1781. Kant.
1800—1835. Schleiermacher, Strauss.

NOTES.

NOTE I., p. 6.—*NATURE AND PERSON*.

"BEFORE the time of Arius the term 'hypostasis' had that meaning, and that only, which is here assigned to it, viz., a 'real personal subsistence.' But the idea of 'reality' also applies to substance and being, and this was the application that Arius gave to it. 'There are three hypostases,' he said, but he meant natures, substances, and that the nature of the Son and Spirit were different from each other and different from the nature of the Father; the nature of the Son is one with the nature of the Father; the Hypostasis of the Son is derived from the Hypostasis of the Father, as Sonship is derivative from Paternity. This Arius denied, and affirmed that the Son was ἐξ ἑτέρας οὐσίας and ἐξ ἑτέρας ὑποστάσεως. Therefore the Council of Nice anathematized in him all who said that the Son was *quâ* nature ἐξ ἑτέρας οὐσίας of any other substance but the One Godhead, or *quâ* Person ἐξ ἑτέρας τινος ὑποστάσεως of any other person save the Person of the Father. Up to this point the language of the Church had always been the same. But the clamorous assertion of three hypostases in an heretical sense by Arius introduced confusion. The Latin Church had hitherto continued free from error. In any case of difficulty the eyes of the Catholic reverted to the 'See of the Apostles.' In this instance, however, it only increased the confusion. 'Persona,' the equivalent for *prosopon*, was the term that expressed to the Western Church the Catholic meaning of *hypostasis*. There was no Latin word for *ousia* until Hilary coined the term '*essentia*;' in the meantime the language of theology could not remain incomplete, and the want was supplied by taking *hypostasis*, the philosophical equivalent for *ousia*, and translating it sometimes as '*substantia*,' sometimes as '*subsistentia*.' Both of these words seem to express with equal accuracy the force of the Greek term; but there is a clear distinction to be observed between them. '*Substantia*' means the essence of a thing, the very root and foundation of its being; whereas in '*subsistere*' is contained the inherent idea of 'check,' 'making a stand,' as we should say. And there is the idea of 'limitation' in 'personality;' it has an 'idiosyncrasy' that is wholly its own. The limitation involved in '*subsistentia*' is the definition that marks the distinction of each Person in the Holy Trinity. The idea of Father is limited by Paternity; that of the Son by Filiation; that of the Holy Spirit by Procession from both Father and Son. So Hooker: 'The substance of God with this property, to be of none, doth make the Person of the Father; the very self-same substance in number with this property to be of the Father maketh the Person of the Son; the same substance having added to it the property of proceeding from the other two, maketh the Holy Ghost. So that in every Person there is implied both the substance of God which is one, and also that property which causeth the same Person to be really and truly to differ from the other two. Every Person hath His own subsistence which no other besides hath, although there be others beside that have the same substance.' [*Eccl. Pol.*, v. 51.] Hence from poverty of language [Basil, Ep. 349, *ad Terent.*] the terminology of the Western Church became confused, '*substantia*' being held to be the equivalent for *hypostasis*, and the confusion did not fail to react upon the East. Thus Athanasius, as standing in close communication with the Roman Church, adopted its mode of speaking, and makes *hypostasis* to be synōnymous with *ousia*; though elsewhere he speaks of three hypostases. The great Council held at Sardica [A.D. 347] allowed the use of *hypostasis* in the sense of *ousia*; for whereas Ursacius and Valens, as Arians, affirmed three hypostases, in the sense of substance, the Council declared that in that sense the Divine Hypostasis was One. In the Meletian schism both that and the Eustathian party were orthodox in their faith; but, while the latter adopted the Roman mode of speaking, and held that there was only one *hypostasis*, meaning substance, in the Deity, the former used the language of primitive antiquity, and declared that there were three *hypostases*, meaning Persons. The Council of Alexandria [A.D. 362], on examining the two parties, affirmed both to be equally orthodox, and that the difference was only verbal; though for the future it ruled that the words as well as the faith of the Nicene Council were to be held binding. Jerome deprecates the use of the expression 'three hypostases' as savouring of Arianism. Perhaps, however, the time from whence uniformity of expression is to be dated is the Council of Alexandria [A.D. 362], where the term *ousia* was applied to 'substance,' and *hypostasis* restricted once more to personal subsistence. The first synodal definition of 'hypostasis' as 'person,' in contradistinction to substance, was at the Council of the Dedication, at Antioch [A.D. 341; Hilary, de Syn., 334]; and the writer who enforced the accurate distinction between οὐσία and ὑπόστασις was Basil [Ep. 349, *ad Terent.*]."—Blunt's *Dict. of Doct. and Hist. Theology*, Art. *Hypostasis*.

"There is a somewhat different sense, or rather a different usage, of the term 'Divine Nature' from that above explained. The distinction may, perhaps, be thus stated: we have used the word thus far as implying 'What God is:' it is used to imply what any one has in virtue of which he is Divine. When we speak of our Lord's Divine Nature, in relation to the Doctrine of the Incarnation, the term is obviously used in a different manner from that in which we say that the Divine Nature includes the Trinity of Persons. In the one case, to say that we are speaking of the Divine Nature means that we are stating essential or analytical judgments of which God is the subject: to say so in the other means that we are speaking of a subject of which Deity may be predicated. In the former case, the Divine Nature is conceived as the whole essence, the sum total (directly or by implication) of all the true propositions that can be made concerning God; in the second, it is (speaking logically) an attribute of the Person of Christ that He is Divine: His Divine Nature is *not* the sum total, but only a part of the qualities in virtue of which He is What He is. It is only necessary to point out the distinction to prevent confusion between the two senses of the term."—Ibid., Art. *Natures Divine.*

The articles in this Dictionary on the various theological terms by which the mysteries of the Trinity and the Person of Christ are formulated are of great value. The above are only extracts, and the references are generally omitted. To other parts of this laborious and learned work less satisfactory reference will have to be made.

NOTE II., p. 8.—*THE SON INCARNATE.*

"Each of these expressions, the 'Word' and the 'Son,' if taken alone, might have led to a fatal misconception. In the language of Church history, the Logos, if unbalanced by the idea of Sonship, might have seemed to sanction Sabellianism. The Son, without the Logos, might have been yet more successfully pressed into the service of Arianism. An Eternal Thought or Reason, even although constantly tending to express Itself in speech, is o Itself too abstract to oblige us to conceive of It as of a Personal Subsistence. On the other hand, the filial relationship carries with it the idea of dependence and of comparatively recent origin, even although it should suggest the reproduction in the Son of all the qualities of the Sire. Certainly St. John's language in his prologue protects the Personality of the Logos, and unless he believed that God could be divided or could have had a beginning, the Apostle teaches that the Son is co-eternal with the Father. Yet the bare metaphors of 'Word' and 'Son' might separately lead divergent thinkers to conceive of Him to Whom they are applied, on the one side as an impersonal quality or faculty of God, on the other as a concrete and personal but inferior and dependent being. But combine them, and each corrects the possible misuse of the other. The Logos, Who is also the Son, cannot be an impersonal and abstract quality ; since such an expression as the Son would be utterly misleading unless it implied at the very least the fact of personal subsistence distinct from that of the Father. On the other hand, the Son, Who is also the Logos, cannot be of more recent origin than the Father ; since the Father cannot be conceived of as subsisting without that Eternal Thought or Reason Which is the Son. Nor may the Son be deemed to be in aught but the order of Divine subsistence inferior to the Father, since He is identical with the Eternal Intellectual Life of the Most High. Each metaphor reinforces, supplements, and protects the other ; and together they exhibit Christ before His incarnation as at once personally distinct from, and yet equal with, the Father ; He is That personally subsisting and Eternal Life Which was with the Father, and was manifested unto us "—Liddon, *Bampton Lectures*, p. 350.

" This is the first instance in John where the Logos is termed *the Son of God*. Seyffarth is mistaken in supposing that the expression merely has reference to the incarnation of the Logos. Schleiermacher expresses himself in a similar manner : 'The Divine alone in Christ could not have been called Son of God, but this term always designates the entire Christ.' Ver. 18 shows the contrary, where the words 'Who is in the bosom of the Father' are to be referred to the eternal existence of the Son with the Father. The difference between this expression and the term Logos consists in this,—that the term ' Son of God ' points out more distinctly and expressly the personality of the Word."—Olshausen, on John i. 14.

NOTE III., p. 10.—*REASONS FOR THE INCARNATION OF THE SON.*

" And the reasons of the fitness and meetness of this Second Person are : First, if we consider the relations of the Three Persons among Themselves, He is of all the fittest to undertake this work. 1. It was meet the *Idiomata*, or the proper titles by which the Persons of the Trinity are distinguished, should be kept and preserved distinct, and no way confounded. He that was to be Mediator it was meet He should be the Son of man, the Son of a woman as His mother, as I shall show anon : and the title and appellation will fitliest become Him that is a Son (though of God) already. 2. It was meet that the Son of God should be this Mediator, that the due order that is between these Three Persons be also kept. The Father is the first, the Son the second, the Holy Ghost the third ; and He that is to be Mediator must be called to it, and sent by another Person, therefore the Father is not to be Mediator . . . . . and therefore He that is to be Mediator to redeem must be the Son, who may send the Holy Ghost to apply His work, who, being the last Person, is to appear last in the world, and take the last work, which redemption is not, but the application of it.

"And, secondly, as thus to preserve the due decorum among the Persons, so also in respect of the work itself, it was most proper to Him. 1. He being the middle Person of the Three bears the best resemblance of the work to be a Mediator. He was from the Father, and the Holy Ghost from Him, and it is He in whom, as it were, the other two are united, and are one, and so He is able to lay hands on both. As the nature of man is a middle nature between the whole creation, earthly and heavenly; and as for one and the same Person to be both God and man was a middle rank between God and us men, so is the Son of God a middle Person between the Persons Themselves."—Thomas Goodwin's Works, vol. v., p. 42. Nichol's Edition.

In his work on "The Knowledge of God the Father and His Son Jesus Christ," the same Puritan divine says, expounding John i. 4:—

"First 'In Him was life, and the life was the light of men.' The evangelist descends from the creation in general unto the giving of life, both of reason and holiness, unto men, at their first creation, whiles they were in innocency. He speaks not of that essential life in Himself; for that which follows in the next words, where he calls Him 'the Life,' is so to be understood. But when here he says, 'in Him was Life,' the meaning is, He was a fountain of Life to us, being first Life in Himself. It is one attribute of Christ's, as He is God-man, yea, as He is man taken up into that union, to have life independently in Himself, even as God the Father hath. Secondly, 'The life was the light of men.' The light, that is, of holiness or God's image. Of men : that is, of men in their primitive state of innocency. For he joins it with the creation of all things, he useth the word *was*, as noting a state past. Now Adam's holiness was from Him: for he was made after God's image. When Adam was created, all the Persons of the Trinity acted their several parts; and the Son acted the part of God-man : and so the Father, eyeing Him as such, and as Him who was in that respect the image of the Godhead, He thereupon says, 'Let us make man after our image,' Christ's human nature being the *prototupon* and exemplar."—Vol. iv., p. 560.

This style of writing may not be altogether according to modern taste. But it at least shows—being only one specimen among multitudes that might easily be presented from Puritan writers—that the men who wrote most about the cross and the atonement had their speculations also about the eternal ideal of man in Christ's Person. In fact, the sentences from above strike a note that is heard in all ages and schools of theology: Irenæus, Clement, and Augustine join with Rupert and Bonaventura; and these again with modern transcendental Christian thinkers in declaring what none have better set forth than our own old English divines of almost every class. These older writers grasped very firmly the principle that the New Testament almost always carries the predicates of the God-man up into eternity,—by a very legitimate application, quite independent of the Lutheran, of the *communicatio idiomatum.* The "Archetypal Man," the "Ideal of Humanity," the "Primordial Ideal of Human Nature," and other such phrases, are but the transcendental perversions of a truth that no theology can dispense with—that man was never in the mind of the Creator apart from Christ.

It will be said that Goodwin and writers of this school speak of the new man as seen or foreseen in Christ. And that is undoubtedly true. But it is hard to deny that behind and beyond the New Man in Christ, man as such was created after His image with special reference to His personality as the Son. Bengel's pithy note on Colossians i. 16, says: "ἐν, *in, denotat prius quiddam, quam mox* διὰ *et* εἰς *: notatur initium, progressus, finis."* All things, and man especially, were in Christ, then through Christ, then for Christ. "He," says Olshausen, "must have been born of the substance of the Father before all the creation, *for* all things are created in Him"—giving this as St. Paul's argument. "In the creation they come forth from Him to an independent existence, in the completion of all things they return to Him."

As to the "First-born of every creature," the elaborate and satisfactory note of Meyer may be read to advantage. "It is," says Dr. Braune, "joined with the first predicate, closely uniting *with* God and distinguishing *from* the creation. *First-begotten* as to God; before *every creature,* when He turns towards the creation, and mankind especially with whom He is for ever allied. It will well repay the reader to study this crucial word thoroughly; for instance in Ellicott, or the German Cremer. The latter says (*Wörterbuch d. N. T. Gräcität*): "Not that He is put on a level with the creature, but because the relation of the creature to Him is defined that without Him the creature would not and could not be. That neither is it said that Christ was 'created,' nor of the creature that he was 'begotten,' is plain from this, that the temporal relation in which He stands to the creature is afterwards expressly introduced: which would have no meaning if the *prototokos* did not refer to Christ's preeminence. 'He is before all things' shows that the point in 'firstborn' has nothing to do with time, as if He were the beginning of the series." The more clearly and precisely these expressions are examined the more certainly is the eternal generation established. And it is an evil that our authorized translation has been so vague. It is satisfactory to be able to confirm most of the substance of this text and note by Canon Liddon's eloquent words (*Bampton Lec.*, p. 475):—

"As the 'Image,' Christ is, in that one substance, the exact likeness of the Father, in all things except being the Father. The Son is the Image of the Father, not as the Father, but as God: the Son is 'the Image of God.' The *Image* is indeed originally God's unbegun, unending reflection of Himself in Himself; but the *Image* is also the Organ whereby God, in His essence invisible, reveals Himself to His creatures. . . . . . . As the Image, Christ is the πρωτότοκος πάσης κτίσεως: that is to say, *not* the First in rank among created beings, *but* begotten before any created beings. . . . . . *In Him*: there was no creative process external to and independent of Him; since the archetypal forms after which the creatures are modelled, and the sources of their strength and consistency of being, eternally reside in Him. *By Him*: the force which has summoned the world out of nothingness into being, and which upholds them in being, is His. *For Him*: He is not, as Arianism afterwards pretended, merely an inferior workman, creating for the glory of a higher Master, for a God superior to Himself. He creates for Himself; He is the end of created things as well as their immediate source; and living for Him is to every creature at once the explanation and the law of its being."

NOTE IV., p. 10.—*THE SON OF GOD AND THE SON OF MAN.*

The articles in Smith's *Dictionary of the Bible* are of great value as to the meaning of these terms severally. Their use in the New Testament may be studied in Schmid's *Biblical Theology.*

" Wherefore our Lord Jesus Christ, the Son of God, may be considered three ways :

" 1. Merely with respect unto His Divine nature. This is one and the same with that of the Father. In this respect the one is not the image of the other, for both are the same.

" 2. With respect unto His Divine Person as the Son of the Father, the only-begotten, the eternal Son of God. Thus He receives, *as* His personality, *so* all Divine excellencies, from the Father ; so He is the essential image of the Father's Person.

" 3. As He took our nature upon Him, or in the assumption of our nature into personal union with Himself, in order unto the work of His mediation. So is He the only representative image of God unto us—in whom alone we see, know, and learn all the Divine excellencies—so as to live unto God, and be directed unto the enjoyment of Him. All this Himself instructs us in."—Owen, *Person of Christ*. (Works, Gold's edit., vol. i., p. 72.)

" When Christ designates Himself the Son of man, He undoubtedly describes His human mode of existence, as in one respect *other* than and *inferior* to, that which was originally His ; for which reason He generally employs this designation in speaking of His sufferings. And yet, on the other hand, He characterises His human mode of existence as the fulfilment of His eternal destination, as the perfection of His glory. When He speaks of the glory which he had with the Father ere the world was, He refers not alone to the pure Divine glory, but to the Divine-human glory on which He was to enter through His resurrection and ascension, and which He possessed eternally in the Divine idea. For it was eternally involved in the idea of the Son that He should become incarnate, that He should become the Head of the kingdom of love. When He says, 'Before Abraham was, I am,' He speaks not merely of the pure glory of the Logos, but of the glory of Christ ; further, not merely of the glory of Christ in the eternal idea, but of the glory which He possessed in the midst of the unbelieving Jews of His own day. As the One, into whom, as the ultimate goal of creation, all things were made, He is the presupposition for Abraham, the presupposition for every period of history. For Him, who is the personal Eternity in the midst of the ages, nay more, in the midst of the entire creation, the sensuous difference between past and future has but a vanishing significance ; for all the ages of the world, all the æons, revolve around Him as around the all-determining centre to which each owes its peculiar character and force."—Martensen's *Christian Dogmatic*, p. 268.

Let us go back again to English Divinity : this time to one equal, though not superior, to Owen, in the exhaustiveness of his treatises on the Incarnation :—

"All those places wherein God promised to be their God; all those sacred hymns and prophecies which instil Him God, even *our* God, in the exquisite or sublime literal sense, refer or drive to that point which we Christians make the foundation and root of our faith, to wit, that He was to be *God with us*, or God in our nature or flesh, God made man of the seed or stock of Abraham, like us in all things, sin excepted. This new and glorious temple was, according to strict propriety, erected *in medio Israel*, or *interiore Israel*, that is, in one that was truly an Israelite, the very centre or foundation of Abraham's seed, or of Jacob's posterity: but being erected in the midst of Israel, or in the seed of Abraham after this sense, it was not erected only for the sons of Abraham, or of Israel by bodily descent, but all were to become true Israelites that should be united by this seed, and worship God in the sanctuary. For in that Jesus Christ was the Son of God, He was more truly the Israel of God than Jacob had been, and all that are engrafted into this temple of God, all that receive life from Him, are more truly the children of Israel than any of Jacob's sons were, which refuse to be united to Him."—Jackson *on the Creed*, Works, vol. vii., p. 28. (Oxford Edition.)

NOTE V., p. 12.—*IMPERSONALITY OF THE HUMAN NATURE.*

"The *anhypostasia, impersonality,* or, to speak more accurately, the *enhypostasia,* of the human nature of Christ. This is a difficult point, but a necessary link in the orthodox doctrine of the one God-man; for otherwise we must have two persons in Christ, and after the incarnation, a fourth person, and that a human, in the Divine Trinity. The impersonality of Christ's human nature, however, is not to be taken as absolute, but relative, as the following considerations will show.

"The centre of personal life in the God-man resides unquestionably in the Logos, who was from eternity the second Person in the Godhead, and could not lose His personality. He united Himself, as has been already observed, not with a human person, but with human nature. The Divine nature is, therefore, the root and basis of the personality of Christ Christ Himself, moreover, always speaks and acts in the full consciousness of His Divine origin and character, as having come from the Father, having been sent by Him, and, even during His earthly life, living in heaven and in unbroken communion with the Father. And the human nature of Christ had no independent personality of its own, besides the Divine; it had no existence at all before the incarnation, but began with this act, and was so incorporated with the pre-existent Logos-personality as to find in this alone its own full self-consciousness, and to be permeated and controlled by it in every stage of its development. But the human nature forms a necessary element in the Divine personality, and in this sense we may say, with the older Protestant theologians, that Christ is a *persona* σύνθετος, which was Divine and human at once.

"Thus interpreted, the church doctrine of enhypostasia presents no very great metaphysical or psychological difficulty. It is true we cannot, according to our modern way of thinking, conceive a complete human nature without personality. We make personality itself consist in intelligence and free will, so that without it the nature sinks to a mere abstraction of powers, qualities, and functions. But the human nature of Jesus never was, in fact, alone; it was from the beginning inseparably united with another nature, which is personal, and which assumed the human into a unity of life with itself. The Logos-personality is in this case the light of self-consciousness, and the impelling power of will, and pervades as well the human nature as the Divine."—Schaff's *History of the Christian Church*, vol. i., p. 757.

"The precise distinction between *nature* and *person*. Nature or substance is the totality of powers and qualities which constitute a being; person is the Ego, the self-conscious, self-asserting and acting subject. There is no person without nature, but there may be nature without person (as in irrational being). The church doctrine distinguishes in the Holy Trinity three Persons (though not in the ordinary human sense of the word) in one Divine nature or substance which they have in common; in its Christology it teaches, conversely, two natures in one person (in the usual sense of person) which pervades both. Therefore it cannot be said that the Logos assumed a human *person*, or united Himself with a definite human individual: for then the God-man would consist of two Persons; but that He took upon Himself the human *nature*, which is common to all men; and therefore He redeemed not a particular man, but all men, as partakers of the same nature or substance. The personal Logos did not become an individual ἄνθρωπος, but σάρξ, flesh, which includes the whole of human nature, body, soul, and spirit. The personal self-conscious Ego resides in the Logos."—Ibid., vol. iii., p. 751.

"The common prevalent expression of it at present in the church is the *hypostatical union*, that is, the union of the Divine and human nature, having no personality nor subsistence of its own.

"With respect unto this union the name of Christ is called 'Wonderful,' as that which hath the pre-eminence in all the effects of Divine wisdom. And it is a singular effect thereof. There is no other union in things Divine or human, in things spiritual or natural, whether substantial or accidental, that is of the same kind with it;—it differs specially from them all.

"(1.) The most glorious union is that of the *Divine Persons* in the same being or nature; the Father in the Son, the Son in the Father, and the

Holy Spirit in them both, and both in Him. But this is a union of distinct Persons in the unity of the same single nature, and this, I confess, is more glorious than that whereof we treat; for it is in God absolutely, it is eternal, of His nature and being. But this union we speak of is not God; it is a creature,—an effect of Divine wisdom and power. And it is different from it herein, inasmuch as that is of *many distinct Persons* in the same nature; this is of *distinct natures* in the same *Person*. That union is *natural*, substantial, essential in the same nature; this as it is not accidental, as we shall show, so it is not properly substantial, because it is not of the same nature, but of diverse in the same person, remaining distinct in their essence and substance, and is, therefore, peculiarly hypostatical or personal. Hence, Austin feared not to say, that '*Homo potius est in Filio Dei quam Filius in Patre:*' De Trin., lib. i., cap. 10. But that is true only in this one respect, that the Son is not so in the Father as to become one Person with Him. In all other respects it must be granted that the inbeing of the Son with the Father,—the union between them, which is natural, essential, and eternal,—doth exceed this in glory, which was a *temporary*, external act of Divine wisdom and grace.

"(2.) The most eminent, *substantial* union in things natural is that of the *soul and body* constituting an individual person.

"There is, I confess, some kind of similitude between this union and that of the different natures in the Person of Christ; but it is not of the same kind or nature. And the dissimilitudes that are between them are more and of greater importance than those things are wherein there seems to be an agreement between them. For,—1st, the soul and body are essential parts of human nature; but complete human nature they are not but by virtue of their union. But the union of the natures in the Person of Christ does not constitute a new nature that either was not, or was not complete before. Each nature remains the same, perfect, complete nature after this union.

"2. The union of the soul and body doth constitute that nature which is made essentially complete thereby,—*a new individual person*, with a subsistence of its own, which neither of them was nor had before that union. But although the Person of Christ, as God and man, be constituted by this union, yet His Person, absolutely, and His individual subsistence, was perfectly, absolutely antecedent unto that union. He did not become a new person, another person than He was before, by virtue of that union; only that Person assumed human nature to itself, to be its own, into personal subsistence.

"3. Soul and body are united *by an external efficient cause*, or the power of God, and not by the act of one of them upon another. But this union is effected by that act of the Divine nature towards the human which we have before described.

"4. Neither soul nor body have any *personal subsistence before* that *union*; but the sole foundation of this union was in this, that the Son of God was a self-subsisting Person from eternity."—Owen's *Person of Christ*, vol. i., p. 228.

"Some school divines and followers of Aquinas will have the former similitude of Athanasius to consist especially in this: that as the reasonable soul doth use the body of man, so the Divine nature of Christ doth use the manhood as its proper united instrument. Every other man besides the Man Christ Jesus, every other creature, is the instrument of God; but all of them such instruments of the Divine nature as the axe or hammer is to the artificer which worketh by them. The most puissant princes, the mightiest conquerors which the world hath seen or felt, could grow no farther in titles than Attilas or Nebuchadnezzar did—*malleus orbis et flagellum Dei*, hammers or scourges of God to chastise or bruise the nations. But the humanity of God doth use such an instrument of the Divine nature in His Person, as the hand of man is to the person or party whose hand it is. And it is well observed, whether by Aquinas himself or no I remember not, but by Viguerius, an accurate summist of Aquinas' sums, that albeit the intellectual part of man be a spiritual substance, and separated from the matter or bodily part, yet is the union betwixt the hand and intellectual part of man no less firm, no less proper, than the union between the feet or other organical part of sensitive creatures and their sensitive souls or mere physical forms. For the intellectual part of man, whether it be the form of man truly, though not merely physical, or rather his essence, not his form at all, doth use his own hand, not as the carpenter doth use his axe, that is, not as an external or separated, but as his proper united instrument: not as the union between the hand, as the instrument and intellective part, as the artificer or commander of it, an union of matter and form, but an union personal, or at the least such an union as resembles the hypostatical union between the Divine and human nature of Christ much better than any material union wherein philosophers or school divines can make instance."—Jackson *on the Creed*, Works, vol. vii., p. 288.

NOTE VI., p. 15.—*ST. JOHN'S INCARNATION-PHRASES.*

It is probable that St. John's First Epistle is the last document of revelation. At any rate, this Epistle, as an appendage of the Gospel, completes the apostolic testimony. In 1 John iv. 2 the confession of faith on which life or death hangs, and by which the extreme antithesis of being in God or in the world or in the devil becomes manifest, lies in the words "Jesus Christ come in the flesh." All are agreed that the general meaning of this formula points to the veritable manhood of Jesus Christ, the true Messiah; but there is the greatest diversity in the exposition of the individual words. It is doubted whether ἐν σαρκί is equivalent simply to εἰς σάρκα. It has also been disputed whether the text does or does not declare the pre-existence of the Logos. The phrase demands a careful consideration in relation to the preposition ἐν, and the participial form ἐληλυθότα. "*In* flesh" might be referred to the incarnation. Düsterdieck, a recent commentator on these Epistles, enters into an elaborate discussion of all extant expositions, and establishes his own conclusion that the confession is of Jesus Christ, who, as true man, has lived, and taught, and laboured upon earth. "But this has meaning only on the supposition that the veritable humanity of this Jesus Christ presupposes something altogether different from that of the common humanity of any other who is flesh, that is, on the supposition that He who appeared in the flesh is the Son of God (chapter iii. 23), who came into the flesh, became flesh, in order afterwards to accomplish His work as One in the flesh. The words 'come in flesh' expressly refer only to the *conversatio Jesu Christi in verâ naturâ humanâ;* but they obviously presuppose the *incarnatio.* But that the incarnation is not meant by the expression itself is evident from 2 John 7, where the word is in the present tense. There the timeless tense suits well enough the whole course of Christ's life, but not the one definite fact of His incarnation. In our present passage it is the perfect participle; in chapter v. 6 it is the aorist." There can be no question of the accuracy of this exposition, if it be understood that the "*come* in the flesh" makes the whole manifestation of Christ nothing more than the full exhibition of the fact that He was incarnate. The word "come" is used by St. John in his Gospel with direct reference to the descent of Christ from heaven. This indeed does not disprove that the whole of His "conversation" on earth is meant, but it lays the stress on His first appearing.

As to St. John's two other phrases, the one, "*became* flesh," has been as unduly exaggerated as the other, "dwelt among us," has been emptied of its meaning. By the Eutychian commentators of all shades "became flesh" has been made to signify "was made, or converted, into flesh." The comment of Meyer is to the point: "The expression *flesh*, not *man*, is purposely chosen; in opposition, not so much to the Divine *idea* of man, which is absent here, but to the *immaterial* nature of the Divine Logos. *He became flesh*, that is, *He became a bodily material nature*, by which it is self-understood that the material *human* existence is meant into which he entered. The same thing is meant by 'came in flesh' in the Epistles, yet, according to the point of view of the *form* of His coming, as conditioned by His becoming flesh. But 'became' shows that He was made what He was not before. The incarnation, therefore, cannot be a mere *accident* of His substantial nature, but is the assumption of another nature, through which the purely Divine Logos-Person became a bodily real personality, that is, the Divine-human Person, Jesus Christ." Meyer goes on to show that the *flesh* does not merely imply the *soul*, but the *spirit* also; that St. John distinctly and repeatedly introduces both: the spirit being the substratum of the human self-consciousness. So far so good; but when he expounds "dwell among us" as limited to the Christian fellowship, in the midst of which the Redeemer displayed His glory—a limitation which is very common among the expositors of this passage — he fails to remember that St. John has given precedence to the universal relations of the Word in his prologue. Not all "beheld His glory," because not all entered the holiest in Christ. But His tabernacle was "with men." Here we must introduce the well-known words of Hooker (*Eccl. Pol.*, book v., chap. lii.):—

"The Word (saith St. John) was made flesh, and dwelt *in us*. The evangelist useth the plural number, *men* for manhood, *us* for the nature whereof we consist, even as the apostle denying the assumption of *angelical nature*, saith likewise in the plural number, 'He took not angels, but the seed of Abraham.' It pleased not the Word, or wisdom of God, to take to some one person amongst men, for then should that one have been advanced which was assumed, and no more; but Wisdom, to the end she might save many, built her house of that nature which is common to all ; she made not *this or that man* her habitation, but dwelt *in us*. .... The seeds of herbs and plants at the first are not in act, but in possibility, that which they afterwards grow to be. If the Son of God had taken to Himself a man now made, and already perfected, it would of necessity follow that there are in Christ two persons, the one assuming, and the other assumed, whereas the Son of God did not assume a man's person unto His own, but a man's nature to His own Person, and therefore took *semen*, the seed of Abraham, the very first original element of our nature, before it was come to have any personal subsistence. The flesh, and the conjunction of the flesh with God, began both at one instant. His making and taking to Himself our flesh was but one act, so that in Christ there is no personal subsistence but one, and that from everlasting. By taking only the nature of men He still continueth one Person, and changeth but the manner of His subsisting, which was before in the mere glory of the Son of God, and is now in the habit of our flesh."

This extract leads to the consideration of the other incarnation-passages to which this note refers. Hooker gives the traditional rendering of Hebrews ii. 16. Strictly speaking the incarnation is not the subject of that passage, save as it follows upon the former, " He likewise Himself took part of the same," that is, of the children's flesh and blood. That Christ, the Son of God, partook verily of the common nature of man that He might effectually " take hold of " and help all who are of the " seed of Abraham " by faith, is the obvious meaning of the words when combined. But they refer rather to the design of the incarnation than to the incarnation itself. The same may be said of the last passage referred to, Galatians iv. 4, where " *made* of a woman " is the same Greek word as " *made* flesh ; " but the saying is introduced for the sake of the redemption and adoption that follow. The passages in St. John remain the specific and distinctive formulæ of the incarnation.

NOTE VII., p. 20.—*APOLLINARIANISM IN MODERN THEOLOGY.*

In Mr. Plumptre's " Boyle Lectures " on *Christ and Christendom*, the human development of our Lord is traced with great care by one who is deeply impressed with the importance of avoiding the error that loses the Man in the God. While reading the early part of this volume the uneasy thought sometimes arises that the author is going towards the opposite error; but the volume read as a whole effectually silences the suspicion. One of the admirable dissertations at the end is on *The Influence of Apollinarianism on Modern Theology;* and I must quote a sentence or two in preference to some rougher notes prepared on the same subject. After a vindication — if such a word may be used — of the Lord's limitation in knowledge, which is not quite satisfactory, the following paragraph occurs :—

"Such has been the history of this attempt to substitute the supposed inferences from a dogmatic truth for the simpler teaching of Scripture. Had the matter rested here, it would have been interesting as an illustration of the intrusive restlessness of the understanding when it enters, even in the spirit of the devoutest reverence, upon speculations which transcend it. But the evil did not end here. In proportion as the influence of Apollinarianism pervaded, however indirectly, the theology of the church, men lost their hold on the truth of the perfect human sympathy of Christ, and turned more and more to one in whom they hoped to find it. If the reaction against Nestorianism was one cause of the growth of Mariolatry, this was undoubtedly another. There was, as Dr. Newman has said, 'a wonder in heaven—a throne far above all created powers, mediatorial, intercessory;' and the thoughts of men turned to her, whom they had before learnt to reverence and love, as being 'the predestined heir of that Majesty.' The human life, even the teaching of Christ, became comparatively subordinate, and the devotion of men turned rather to the beginning and the end—the Infancy and the Crucifixion. Doubtless, at the worst of times, and under the fullest *cultus* of the Virgin, the other and truer thought was at times awakened into life. Men have sung of the love of Jesus, and found their refuge in the heart of Christ. But in the popular religion of the Latin Church men and women have turned to the Virgin mother rather than to the Son, as believing that they would there find a fuller sympathy, and a more benignant reception of their prayers.

"With others, the reaction against the unreality which the adoption, partial or complete, of Apollinarian thought has led them to feel in popular statements as to the gospel history, has taken another form. Not having been taught to feel that it was a human Mind and a human Heart that spoke to their minds and hearts there, they have turned with an eagerness which we ought to welcome, to those who have restored the humanity of Christ to its life and power, even when, in doing this, they have sacrificed the truth of His being also the Eternal Word. In proportion as any Life of Jesus has brought this as a living reality before men, they have welcomed and accepted it. In the language of current theology they could trace no recognition of the growth in wisdom, no pattern life unfolding in affections, intellect, wisdom, as ours unfolds, brought by degrees into fullest fellowship with the Divine Nature, illuminated by the pervading presence of the eternal Light, and growing, as our nature grows, in the power of receiving and transmitting it ; and so they have found what met the cravings of their hearts in the clearer, more vivid pictures, of those, even, who thought of the Christ, not as manifesting His Father in heaven, but as being altogether, even in ignorance of truth, and infirmity of purpose, and acquiescence in evil, such an one as themselves. The remedy for that perversion or denial of the truth—the safeguard against that danger—are to be found, not in falling back upon the partial suppression of the truth, the history of which has been here traced, but in proclaiming in its fulness the church's faith—that in that union of the Godhead and the manhood the latter is indeed taken into the former, yet not so as to lose its distinctness. The Christ is ' perfect God and perfect man, of a reasonable soul, and human flesh subsisting.' " (p. 371.)

These hints are suggestive as to some special aspects of the Apollinarian tendency. The following extract may well give a glance of its unconscious influence on the exposition of Scripture. It occurs in the *Biblical Studies* of the late Rev. W. Robinson, of Cambridge,—an able and suggestive work :—

" Without controversy, great is the mystery of the eternal Word ; but not greater than the mystery of the incarnation of our own spirits. The former surprises us much more than the latter, but is not more truly out of the reach of our understanding. Mr. Watson pleads warmly against the notion that the Sonship of our Lord is a merely human distinction ; or, to use his own words, against the supposition that it refers 'to the immediate production of the humanity by Divine power.' And, so far, he has Scripture to sustain him. The flesh is not the Son of God. That designation denotes the Word made flesh. But there is no part of Scripture which says that the Word of God was the Son of God. Of the origin of the existence of the Word of God, by whom the Father made the worlds, we are left in ignorance. It may be given us in another world to know that the Nicene inquirers came as near to the truth as in this world men can ; or we may hereafter find that their theory of eternal Sonship is wholly baseless. On such a subject, unless revelation be indisputably plain, man cannot innocently be confident. Deeply therefore is it to be regretted that the bald dogmatism of the Nicene era should be thrust into popular confessions of faith, or, indeed, into any confessions. How long will the people, parrot-like, follow the priest as he says, 'I believe in one Lord, Jesus Christ, begotten of the Father before all worlds?' Let all who are alive to their own responsibility to God, as the God of truth, remember that the standard of faith is the Bible; not the Bible supplemented by the Nicene Creed. If the doctrine of eternal Sonship be not taught in Scripture, the utterance of that creed is superstition and sin.

"It perhaps deserves serious consideration whether the Nicene dogma have not the effect of thrusting out of sight one of the most wonderful facts disclosed by Divine revelation; for the testimony of Scripture is, that the human body, born of Mary, was, through the wonder-working power of God, to whom all things are possible, animated by the Word of God. 'The Word was made flesh, ... and we beheld ... the glory of the only begotten of the Father.' Men have added to this statement, and maintained that our Saviour had not only a body made in the likeness of sinful flesh, but a human soul; whereas, according to Scripture, Jesus of Nazareth was not the son of Joseph and Mary, but the incarnation of the Word, which was in the beginning with God. How the two—the human and the Divine—should dwell together in such combination we know not; but we may reasonably expect to gain some further light on this mysterious subject, as the result of our future experience; and, while we are here, let the faith firmly grasp such suggestions as the word of God contains, and wait for the grand discoveries of eternity. There is 'one Mediator between God and man, the Man Christ Jesus:' which must not be interpreted to mean that the mediation is by humanity alone; for the Man Christ Jesus was the Word made flesh. So when we read that He who was in the form of God was made in the likeness of man we have probably before us the most wonderful of facts. It was not in a figure, but really, that 'He who was rich for our sakes became poor;' nor is the Immanuel of Scripture two persons, but one person. 'In the beginning was the Word;' by Him the Father made the worlds: without Him was not anything made that was made. He, the Word Divine and everlasting, was made in the likeness of sinful flesh. In Him dwelt all the fulness of the Godhead bodily, and, having given Himself for our sins, He rose to reign 'God over all things.' Without controversy, 'great is the mystery of godliness.' 'The Word was made flesh.'"—*Biblical Studies*, p. 116.

Without the aid of the Nicene Creed we know the origin of the Word and Image of God (John i. 18, Colossians i. 15, Hebrews i. 2). See Note II.

NOTE VIII., p. 22.—"*THE EXINANITION.*"

"That we rightly understand the use made of the example of Christ, as the model after which the Christian life is formed, we must first endeavour to bring the model itself clearly and distinctly before our minds. Before the eye of the apostle stands the image of *the Whole Christ*, the Son of God, appearing in the flesh, manifesting Himself in human nature. From the human manifestation he rises to the Eternal Word (as John expresses it), that Word which was before the appearance of the Son of God in time—yea, before the *worlds* were made ; in whom, before all time, God beheld and imaged Himself: as Paul, in the Epistle to the Colossians calls Him, in this view, the Image of the Invisible, *i.e.* 'the incomprehensible God.' Then, after this upward glance of his spiritual eye, he descends again into the depths of the human life, in which the Eternal Word appears as man. He expresses this in the language of immediate perception, beholding the Divine and the human as one ; not in the form of abstract truth, attained by a mental analysis of the direct object of thought. Thus he contemplates the entrance of the Son of God into the form of humanity as a self-abasement—a self-renunciation—for the salvation of those whose low estate He stooped to share. He, whose state of being was Divine—who was exalted above all the wants and limitations of the finite and earthly existence—did not eagerly claim this equality with God which He possessed ; but, on the contrary, He concealed and disowned it in human abasement, and in the form of human dependence. And as the whole of the human life of Christ proceeded from such an act of self-renunciation and self-abasement, so did His whole earthly life correspond to this one act, even to His death—the consciousness, on the one hand, of Divine dignity, which it was in His power to claim ; and on the other, the concealment—the renunciation of this—in every form of humiliation and dependence belonging to the earthly life of man. The crowning point appears in His death—the ignominious and agonising death of the cross. Paul then proceeds to show what Christ attained by such self-renunciation, thus carried on to the utmost limit by such submissive obedience, in the form of a servant ; the reward which he received in return ; the dignity which was conferred upon Him. Here too is presented the universal law, laid down by Christ Himself, that whoso humbles himself, and in proportion as he humbles himself, shall be exalted."—Neander on Philippians ii. 7, 8.

This extract gives a good specimen of the temperate treatment of a subject which, as the next note will show, has been very rashly handled in Germany and France. It will bear study as well as reading. For the exegesis of the great kenosis passage—Philippians ii. 7–9—on which a little library of monographs have been written, besides the dissertations in the Commentaries, the reader cannot be directed to a safer and more exhaustive dissertation than that contained in Dr. Lightfoot's recent *Commentary on the Philippians.* The two instalments of St. Paul's Epistles which this faithful and evangelical scholar has issued have excited great expectation as to the still more important sequel.

NOTE IX., p. 24.—*DEPOTENTIATION.*

The modern theory of a Depotentiation of the Eternal Son, in which His incarnation is the passing out of one condition (the Divine) into another (the human), has been referred to at some length in the preceding History of the Doctrine of Christ's Person. A few illustrations of the manner in which the theory is applied to the New-Testament exhibition of Christ Incarnate will here be added. In his *Commentaire sur l'Evangile de Saint-Jean,* M. Godet thus writes on chapter i. 14 :—

"Protestant orthodoxy, whether Lutheran or Reformed, refuses to take the term ἐγένετο in its full force. The former eludes it by the *Communicatio Idiomatum,* by virtue of which the Divine Subject, the Word, alternating in some way between the two modes—Divine and human—of existence, lends at will the attributes of each nature to the other. The latter maintains strictly the distinction of the two natures, and, placing them in juxtaposition in one and the same Subject, thinks it has satisfied the meaning of the word '*became* flesh.' It seems to us that these methods do violence to the text, instead of developing it. The term 'was made flesh' includes more than the fact of becoming visible ; it indicates the entrance into a mode of being and of development entirely human. It excludes, as I think, no less positively, the co-existence of two opposed natures, alternating or simultaneous, in the same subject. The natural sense of this proposition is, that the Divine Subject entered into the mode of human being after having renounced the mode of Divine being. . . . . If it is asked how a fact so prodigious as that of the passage of a Divine Subject into a state really human was possible, we reply that, the Word having impressed His own type on humanity in creating it, there was, in this primordial homogeneity, the condition of the real and organic union between Him and man which is taught by the sacred writers, and supposed by the whole evangelical history."

Here it is plain that the expositor is, in reality, paying homage to the doctrine of two natures in one Person, without denying it in words. He cannot mean that the Logos renounced His *nature* when He laid aside the glorious manifestations of His nature. M. Godet dwells much on His baptism as the restoration to the Incarnate Lord of the consciousness of Himself as Son : " He could say what He could not previously have said, 'Before Abraham was, I am ;' " but he forgets the deep significance of the word in the temple in His twelfth year, and that the fact that throughout—before St. John begins his narrative of the Son's revelation of the Father—he declares that "*He is*" essentially and eternally "in the bosom of the Father." This writer I quote, because he is the clearest and best example among a number of expositors who base their exposition on this view. He illustrates the delusion under which they all write: the delusion, namely, that something is gained by a rejection of the ancient doctrine, and that this vague and indefinite idea of the descent of the Logos out of Divinity for a season is the solution of an immense difficulty. What then means such a sentence as this, "The notion expressed by the title of *Son of God* is simply that of a personal and mysterious relation between this infant and the Divine Being" ? But the paragraph in which M. Godet dismisses the subject convicts his hypothesis of unreasonableness :—

" It is impossible to see in what this conception of the incarnation wounds the true humanity of our Lord. Man is a vessel destined to receive God, but in time, and in the way of a free progress. It is a vessel which enlarges in the measure that it is filled, and which must be filled in the measure that it is enlarged. The Logos is also the vessel of the Divinity, but eternally equal to Himself, and perfectly filled. Conformably with this affinity, and this difference between the Logos and man, the following is the formula of the Incarnation, as St. John teaches it :—*The Logos has realised in Jesus, under the form of human existence subjected to the law of development and progress, that relation of dependence and of filial communion which He realised in heaven under the immutable form of the life Divine.*"

These are beautiful words, and true. But the two *vessels* must, by the proposition, be always distinct while united, and thus the natures are for ever Two.

Let us turn from the evangelical M. Godet to a theologian of a far more liberal type, and see how he brings out the truth. The following is on *The Relation between the Condition of the Logos in the Flesh and His condition as Pre-existent*, from Köstlin, *Der Lehrbegriff des Evangeliums und der Briefe Johannis :*—

"While His opponents knew not whence He came, and whither He was going, and therefore could give to themselves no account of His person, He Himself knew, and could cut off all contradiction by His *I know* (chap. viii. 14). He is related to men as the heavenly to the earthly (chap. viii. 23), as the spirit to the flesh (chap. viii. 14, 15), only with the difference that the Higher in Him is not only by nature distinguished from the earthly, but at the same time what is, as to before and behind, infinitely above it (chap. viii. 58). Hence the immediate vision of God which, before His incarnation, He enjoyed (chap. iii. 32). But there are also passages in which the Son even now seeth the Father in an absolutely immediate manner (chap. v. 19). In fact the distinction between the existence of Jesus before and His existence after the incarnation sinks to a minimum, and absolutely vanishes. Jesus does not use the term Logos of Himself, but 'The only begotten Son, which is in the bosom of the Father,' is used at once of the pre-existing and the manifested Logos. It is said in ver. 14 that we had 'beheld the glory of Him,' the Logos, and that the Only-begotten, in the bosom of the Father, revealed Him ; hence the same 'Only-begotten' has two predicates, one pre-historical, 'in the bosom,' and one historical, 'hath declared.' So in the First Epistle, 'Jesus Christ come in flesh' admits of no distinction between the Logos and Jesus. In John iii. 13 there is ascribed to the Son of Man a perennial being in heaven. The Son of Man, or Christ, during all His life upon earth, is at the same time in heaven, with or in the Father. By His descent from heaven He left not the Father, for with Him, as with God, the relations of space have no application. So the Father is in Him, and He in the Father. According to chap. vi. 62, the Son of Man goeth up whither He was before ; the Logos, therefore, may bear this name even before His incarnation. But the former estate was one of δόξα, the fulness of Divine *glory*. We find no trace that Christ's 'becoming flesh' was in itself a humiliation (Philippians ii. 8). Christ rather is a man, 'glorious,' 'full,' not 'emptied,' 'equal with God,' and not robbed of that equality. Even in His death we see only in John the dignity of glory, and, during His whole presence among us, all the finite and limited among men vanishes. Especially is there no idea of development; He learned nothing (chap. vii. 15), but *is* the Logos who hath seen God, and always seeth Him. Thus only can we understand the ascending and descending of the angels on the Son of Man (chap. i. 51). In the Old Testament (Genesis xxviii. 12) angels accompany the Divine glory between heaven and earth; but there the glory is above, while in the New Testament it is below, and upon earth."

This goes to the other extreme. It must not be forgotten that it is St. John who records the Lord's prayer for the restoration of His glory; that it is St. John who gives us the most affecting record of our Saviour's pure humanity (chap. xi.); and that the human agony of Christ is in no gospel more affectingly recorded. There is absolutely no contrariety between St. John and St. Paul in their view of the Exinanition, nor between St. John and the Synoptists in their view of Christ's purely human development. Remembering this abatement, nothing can be nobler than Köstlin's tribute to the unity of our Saviour's Divine and human manifestation. The refutation of the Depotentiation theory is, by implication, complete.

One of the ablest essays which the subject has called forth is *Das Dogma vom Gottmenschen*, by Woldemar Schmidt. After giving a sketch of the various theories lately propounded, he turns to the Scripture itself for a solution, and comes to the only sound conclusion, which he gives in very well selected words. With them we also shall drop the subject :—

"If we establish that at the very beginning of the life of Jesus the perfect unity of the Divine and the human took place in the manner stated, then will all in the process of it appear to be Divine, and yet human, the Divine in the human, and the human in the Divine, in all the stages of His development. The passages which speak of the Son's 'coming forth from the Father,' 'coming down into the world,' 'being given and sent of the Father,' declare that the Eternal Son, distinguished from the Father as a Recipient, enters into time and its belongings, and suffers Himself to be affected by human things. Hence when He says, 'The Father is greater than I,' or, 'One only is good, that is, God,' when He cries, 'Not as I will, but as Thou wilt,' when generally he prays to God, we must understand all this of his Divine-human person. The Son of God can and will be what He became in the incarnation, flesh of our flesh, and blood of our blood. . . . . [But in all the acts of His life of submission He remains the same that He was from eternity, only it was His will to receive in time what was still His own from eternity."

NOTE X., p. 25.—*THE UNCHANGED MANHOOD.*

See the "History of Doctrine," V. The Lutheran theology surpasses all other in the precision of its statements regarding the two estates of Christ, that of His humiliation, and that of His exaltation. The necessity of their sacramental doctrine required the Lutherans to etherealise, as it were, the Saviour's human nature, and make it the physical nourishment of His saints. However incongruous their doctrine appears when thus stated, the theory of Lutheranism was faithful to the continuance of our Lord's true humanity. For it was only the Divine ubiquity which thus diffused the unchanged body of Christ. On Hebrews ii., the great Manhood chapter in New-Testament Christology, Dr. Wordsworth and Delitzsch seem to me by far the best expositors; and with deep earnestness should that chapter be studied.

NOTE XI., p. 39.—*BIBLICAL THEOLOGY.*

The study of the doctrine of our Saviour's Person as the Incarnate Son, who is, strictly speaking, known to theology only as One Christ, must, of course, be supremely a Biblical study. Traced first in the sacred Record, where it has a rich development, it then is carried into dogmatic theology, where its influence is seen in the construction of every department of Christ's saving work. This already opens up the controversial history of the Doctrine in what may be termed Historical Theology. The present Essay has traced the subject through these three theological courses of study severally, but only in a cursory and suggestive manner. The development of the doctrine in Scripture is a branch of the subject to which the student is bound to give his best attention. It will yield him inexhaustible fruit. But he must clearly understand what it is that he is to trace in the Scripture.

1. It is not the proof of the Divinity of our Lord so much as the specific characteristics of that Divine Person, who in the mystery of the redemption became man, and whose names as the Divine Incarnate Person are peculiarly His own. It is not, therefore, the Godhead of Christ generally that should be elaborately deduced from the Bible, but the Godhead of the God-man. There is no section of Scripture consecrated to the proof that Christ was God, but every section of its Christology declares that Christ, as the Son of God incarnate, is Divine. Hence the extreme importance of weighing well and carefully classifying the specific terms that bear the weight of our Lord's Divinity. The unbeliever may be able to contest the direct application to Christ of the few passages in which, as we believe, He is named God absolutely. Biblical criticism may render one or two of them doubtful, and scepticism may smile at the credulity which rests the belief of so stupendous a doctrine on a single passage in St. John, or St. Paul, or the Epistle to the Hebrews. The fact is, that the strength of our argument does not lie there; of our *argument*, I say, for our own tranquil faith rejoices greatly over these single sayings in which the absolute Divinity of our Lord cannot be hid. But the defender of Christian doctrine must learn to feel in their full strength that he may urge with irresistible force the names of our Lord's glorious pre-existence, "the Son," "the Image," "the Word," "the Only-begotten," "the First-begotten before every creature, the πρωτότοκος, before the πρωτόκτιστος or the πρωτόπλασμα, before that first personal or inanimate creature, be it who or what it may."

2. He must learn also to perceive and state clearly the fact that the Incarnate Person is the *only Christ that the Scripture knows*. There is not a sentence in the Bible that rests for a moment—if a moment, it is no more—upon the Divine Second Person as such and alone. "The Word was God" seems the only exception; and there the evangelist lingers on that supernal thought only long enough to prepare our minds for the counterpart of the sentence, "the Word was made flesh." Hence there is found what I may call a *communicatio idiomatum* among the names of the

Incarnate as belonging respectively to eternity and to time. The "Word" belongs to both, as we see in comparing the exordium of St. John's Gospel with that of his Epistle. The "Son" belongs to both, and with such literal undistinguishableness that the doctrine of the Eternal Sonship has been impugned by some who accept the Eternal Word. The "Image" belongs to both, for the "glory of God is seen in the face of Christ Jesus" in the Gospel.

3. Once more, he must imprint upon his mind by careful, very careful, study the fact that with all their abundant variations of statement there is but One Form evidently set forth throughout the Scriptures. A casual glance may observe differences between the Three and the One in the four Gospels; between these four and the Acts; between St. Paul's, and St. Peter's, and St. James's Person of Christ; between St. Paul's in the Romans and St. Paul's in the Colossians. But an intent scrutiny shows that they are all "gathered up into one" by a wonderful ἀνακεφαλαίωσις. If we retreat to a little distance and look, there is but one outline, the Figure of Him whom, if our eyes be not holden, we know to be the Son of God incarnate.

As aids to this manifold task, the reader may be directed to the Introduction of Dorner's History, and to the *Biblical Theology* of Schmid: I cannot add any home-born English work. But his best help will be the inexhaustible *Greek-Testament Concordance.*

NOTE XII., p. 43.—*REVELATION.*

"The conception of sacred history is inseparable from that of miracles. The full discussion of this subject must be reserved for the dogmatic system itself; but we may here, in general terms, designate the miracle of the *incarnation*—of God becoming man in Christ—as the fundamental miracle of Christianity. Christ Himself is the prime miracle of Christianity, since His coming is the absolutely *new beginning* of a spiritual creation in the human race, a beginning whose significance is not only ethical, but cosmical. The Person of Christ is not only a *historical* miracle—not merely a new starting point in the world's moral development; as such it would be only relatively a miracle, a wonder, in the same sense as the appearance of every great genius may be so termed, not being analogous to anything preceding. But Christ is something *new* in the race. He is not a mere moral and religious genius, but the new Man, the new *Adam*, whose appearance in the midst of our race has a profound bearing, not only on the moral, but on the *natural* world. He is not a mere prophet, endowed with the Spirit and power of God, but God's only-begotten Son, the brightness of His glory, and the express Image of His Person, for whose redemptive appearance not only man, but nature waits. The Person of Christ is, therefore, not only a historical, but a *cosmical* miracle; not to be explained by the laws and forms of this world, this world's history, and natural phenomena. But in order to be able to appropriate to itself the new revelation in Christ, the human race must receive a new sense, a new spirit. The Spirit of Christ must enter into a permanent union with man, as the principle of a new development, a development conceivable only as proceeding from an absolutely new beginning in the conscious life of the race.

"The miracle of the Incarnation is hence inseparable from that of Inspiration, or the outpouring of the Spirit on the day of Pentecost, through which the principle of the new development is implanted in the human race, and from which the new life of fellowship and the new sense of fellowship take their rise. The miracle of inspiration is the same in the subjective, as the miracle of the revelation of Christ in the objective, sphere. To these two new commencements, which form two sides of one and the same fundamental miracle, the miracle of the new creation, the Christian church traces its origin. All the individual miracles of the New Testament are simply evolutions of this one; and all the Old-Testament miracles are only foretokens, anticipatory indications of the new creating activity, which, in the fulness of time, is concentrated in the miracle of the incarnation, and of the founding of the church."— Martensen, *Christian Dogmatics*, p. 18.

NOTE XIII., p. 46.—*LATITUDINARIAN THEORIES*.

An excellent examination of modern Latitudinarian theories will be found in Dr. Fairbairn's Appendix to Dorner's *History of the Development of the Doctrine of Christ's Person:* an Appendix which adds much to the value of that work. Professor Smeaton's two Treatises on the *Doctrine of the Atonement* may be read with advantage. They are books of great value in the department of Biblical Theology, and the references to modern theories are terse and good. Dr. Crawford's recent work on the Atonement contains an exhaustive examination of these modern theories, and, as a whole, leaves nothing to be desired. But there are some aspects of the question, in the treatment of which my friend Dr. Rigg's *Modern Anglican Theology* still holds the first place.

NOTE XIV., p. 47.—*MODERN THEOPASCHITISM.*

The name of Thomasius has been mentioned as connected with this subject. His treatise on the Person and Work of Christ is the ablest and most comprehensive on the subject that Lutheran divinity has latterly produced. The following passages will be found interesting as giving a view hitherto unnoticed :—

" The entirety of these acts we call the *humiliation*. In it the Divine act of the beginning became the *Divine-human act of His whole life*. The difference between this and the self-limitation involved in the incarnation itself consists in the fact, that it has for its object not the Logos unincarnate, but the Logos in the flesh, that is, the whole Incarnate Person : it is the Divine-human continuation of that original self-limitation into the way of humiliation and suffering, into the way of the cross, and thus only more deeply into the course that began in the incarnation. It was not absolutely necessary that the Mediator should pursue this way : He might even as man have walked otherwise through life. But He surrendered Himself voluntarily to the way of sorrow, because it was required by the atoning design ; or, rather, all this was already bound up in that *one voluntary act* of the exinanition. Hence it might be said that there was an *ethical* necessity for the assumption of all the forms of sorrow, a necessity of freedom. Thus, as the *ethical*, not the physical, *act* of holy obedience and compassionate love, must the whole course of humiliation be viewed.

" From this arises the wonderful peculiarity which the whole earthly life of the Redeemer exhibits. As the Divine-human continuation of the incarnation it is at once revelation and exinanition.

" It is a *revelation of the immanent Divine properties*, of absolute might, truth, holiness, and love. For, as the Son did not in the incarnation surrender these Divine essential properties, which as such are inseparable from the essence of God, so He does not as the Incarnate refrain from their use ; they shine forth through His whole self-manifestation, and diffuse over His life in the flesh that heavenly radiance which beams clear and bright even through poverty and humiliation. And this applies not merely to the last two of those perfections, holiness and love, but to the former also, power and truth; absolute might, as the freedom of self-determination, as the will perfectly commanding itself; absolute truth, as the clear knowledge of the Divine concerning itself, more particularly as the knowledge of the Incarnate concerning His own being and the Father's will. He learned not this in any human school; internally, by virtue of His unity with the Father, He beholds His eternal thoughts, which He speaks of as objects of His own immediate contemplation. For if it is said that these Divine thoughts come gradually into His consciousness through the mediation of the Holy Ghost, that is only the development of what is already bound up in His own essence: in the form of human knowledge it so becomes gradual. As His word, so also His whole self-testimony, yea His whole manifestation, is the revelation of that essential communion which He has with God.

"But not the less is the humiliation at the same time a *self-exinanition*, a continuous renunciation of the Divine manner of existence which He gave up in the incarnation, and of the *relative Divine attributes* in which the immanent properties manifest themselves outwardly—omnipotence, omniscience, omnipresence . . . . . He renounces possession of these properties . . . . . The Divine omnipotence He neither used nor possessed; He did not actually rule the world while He walked upon earth as man; He exercised no other dominion than the ethical one of truth and love, and used no other means than the word of the gospel for the establishment of His kingdom. Not as if He ruled the universe in a hidden manner, He used the absolute power which dwelt in Him only for His mediatorial calling. He could not because He should not. He was not an Almighty Man. Even the miracles which He performed are no argument to the contrary: they are among the works of His vocation for which His humanity was anointed by the Holy Ghost. Not otherwise with His *knowledge*. The penetrating insight into the being of nature and the deep knowledge of human hearts which He exhibits, is not Divine omniscience. It grew with His growth, and ripened under natural instrumentalities and conditions, and had its limits in the mature man. The Mediator was not an omniscient Man. So also with His *omnipresence* . . . . . . Accordingly the humiliation was not a mere concealment, but an actual *kenosis*, not only of the use of those relative perfections, but in their *possession*: the distinction is not applicable here. Surrender of the use is also surrender of the possession of omniscience and omnipresence. The Redeemer during His earthly life was neither almighty, nor omniscient, nor everywhere present.

"But all this we say of the *whole undivided Person*. No distinction can be made between the manhood which renounced, and the Godhead which exercised them still. Otherwise the self-consciousness of the Logos and that of the man fall asunder: and the result would be a man in whom

God dwells. So far as the God-*man* renounced the Divine glory, the *God*-man also renounced it . . . . . . The distinction between the absolute and the relative perfections must be maintained : it is necessary if God is not to be made dependent on the world. Omnipotence is no *plus* of absolute power, omniscience is not an extension of the immanent Divine knowledge ; and when the Son as man renounced these attributes, He deprived Himself of nothing which is *essentially necessary to God in order that He be God*. And it was His own Divine free determination to renounce them : thus He was not almighty, not omnipresent, not omniscient— *because He willed not to be so."*

An immense amount of reasoning has been expended upon the question of the immanence and relativity of the Divine attributes. But it must appear obvious to every one who thinks that the matter is literally unsearchable by our faculties. How this great master of the modern German Christological theosophy feels the pressure will appear from the concluding extract :—

" The difficulty lies in another direction : in this, that the Divine-human consciousness of the Redeemer absolutely ceases sometimes,—whether for a longer or shorter time is indifferent—for example, in sleep, or in the first beginnings of His Divine-human life, or in death. The last two especially bring out the difficulty. For, in the former, while He ripened unto birth, the self-consciousness is present only as a potence, which comes to effect afterwards ; in the latter it sinks into the night of death, goes out as an extinguished light, though but for a moment. These are facts which we must acknowledge, unless we give the Lord's life a Docetic appearance, and deny the reality of His birth and of His death. But these facts of perfect passivity are at the same time the *supreme points of His activity :* they are the highest expressions of His obedience to God, the *great acts* of His redeeming love, by Himself conceived, and willed, and done. There are no others in which the energy of His Divine-human will could have more strongly and gloriously approved themselves, none in which it could have more absolutely declared its independent power : in this will they had their ground. Thus we may say with regard to this, as with regard to the incarnation, that in the profoundest self-surrender the Subject remains the same, Himself ; and if the *how* is concealed from our view, the fact itself is firm, that what, from without, seems to be the extremest subjection is in its deep significance the highest freedom.

" Both may be included and summed up in the idea of the Potence, concerning which we said that the Logos, becoming man, constricted Himself into it. For the Potence is, as the expression itself means, not anything powerless and empty, but Being condensed into its inmost element and principle ...... It is involved in the free act of will, by force of which the God-man gives Himself up for the world."—Thomasius: *Christi Person und Werk*, T. ii., s. 141.

NOTE XV. AND XIX., pp. 53, 79.—*THE SINLESSNESS OF JESUS.*

The question ever arises : Did the veritable temptation of Christ infer the possibility of His sinning? Does the unity of our Saviour's Person render His sinning absolutely impossible ? If so, must we not assume that, so far as Christ's conflict with Satan was an example, it was an example to show us in whose strength we must conquer, not the example of One who conquers as we must conquer? The fallacy that the Messianic tribulation and trial included the victory over the possibility of sinning—a possibility removed by the very fact of the Incarnation—runs through nearly all modern German theology. Take the following words from an untranslated work of the late Dr. Stier :—

"What does it mean that Christ became man, and not an angel? Because He *laid hold of* man, and not the angels, for salvation ? There is a human nature which is compared with the angelic, when the Saviour says of the children of the resurrection, '*They are like the angels*' (Luke xx. 36). But He assumed not that, for to bring us children of death to that glory He died for us in that humanity which may die, and *to that end* was born. We further avow that He was born of the Virgin, and exclude all inherited sin thereby ; but the Virgin was also a woman, and the apostolic word lays stress upon this, that God sent His Son *born of a woman* (Gal. iv. 4). And do we not know what man's inheritance is, as born of a woman ? .... It is wrong, though rightly intended, and leads to pernicious consequences, when some good men say that Christ bore in Himself the *sinfulness* of our human nature that He might destroy it. The apostle carefully chooses His expression that He came '*in the likeness* of sinful flesh' (Rom. viii. 3)—not in the *form*, but in the *likeness*; as the brazen serpent was not a real, poisonous serpent. But that *weakness*, though having in it no sin, had, as weakness, the *susceptibility* for the seduction of sin. He was so fashioned in our flesh, as it became after the fall, that actually all which excites sin in us could solicit Him with the possibility of sin. Hence in Him the striving *against* sin—that word denying, however, any participation in it—*even unto blood* (Heb. xii. 4). For, though our Lord had no positive tendency to sin, yet there was in Him a sluggishness and slowness [*Trägheit und Unlust zum Gehorsam*, which the translation understates] of inclination to the obedience of the Eternal Spirit, in His spirit, which His wrestling soul must overcome. If we do not admit this contest, we fail to understand the Lord's life from beginning to end. Yea, verily, in His whole life, from childhood, this was His task, to become *strong in spirit* through the overcoming of the flesh."

Injustice is necessarily done to Stier's presentation of the case by giving these extracts without their abundant illustrations. But we have only to do with the issue of all, which is this:—

"Yet more: a power must be given to Him who renews the great temptation, greater than Adam's race had known before; for the higher the incarnate Son of God stood through the indwelling Godhead, the more pressing must the legitimate testing of this God-man be. Because all that He obtained through His endurance and victory was to avail for all men, it must become a *merit* that should defy all the objections and protests of hell. So *must* it be, in order that no Satan might blaspheme in eternity and say: God did not exercise the right that my sin experienced in the sin of man; if the Redeemer had encountered this or that, He might have fallen into my power, and been put to shame! We go far, dear readers, with our poor thoughts, but not beyond Scripture. And the tremendous question rises here to our thoughts on this dizzy height: *Could* then Christ, the Son of God in the flesh, have been put to shame, and fallen before temptation? And we dare not shrink from the bold answer, *Yes*, He could have fallen. For, to say it once more, temptation without the possibility of fall is no temptation; and the full eternal value of the victory of Jesus Christ would vanish if this victory was a self-understood necessity. Among all the dark possibilities which the abyss holds, this is the most fearful, that the Second Adam might have fallen even as the first did. What then would have become of the human race,—what judgment would have passed upon the man Jesus, whose union with the Eternal Son the first actual sin had broken—we need not ask; but rather exult in the triumphant thought, that He has conquered."—Stier, *Der Brief an die Hebräer*, ch. ii. 14-18.

Stier was a profoundly reverent author. He went no farther than his theory carried him. But his theory was wrong; and that it was wrong is proved by the healthy recoil of every

Christian heart, his own evidently included, from the conclusion to which he here gives expression. Difficulties there are doubtless in the temptation of our Lord ; but not so many difficulties in the scriptural account itself as dogmatic prepossessions find in it. We never read that as Christ conquered we must conquer ; that He is the pattern of our victory, or anything of that kind. He was tempted in all points as we are, so far as " without sin " and " separate from sinners" He might be tempted. Surely the agony of a perfectly sinless Being must be very different from the struggle of one in whom the germ of sin has burst into development. Hence to be consistent, one step more must be taken,— from Stier to Irving.

Edward Irving published, in 1828, a volume of sermons on the Incarnation, in which he asserted that the Son assumed our nature in its fallen sinful state ; that the flesh of Christ was in its proper nature mortal and corruptible ; that it was liable to sin, nay, was " instinct with every form of sin." Its incorruption and its sinlessness were imparted " by the indwelling of the Holy Ghost." The eloquent unreason which bewilders this subject in Irving's pages we have nothing to do with : suffice that the incarnation is entirely lost as the union of the Divine and human at the outset of the Incarnate Person's history. The reconciliation between heaven and earth was not so properly wrought by Christ as " wrought in Him, while tabernacling in flesh, and wrestling with its infirmities." As his chimaera leads him hither and thither, the hallucinations of Mr. Irving assume the forms of most of the heresies that have been condemned by the Christian church. But all that he says or dreams is justified on the assumption that our Lord took into alliance with Himself a human person in whom He wrestled with the sin of our race.

The noblest book written on the sinlessness of our Lord—a subject with which we have only indirectly to do—is that of Ullmann, the translation of which in the recent edition is a book for which the English theologian ought to be very grateful. If not sustaining the very highest theory, this volume practically establishes all we could desire.

NOTE XVI., p. 54.—*THE EXINANITION INCOMPREHENSIBLE.*

Woldemar Schmidt says very forcibly :—

"Our age groans beyond any other under the burden of distortions of our Lord's life. Some bring Him down to what has no semblance of it, of true humanity, others rob Him of the glory of His Divinity ; not to mention those who resolve the life into fable and myth, and the Docetism which is often found united with the most repulsive forms of Ebionism. If we look at the consequences of both tendencies of thought, we must regard them as equally dangerous ; for peace and reconciliation are only to be found in the God-man. Luther's saying, 'The Saviour would be a poor Saviour if He had only suffered for me in the human nature,' he joined to another, ' If Christ were a hundred times God, and not true man also, it would be of no use ; for then He would not be ours, not our fellow in all things excepting sin.' If we are to learn anything from the struggles of the last century, it is we think this, that the perils of our church are not to be obviated by the labours of a purely historical criticism, which looks at the matter externally, but by the study of the Sacred Form as presented in our most holy faith as not merely ideal but historical. The problem which this sets before us is the problem of the entire gospel. Melanchthon on his death-bed longed for eternity, because he hoped it would solve this problem for him. We say with Dorner : ' We stammer before this centre of wonder. But only by stammering do we learn to speak. And the Word made flesh, as the highest speech of God to man, will give the evermore perfect knowledge of Himself, and effect that language concerning Him shall more clearly reflect His Person and more harmoniously speak concerning it ; yea, shall hear and receive it as the thankful answer of mankind made blessed in faith."—*Das Dogma vom Gottmenschen*, p. 23.

NOTE XVII., p. 66.—*THE SACRAMENTAL PRESENCE.*

The relation of our Lord's Divine-human Person to the Eucharistic Memorial is the test of all the sacramental theories that have been current in the church. A few illustrations may here be given of the simple statements in the text.

The doctrine of Transubstantiation—a word which for the present purpose may stand for the whole theory of which it is the centre—carries out with a perfect consistency the idea that Christ gives Himself and all the benefit of His redeeming Person to the recipient who partakes of what has the appearance of bread and wine. The word Transubstantiation strictly and primarily has the meaning assigned to it by the Council of Trent. The Thirteenth Anathema reads thus: " Whosoever shall say, that in the holy sacrament of the Eucharist the substance of bread and wine remains, together with the substance of the body and blood of our Lord Jesus Christ, and shall deny that wonderful and singular change of the whole substance of the bread into the body, and of the whole substance of the wine into the blood, the species of bread and wine still remaining, which change the Catholic church very fitly calleth Transubstantiation: let him be accursed." There lies the real conversion from which the word is derived; but the formation of the doctrine had been conducted by men whose doctrine of the unity of the One Person had been won at a great cost, and was jealously guarded. Hence we find the Twelfth Anathema of the Tridentine Council, preceding that which has just been quoted, as follows: " Whosoever shall deny, that in the most holy sacrament of the Eucharist, the body and blood, together with the soul and Divinity of our Lord Jesus Christ, and, consequently, the whole of CHRIST, are truly, really, and substantially contained; but shall say that they are there only symbolically, figuratively, or virtually: let him be accursed." This is clear, consistent, intelligible, and incredible.

The theory of Consubstantiation, into which the former was converted by Lutheranism, is, like all other modifications of it, a mere Apollinarian progeny—the body without the soul of the physical Christ in the Eucharist. Instead of investigating the Lutheran confessional formulæ—already referred to in the preceding Historical Sketch—I will quote Olshausen, one of the most luminous defenders of the modified theory established by the German Reformation, with special reference to our present doctrine of Christ's Person. He says (in his commentary on Matthew

xxvi. 26) : " One of the deepest metaphysical problems—the question of the relation of spirit to matter—comes under discussion in the doctrine of the Holy Supper ; as it does eminently in the doctrines of the resurrection and glorification of the flesh. From the various principal views concerning this doctrine arise also, on account of their number and variety, the several theories regarding the Supper. *Idealism* appears in the Roman Catholic doctrine of Transubstantiation, in which the matter is volatilized into spirit. *Dualism* is expressed in the view of Zwinglius, in which spirit and matter are rigidly and absolutely dissevered. *Realism* distinguishes, on the contrary, the Luthero-Calvinistic interpretation, which conceives spirit and matter as neither changed nor dissevered, but as both existing in their true connection and mutual dependence. The doctrine of the two natures in Christ is, accordingly, the antitype for the doctrine of the *higher* and *lower* on the Supper. As in Christ Divinity and humanity are united, without the one being deprived of its identical nature by the other, so also in the Supper the Word of God attaches itself to the matter, and consecrates it to the sacrament. '*Accedit verbum ad elementum et fit sacramentum.*' In these words of Augustine rests the only true canon for the doctrine of the sacraments."

This is consistent with the tendency of the Lutheran doctrine which makes corporeity, as one said, "the end of all the ways of God ; " but it entirely subverts the design of the institution. At the outset, it is not true that the relation of spirit to matter enters into the sacramental idea : the flesh and blood of Christ remain matter still, since the identity of the crucified body and the body glorified and present in the Eucharist is assumed : it is as matter still, though glorified, that the flesh of Christ is supposed to feed the soul. Here, as in Transubstantiation, there is an incomprehensible confusion, rather, of matter and spirit. Nor is it easy to see how the Transubstantiation theory is idealistic, since there also the very substance of flesh and blood is supposed to be present under the accidence of another substance. As to the Dualism of Zwingli's view, that also is an inapplicable notion ; for that view does not concern itself with the relations of matter and spirit at all, there is no connection whatever established between them.

But there is Dualism, or rather for the present purpose it may be said Nestorianism, in the Lutheran doctrine which brings the glorified flesh and blood into presence *with* and *under* the earthly substances. But, passing by all this, the relation between the Divinity and the humanity of Christ, and the higher and lower in the sacrament, is misunderstood. It would seem that the elements in the Supper are the humanity, and the Divinity the glorified flesh and blood : which is contrary to every true conception of the Lord's Person. Moreover, if it is the access of the Word that makes the Sacrament, it is not the presence of the flesh and blood ; and the Zwinglian hypothesis is approached. In fact, by no artifice can the doctrine of Consubstantiation be rescued from the charge of dividing the Christ. Whatever may be meant by the glorified corporeality diffused by Omnipotent virtue from heaven through the bodies and souls of believers, it is only the human nature of the Lord after all ; and glorified corporeality cannot nourish the spirit which is incorporeal. *Is Christ divided ?* He that eateth ME shall live by ME !

If the reader will turn the page of Olshausen's Commentary, he will see in what difficulty this theory is involved when viewed in the light of the institution itself. " It appears difficult, concerning the first Supper, to retain firmly the full signification of the sacrament ; since, as the work of Christ was not yet completed, His body not yet thoroughly glorified, the Holy Ghost not yet shed abroad, we might believe that this first participation possessed only a representative character ; that it was after the resurrection the entire power was for the first time to be experienced in the ordinance. A remembrance of the Lord's death could not have place in the first supper ; for the event was still prospective. The breaking of the bread and the distributing of the cup possessed more of a prophetic character. It was, in the first instance, an ante-type, after the death only became an after-type . . . . To those who admit that the glorification of the humanity of Christ did not begin till the resurrection or ascension to heaven, it is really incomprehensible how Jesus, before His passion, could have dispensed His flesh and blood. To them nothing remains but to say ' that Christ created His own flesh and blood out of nothing.

According to our view of the glorified humanity—a view which appears to us to grow continually clearer upon closer examination—the true nature of the first Supper becomes completely obvious. The Saviour already bore the glorified body within Himself. The model body enveloped it as the shell does the kernel. Therefore the influence of this glorified corporeity might even then have proceeded from Him."

Before leaving Olshausen, it may be observed that he is one of those Lutherans who deeply felt the difficulty of excluding the Whole Christ from the Supper. And why? Because, on the theory of an impartation of the glorified corporeal element, the doctrine of the communication of Divine properties to the humanity must be maintained; and this he could not admit. Hence, rejecting the *communicatio idiomatum*, he discriminates "between the individual personality of the God-man and the efficiency proceeding from Him;" and says that "everything proceeding from Him, even His divinely human efficiency, partakes of His nature." The subject may be dismissed with a single question: What is the efficiency of the Divine-human Person, but the Holy Ghost? What did He shed forth on His ascension? The boundless wealth of His glorified substance, or the Eternal Spirit common to His Person and the persons of His saints? *He hath shed forth this*, says St. Peter, and this he spake of the Holy Ghost which, Jesus being glorified, His church should receive.

There is much here that reminds me of Dr. Thomas Jackson, to whom let us turn, as he expresses the Anglican view, and far more thoroughly and consistently than the moderns:—

" This is a point which every Christian is bound expressly to believe—that God the Father doth neither forgive sins, nor vouchsafe any term or plea of reconciliation, but only for the merits and satisfaction made by the sacrifice of the Son of God, who, by the Eternal Spirit, offered Himself in our human nature upon the cross. In the next place we are to believe and acknowledge that, as God the Father doth neither forgive nor vouchsafe reconciliation, but for the merits and satisfaction of His only Son, so neither will He vouchsafe to convey this or any other blessing unto us which His Son has purchased for us, but only through His Son; not only through Him as our Advocate and Intercessor, but through Him as our Mediator, that is, through His humanity as the organ or conduit, or as the only bond by which we are united and reconciled unto the Divine nature. For although the Holy Spirit, or Third Person in Trinity, doth immediately, and by personal propriety, work faith and other spiritual graces in our souls, yet doth He not by these spiritual graces unite our souls or spirits immediately unto Himself, but unto Christ's human nature. He doth, as it were, till the ground of our hearts, and make it fit to receive the seed of life; but this seed of righteousness immediately flows from the Sun of Righteousness, whose sweet influence likewise it is which doth immediately season, cherish, and ripen it. The Spirit of Life, whereby our adoption and election is sealed unto us, is the real participation of Christ's body, which was broken, and of Christ's blood, which was shed for us. This is the true and punctual meaning of our apostle's speech (1 Corinthians xv. 45):—'*The first man, Adam, was made a living soul,*' or, as the Syriac has it, *animale corpus*, 'an enlivened body;' but *the last Adam was made 'a quickening Spirit,*' and immediately becometh such to all those which as truly bear His Image by the Spirit of Regeneration, which issues from Him, as they have borne the image of the first Adam by natural propagation. And this is again the true and punctual meaning of our Saviour's words (John vi. 63):—'*It is the Spirit that quickeneth; the flesh profiteth nothing. The words that I speak unto you, they are Spirit, and they are life.*' For so He had said in the verses before to such as were offended at His words, '*What and if ye shall see the Son of Man ascend up where He was before?*' The implication contained in the connection between these two verses and the precedent is this—That Christ's virtual presence, or the influence of life, which His human nature was to distil from His heavenly throne, should be more profitable to such as were capable of it than His bodily presence, than the bodily eating of His flesh and blood could be although it had been convertible into their bodily substance. This distillation of life and immortality from His glorified human nature is that which the ancient and orthodoxal church did mean in their figurative and lofty speeches of Christ's real presence, or of eating His very flesh and drinking His very blood in the sacrament. And the sacramental bread is called *His body*, and the sacramental wine *His blood*. As for other reasons, so especially for this, that the virtue or influence of His bloody sacrifice is most plentifully and most effectually distilled from heaven unto the worthy receivers of the Eucharist; and unto this point, and no further, will most of the testimonies reach, which Bellarmine, in his books of the Sacraments, or Maldonate, in his '*Comments upon the Sixth of St. John,*' do quote out of the fathers for Christ's real presence by transubstantiation, or which Chemnitius, that learned Lutheran, in his books, *De Duabus in Christo Naturis*, and *De Fundamentis sanæ Doctrinæ*, doth avouch for Consubstantiation. And if thus much had been as distinctly granted to the ancient Lutherans, as Calvin in some places doth, the controversy between the Lutheran and other reformed churches had been at an end when it first began, both parties acknowledging St. Cyril to be the fittest umpire in this controversy."—Jackson, *On the Creed.* "Works," x. 40.

Here it will be obvious that there is a common element of doctrine between the Anglican Real Presence and the Lutheran, and the remarks already made will apply to both. But with all the stress laid upon the exclusiveness of the sacrament as the only ordinary channel of the bestowment of life, there is observable in this extract, and in the earlier theologians generally, a strong assertion of the direct agency of the Holy Spirit in this bestowment. Obviously these writers are embarrassed by the abundant teaching of Scripture as to the relation of the Spirit to the whole Christ, and by the fact that never is His agency connected with our Lord's lower nature alone. Upon this depends the whole controversy. "The flesh profiteth nothing," even the flesh of Christ, save as belonging to the Indivisible Person, whose merit, grace, and mysterious communication of Himself is committed to the dispensation of the Holy Spirit. He distributeth to each severally the Whole Christ.

Let the following words of Hooker be weighed in their full significance :—

"The first thing of His so infused into our hearts in this life is the Spirit of Christ, whereupon, because the rest, of what kind soever, do all both necessarily depend, and infallibly also ensue, therefore the apostles term it sometime 'the seed of God,' sometime 'the pledge of an heavenly inheritance,' sometime 'the handsel,' or earnest, of that which is to come. From hence it is that they which belong to the mystical body of our Saviour, Christ, and be in number as the stars of heaven, divided successively, by reason of their mortal condition, into many generations, are, notwithstanding, coupled, every one, to Christ, their Head, and all unto every particular person amongst themselves, inasmuch as the same Spirit which anointed the blessed soul of our Saviour, Christ, doth so formalize, unite, and actuate His whole race, as if both He and they were so many limbs compacted into one body, by being quickened all with one and the same soul."—*Eccl. Pol.,* v. 56.

The same writer guards his doctrine—albeit vainly, so far, as its general results go—with such sentences as these, which are detached indeed, but not unfairly so, as each having its own weight :—

"Thus much no Christian man will deny, that when Christ sanctified His own flesh, giving as God, and taking as man, the Holy Ghost, He did this not for Himself only, but for our sakes, that the grace of sanctification and life, which was first received in Him, might pass from Him to His whole race, as malediction came from Adam unto all mankind. Howbeit, because the work of His Spirit to those effects is in us prevented by sin and death possessing us before, it is of necessity that, as well our present sanctification unto newness of life, as the future restoration of our bodies, should pre-suppose a participation of the grace, efficacy, merit, or virtue of His body and blood, without which foundation first laid there is no place for those other operations of the Spirit of Christ to ensue. So that Christ imparteth plainly Himself by degrees."

HIMSELF : not "His flesh" was sanctified, but Himself. He received the Spirit, not His human nature only, which had its fulness in the incarnation act already ; and grace, efficacy, merit, or virtue, are never in all the Scripture assigned to His "body and blood," but to HIMSELF. And, to conclude :—

"Thus, therefore, we see how the Father is in the Son, and the Son in the Father ; how they both are in all things, and all things in them : what communion Christ hath with His church ; how His church, and every member thereof, is in Him by original derivation, and He personally in them by way of mystical association, wrought through the gift of the Holy Ghost, which they that are His receive from Him, and, together with the same, what benefit soever the vital force of His body and blood may yield ; yea, by steps and degrees they receive the complete measure of all such Divine grace as doth sanctify and save throughout, till the day of their final exaltation to a state of fellowship in glory with Him, whose partakers they are now in those things that tend to glory. As for any mixture of the substance of His flesh with ours, the participation which we have of Christ includeth no such kind of gross surmise."

Reserving some remarks on the disparagement of the Holy Spirit's agency in the developments of modern doctrine, I close with the words of Irenæus, not omitting the peculiar Patristic theory of the Atonement with which they commence :—

"The powerful Word and true Man, reasonably redeeming us by His blood, gave Himself a ransom for those who had been led into captivity.

And since the apostasy unjustly ruled us, and when we belonged by nature to Almighty God, alienated us against nature, and made us His own disciples, the Word of God, being all-powerful, and not wanting in justice, dealt justly even with the apostasy itself, buying back from it that which was His own; not violently, as He had first gained dominion over us by snatching greedily what did not belong to Him, but by persuasion (or demonstration), as it became God to receive what He willed by persuasion, and not by force, so that neither might justice be violated, nor God's ancient creation perish. The Lord, therefore, redeemed us by His own blood, and gave His soul for our souls, and His flesh for our flesh, and poured out the Spirit of the Father for the union and communion of God and man, bringing down God to men through the Spirit, raising men to God through His incarnation, and firmly and truly giving us incorruption in His advent through communion with God."

Canon Liddon, in his *Bampton Lectures*, is neither clear in the statement of his own doctrine nor just to those whom he deems his opponents. As to the former, the phrases "life-giving Humanity," "channels of grace that flow from His Manhood," applied to both sacraments, "Sacramental joints and bands," as expository of Colossians ii. 19, Ephesians iv. 16, are loose and indeterminate phrases. The strength of the argument from the Eucharist to the Divinity of Christ is undeniable, and might have been put much more strongly than it is if the Divinity of the Incarnate *Person* has been the great idea distinctively seized. But it is an argument that does not require the theory of a sacramental union with Christ, understanding by union the fellowship of His glorified flesh and blood. If instituted as a symbol, the Eucharist would imply a life of Christ imparted that none but a Divine Person could impart. If only a "sign" of our nourishment through the gift of Christ, it would require the "thing signified" to be Divine. It is not true that this low, and in itself unworthy view, led Zwingli to waver in his confession of Christ's Divinity, nor that Calvin's doctrine, which undeniably is at least as high as that which the Church of England, after a just balance struck between her formulæ, can be said to teach, led him, or has led his followers, to abandon the faith. The doctrine of the Eucharist held among the various sections of the Protestant Church, which do not hold the Sacramental theory, so-called, runs through a wide range of phases—from the very borders of that theory down to the Zwinglian, and even lower; but it is not seen that the measure of faith in the Holy Trinity fluctuates with the fluctuations of these views. Thousands of readers, whose hearts Canon Liddon causes to glow within them by his advocacy of their Saviour's Godhead, feel deeply grieved by language which classes Zwinglian and Socinian together, many of those readers being Zwinglian in their opinion of the Eucharist, but as little Socinian as the Bampton Lecturer could wish them. Moreover, it is unfair to speak constantly of the opponents of the "Real Presence" as denying the "reality of sacramental grace," or "depreciating the sacraments." Let Canon Liddon revive his remembrance of the Westminster Confession, or go for once into the congregation whose fenced ceremonial embodies the doctrine of that Confession, and he will modify his censure. "1. Sacraments are holy signs and seals of the covenant of grace immediately instituted by God to represent Christ and His benefits, and to confirm our interest in Him, as also to put a visible difference between those that belong unto the church and the rest of the world, and solemnly to engage them to the service of God in Christ, according to His word. 2. There is in every sacrament a spiritual relation or sacramental union between the sign and the thing signified, whence it comes to pass that the names and effects of the one are attributed to the other. 3. The grace which is exhibited in or by the sacraments, rightly used, is not confined by any power in them, neither doth the efficacy of a sacrament depend upon the piety or intention of him that doth administer it, but upon the work of the Spirit, and the word of institution, which contains, together with a precept authorizing the use thereof, a promise of benefit to worthy receivers."—*Westminster Confession of Faith*, chapter xxvii.

Finally, when Canon Liddon pointed to the downward course of the old Presbyterian congregations, he should not have forgotten that a large number of the members of the Establishment have not been kept by sound sacramental formularies from the error that denies the Lord's Divinity; witness the clerical author of *An Examination of Canon Liddon's Bampton Lectures*,

NOTE XVIII., p. 67.—*THE REAL PRESENCE BY THE SPIRIT.*

"It has been a peculiar feature of English religion, and of many English theologians, to understand the presence of God Incarnate as the means of human sanctification, and to speak of the Holy Ghost in such a manner as to imply that, although He never became united to human nature by incarnation, yet there is some means by which He comes into direct union with it, and 'dwells in' each sanctified person. Hence there has been a tendency to interpret the word πνεῦμα as referring to God the Holy Spirit, wherever it is used in association with the idea of sanctification; and the tripartite nature of perfected human nature has been altogether ignored, the 'spirit' of man being taken as a synonym for the 'soul' of man, or for that portion of his nature which is not corporeal. A more exact theology recognises the incarnation of God as the means by which God and man were brought into union in the Person of the Son of God; the mediation of Christ as the means by which that union is realised in the persons of Christians; the Holy Spirit as that Person of the Blessed Trinity who effected the union in our Lord by a miraculous conception, and who effects it in Christians by the work of sanctification; and the human 'spirit' as the result of the Divine Spirit's work—the 'building up' of a 'new man,' the development of Christ's 'indwelling' in the soul."—Blunt's *Dict. of Doct. and Hist. Theo.*, Art. Spirit.

It is not necessary now to prove that there is much confusion here, in fact as many misconceptions as there are sentences. Let him who fails to see that read the passage again, noting especially "some means by which the Spirit comes into union with human nature," and the "spirit in man" being taken from man's nature, leaving him body and sensibility alone. The passage is quoted for the sake of its quiet little appendage in the note. "It is a popular idea that there is a great deal about the indwelling of the Holy Spirit in the soul to be found in the New Testament, but this idea is dissipated by an examination of the New Testament itself. There are about sixty-four passages in all, which express, in some form or other, the idea of God abiding with Christians in the sense of indwelling, which can thus be classed." Then follows the classification, with which great pains have been taken. Result : The indwelling of God the Father, or the whole Blessed Trinity, ten times in the church, twice in the individual ; the indwelling of God the Son six times in the church, twenty-five times in the individual ; the indwelling of God the Holy Ghost ten times in the church, and in the individual NONE.

The reader will be much amazed to find that the "spirit" is that element of human nature which was lost in the fall ; especially as the term, with some of its correlatives indicating man's rational nature, is used with regard to "man" generally, renewed and unrenewed, throughout the Scriptures. That the term "spirit" is occasionally employed by St. Paul with relation to the renewed nature cannot be absolutely disproved, but the sweeping assertion above is not "good divinity." Passing that by, however, a few words must be said as to the indwelling Spirit— only a few words, as the subject lies rather wide of our proper scope. Not to speak of the *periphrasis* by which the Holy Spirit in the Trinity must be a spirit within the individual Christian—not denied, indeed, by this theory—the assertion that the Holy Ghost is not indwelling in the believer is simply incorrect. The peculiar indwelling term is used in many passages, and although "in you" follows, the context imperatively requires that this "you" be individualised. The reader must, by the aid of his Concordance, verify this in the Greek Testament, and especially in the great chapter of the Spirit, Romans viii. The central saying of that chapter makes the Holy Ghost our Intercessor within us ; *within*, for " He that searcheth *the hearts* " requires this internal meaning. Though the gifts of the Spirit are distributed by Himself as central in the body, some of those gifts are meaningless if they are not regarded as an internal benediction. The Holy Ghost is a witness within. Where else can His testimony be given as the "Spirit of the Son," the "Spirit of our sonship?" The "sealing" might be forced into an external meaning, but surely not the "earnest." When the Saviour spake of the Spirit coming after His own glorification, His words were, "Out of his belly shall flow rivers of living water," and this is the flow of an internal fountain. But the Spirit's own Pentecostal day proclaims the fallacy of this sweeping generalization. After the distributed tongues resting *on* the believers came the entrance into their hearts: "They were all filled with the Holy Ghost."

Dr. Moberly has made himself a high, though not always sound, authority on this question. Let him rebuke his fellows :—

"All this, and much more than can be specified, is his, because of his personal priestliness; and the secret origin of all this heavenly power—the real and only source of it—is in the undoubted presence of the Almighty Spirit of God in his separate soul, as he is a member of the Spirit-bearing body of Christ. The single soul of the Christian man, duly planted into the Divine body, is a temple of God, or shall I call it a chamber of the temple of God upon the earth, wherein His sacred presence dwelleth. . . . As Christ walketh in the midst of His great temple built up of lively spiritual stones, so is each single stone instinct with that living Spirit, and the Christian man, whosoever and wheresoever he be, and whatsoever he doeth, cannot, if he would, flee from the Almighty presence. . . . The faith in his heart—in the strength of which he puts his whole trust and confidence in God, in Christ—the devout study and inward digesting of the Holy Scriptures, the secret, sacred meditations upon the holy mysteries of the revelation of the name of God, the heart-deep confessions, the true, outpoured prayers, whether personal or intercessory, are but the details of that great inward activity and work wherein the conscious and willing spirit of a man, sanctified, lifted, ennobled, glorified if I may say so, by the indwelling Spirit of the most high God, is continually rising to a nearness and closeness to God, which is itself the essence and perfection of the priestly condition. Won for him by the great *sacrifice* of the cross—brought home to himself through the agency of the organized body of Christ, the church—yet so won, and so brought home to him, it is absolutely his. The Spirit of God itself from his heart maketh intercession for him too profound, too Divine, too infinitely various, mingled, subtle, and delicate, to be capable of any adequate utterance in human words. 'And He that searcheth the heart knoweth what is the mind of the Spirit; that He maketh intercession for the saints according to the will of God.'"—Moberly's Bampton Lecture on *The Administration of the Holy Spirit*, p. 257.

To the same effect, Alexander Knox, one of the fathers of modern Sacramentalism :—

"As this operation, therefore, of the Holy Spirit, is, self-evidently, the noblest and the most valuable which can be conceived in this stage of our existence; so to this must we refer all that is said in the New Testament respecting the gift of the Holy Ghost, which was to distinguish the gospel dispensation. Whatever else may be included in that gift, or by whatever sensible demonstrations of omnipotence it was to be verified or signalized, still we must conclude from the whole tenour of the New Testament that the essence of that Divine gift was spiritual and heavenly; and that it was to consist in the accomplishment, through the Spirit of God, in our inner man, of all that had been purposed and provided for in the incarnation and mysterious ministry of the Son of God. Nothing short of this could glorify the Redeemer, or constitute the sealing of 'the spirit unto the day of redemption;' and thus only could Christians be so strengthened with might by the Spirit, in the inner man, that Christ should (as it were) dwell in their hearts by faith, and that they should be rooted and grounded in the love of God."—*Remains*, vol. ii., p. 49.

The secret of this anxiety to lower and limit the Holy Spirit's function is the difficulty of finding a place for Him in the human spirit, as the Indwelling God, if the glorified human nature of our Lord is the sole sanctifying Occupant: the two are incompatible. One or other must be chosen: either the whole Christ, as represented by the Holy Spirit, is imparted; or we have a sacramental religion of carnal and mechanical and Capernaite materialism, which knows not the Trinity, and needs not a distinct and personal Holy Spirit of God. There is something that may be tolerated, and reasoned with, in the theory of a glorified humanity imparted through sacramental emblems by the power of the Holy Ghost within, taking of those "things of Christ." The unscripturalness of the doctrine that made the sacrament the only channel might be forgiven or rendered innocuous so long as, after all, the Holy Ghost was the indwelling Vivifier of the sacred elements. But when the Holy Ghost is excluded from the sanctuary of man's spirit, and made only the Doorkeeper of the heart, into which the Lord's humanity alone may enter, and thus dishonoured in His own dispensation, we can only wonder what further outrage can be offered to the truth as it is in Jesus. This evil note has been of late sounded out very clearly, and we are on our guard. Long has there been obvious a certain undefinable lowering of the doctrine of the Divine Spirit in works of that pseudo-sacramental tendency: a defect rather to be felt than described. But such plain language as the above throws all disguise away, and we know what to be prepared for.

In Romanist works the function of the Spirit is much limited to His office as towards the mystical Body. Archbishop Manning's work on the *Temporal Mission of the Holy Ghost* contains not three sentences that directly concern the Spirit's indwelling in the believer. The fifth chapter of the first book has this for its thesis : " Before the Incarnation the Holy Ghost taught and sanctified individuals, but with an intermitted exercise of His visitations ; now He teaches and sanctifies the Body of the Church permanently." The treatment of this most carefully avoids any reference to the individual sealing of the Spirit : so carefully that none but a suspicious eye would detect the absence. When quotations from the Fathers are abundant, the truth cannot always be suppressed : hence a few rich sentences occur which will not be hid. For instance :

" S. Gregory the Great says : ' For the Mediator between God and men, the man Christ Jesus, was present always and in all things. Him who also proceeds from Himself by substance, namely, the same Spirit, in the saints who declare Him He abides, but in the Mediator He abides in fulness. Because in them He abides by grace for a special purpose, but in Him He abides by substance and for all things." Such a sentence as this is utterly out of harmony with the rest of the book : we claim it as our own. It is, however, the only sentence in the whole of this elaborate volume that mentions the personal indwelling of the Holy Ghost.

But in the Archbishop's doctrine there is a consistency which is utterly wanting in the Anglican. " The Holy Spirit, through the church, enunciates to this day the original revelation with an articulate voice, which never varies or falters. Its voice to-day is identical with the voice of every age, and is therefore identical with the voice of Jesus Christ. ' He that heareth you heareth Me.' It is the voice of Jesus Christ Himself, for the Holy Ghost ' receives' of the Son that which ' He shows to us.' "

Long may the " popular feature " remain in English theology.

NOTE XIX., p. 84.—*CONTROVERSY ON THE ETERNAL SONSHIP.*

In the Appendix to Dorner, already referred to as containing the recent English history of the doctrine, Dr. Fairbairn gives a statement of this controversy which I shall thankfully borrow:—

"Several respectable theologians, not doubting the article of our Lord's proper Divinity, yet began to dispute the fitness of the term 'Eternal Sonship,' nay, argued the incompatibility of the term with Deity in the stricter sense, and explained it, where it occurs in Scripture, of His incarnation, or what belonged to Him as the Divinely constituted Mediator. Of this class were the commentator Adam Clarke, Drew, Moses Stuart, and several others. The leading argument of all these writers (as indeed of the Arians and Socinians before them) was, that generation necessarily implies production, or a beginning in time; father implies precedency in time, or priority in being, with reference to son; so that eternity is excluded by the very form of the statement. Stuart, however, who was certainly the most learned and ablest of the writers who took this line of objection, did not go quite so far as the others; but he disliked the mode of representation, partly on account of what it seemed to imply, and of its apparent unintelligibility; but he did not absolutely reject it. 'If the phrase *eternal generation,*' he said, 'is to be vindicated, it is only on the ground that it is figuratively used to describe an indefinable connection and discrimination between the Father and Son, which is from everlasting. It is not well chosen, however, for this purpose; because it necessarily, even in its figurative use, carries along with it an idea which is at variance with the self-existence and independence of Christ as Divine; and, of course, in so far as it does this, it seems to detract from His real Divinity.'

"It is to such statements, which had a certain superficial plausibility about them, and appeared to be producing some impression upon orthodox believers, that we owe the excellent treatise of Mr. Treffry, on the *Eternal Sonship of our Lord Jesus Christ.* It was written specially to meet this phase of incorrect representation, which would soon have glided into actual error, and is the fullest and most satisfactory vindication that has come from an English theologian, of the truth of Christ's Sonship, not as Messiah merely, but as the Second in the adorable Godhead. With the exception of some imperfect and partially mistaken representations concerning the views of Philo, the learning exhibited in the work, though not profound, was respectable, and adequate to the task which the author aimed at establishing ; and as a controversial treatise the work is well entitled to commendation, both for the sound judgment and the Christian temper displayed in it. In regard to the specific point under discussion, Mr. Treffry shows that the exception taken by Trinitarians to the Eternal Sonship arises partly from pressing the human analogy too far, and partly from a want of discrimination in respect to the senses in which self-existence is predicable of the Three in the Godhead. There is much, he justly observes, in analogies derived from earthly relations that is wholly inapplicable to the Divine character; and priority of being, and pre-agency, which are inseparable from human paternity, having their ground in men's animal natures, cannot possibly have place with God. 'The essential ideas here are generative production, identity of nature, inferiority of relation, and tender endearment. These may all exist irrespective of time. When generation has a beginning, it is either because the generator is not eternal, or because he must exist previously to generation. But if he has himself no beginning, and if there is no evidence that a generative emanation may not be essential to his nature, it is clear that generation does not necessarily imply beginning. God is eternal ; and Divine generation, for aught that can be alleged to the contrary, may be essential to the Deity.' On the point of self-existence Mr. Treffry showed how Stuart and others failed to discriminate between self-existence as predicable of each Person of the Godhead, and the same as capable of being attributed only to the Divine essence and unity. ' In the one case, the term is equivalent to necessary existence, and is true in application to the Divine subsistences severally considered. In the other, it signifies existence in absolute and separate independency, and is not correct except as spoken of the entire Deity. For the Father is not without the Son, nor the Son without the Spirit. The attribution to each Person (namely, as apart from the others) of absolute independence and self-existence, is, in effect, the denial of all necessary and eternal relation in the Deity.' "—Dorner, *Doct. of the Person of Christ*, v. 425.

NOTE XX., p. 111.—*THE ANGEL OF JEHOVAH.*

No question has occupied more attention and none been more variously decided than this. The New Testament does not give its usual help, no direct reference being found to the Angel of the Lord. The view taken in the Lecture seems on the whole the only one that is consistent with all the facts ; and it has this recommendation, that it supplies the missing evidence of the Divinity of the Divine-human Person whose humanity is so abundantly referred to. If the Angel of Jehovah was not the Second Person of the Holy Trinity we have to wait until the prophecies of Isaiah for the first express declaration of the Divine nature of our Lord in the Old Testament. Moreover, the term prepares for the mediatorial subordination of that God who is also the Servant of God. Apart from the scriptural evidence alluded to in the text, the reference to our Saviour's preexistent Godhead recommends itself to the Christian's sense of the law of development in Scripture. There is something, moreover, inexpressibly attractive in the thought that that sacred Personage was the as yet unincarnate Lord. But the importance of the subject justifies a slight exhibition of the varieties of opinion held on it. Two general views have been held: the following is abridged from Oehler's recent work on the *Theology of the Old Testament*:—

"The first view was followed in the early ages by Augustine, Jerome, and Gregory the Great: that it was an angel in the narrower sense, a finite spirit under subjection to God. The words and acts of such a messenger belong to Him whom he represents: just as in the case of the prophets, and in the case of the angels in the New Testament. But the Old-Testament angel does not say *Thus saith the Lord*, nor does he deprecate worship like the angel in the Apocalypse. He accepts it (Joshua v. 14), and even a sacrifice (Judges vi. 19). This view appears in two forms: according to one, the angel is deputed on each occasion; according to the other, it is always one and the same special angel, the archangel of the book of Daniel. As to another point, it is to be noted in general that the notion that the Mal'ach of the Pentateuch must be explained by the Angel of the Lord in the New Testament forgets the gradual progress of revelation, which advances from the theophany to revelation through Divine organs and through the Spirit. To this is to be added that the same expressions are used concerning the Mal'ach and the Divine indwelling in the sanctuary; in both is the Divine name and the Divine face.

"The second view is that the Angel is a self-manifestation of Jehovah entering into the sphere of the creature: one in essence with Jehovah but yet different from Him. Of this view there are three modifications. First, the Angel is the Logos. This was the view of most of the Greek Fathers, of Justin, Irenaeus, Tertullian, Cyprian, Eusebius. Secondly, the Angel is a created being, with which, however, the uncreated Logos was personally connected. Thirdly, the Angel was God, but not hypostatical, only an unsubstantial manifestation : a transient visibility, a *mission* or angelic effluence returning again to the Divine Being."

After considering and admitting the force of every objection against each of these views, Oehler ends by leaving the subject where it must be left: the Old-Testament Angel can be explained only by the New Testament :—

"It must be acknowledged then that no one of the various views quite does justice to all the passages ; that the doctrine of the Mal'ach in the Old Testament vacillates in a peculiar manner between a Sabellian and a Hypostatic conception of the Angel, so that it seems impossible to bring the matter to a definite intelligible expression. But the matter has a different aspect from the standpoint of the New Testament. From this (see especially 1 Corinthians x. 4) it is the Logos, the Son of God, through whom revelations to Israel are mediated, and who therefore works in the Mal'ach. But in the New Testament the Son of God is nowhere so identified with the Mal'ach as if His incarnation had been preceded by His permanently becoming an angel ; but the Logos, according to the New-Testament view, works in all the other forms of Old Covenant revelation in just the same way as in the form of the Mal'ach."

To this it ought to be added that the Angel form and designation had more express reference than any other to the future subordination of the Incarnate Servant or Messenger of the Covenant. This is remembered in the following extract from the *Speaker's Commentary* on the prominent passages in Genesis :—

(Genesis xvii. 1.) "*And the Lord appeared unto Abram.*
"This is the first mention of a distinct appearance of the Lord to man. His voice is heard by Adam, and He is said to have spoken to Noah and to Abram : but here is a visible manifestation. The following questions naturally arise :—i. Was this a direct vision of Jehovah in bodily shape ? ii. Was it an impression produced on the mind of the seer, but not a true vision of God ? iii. Was it an angel personating God ? iv. Was it a manifestation of the Son of God, a Theophania, in some measure anticipating the Incarnation ? (i.) The first question seems answered by St. John (John i. 18), ' No man hath seen God (the Father) at any time.' (ii.) The second to a certain extent follows the first. Whether there was a manifestation of an objective reality, or merely an impression on the senses, we cannot possibly judge ; but the vision, whether seen in sleep or waking, cannot have been a vision of God the Father. (iii.) The third question has been answered by many in the affirmative, it being concluded that 'the Angel of the Lord,' a created

Angel, was always the means of communication between God and man in the Old Testament. The great supporter of this opinion in early times was St. Augustine (*De Trin.* iii. c. xi. Tom. viii. pp. 805—810), the chief arguments in its favour being the statements of the New Testament that the law was given 'by disposition of angels,' 'spoken by angels,' &c. (Acts vii. 53; Galatians iii. 19; Hebrews ii. 2.2). It is further argued by the supporters of this view, that 'the Angel of the Lord' is in some passages in the Old Testament, and always in the New Testament, clearly a created angel (*e.g.* Zechariah i. 11, 12, &c.; Luke i. 11; Acts xii. 23); and that therefore it is not to be supposed that any of these manifestations of the Angel of God or Angel of the Lord, which seem so markedly Divine, should have been anything more than the appearance of a created angel personating the Most High. (iv.) The affirmative of the fourth opinion was held by the great majority of the Fathers from the very first (see, for instance, Justin, *Dial.*, pp. 280—284; Tertull., *Adv. Prax.* c. 16; Athanas., *Cont. Arian.* iv. pp. 464, 465 (Ed. Col.); Basil, *Adv. Eunom.* ii. 18; Theodoret, *Qu. V. in Exod.*). The teaching of the Fathers on this head is investigated by Bp. Bull, *F. N. D.* iv. 3. In like manner the ancient Jews had referred the manifestation of God in visible form to the *Shechinah*, the *Metatron*, or the *Memra de Jah*, apparently an emanation from God, having a semblance of diversity, yet really one with Him, coming forth to reveal Him, but not truly distinct from Him. The fact, that the name *Angel of the Lord* is sometimes used of a created Angel, is not proof enough that it may not be also used of Him who is called 'the Angel of mighty counsel' (μεγάλης βουλῆς Ἄγγελος, Isaiah ix. 6, Sept. Trans.), and 'the Angel of the covenant' (Malachi iii. 1): and the apparent identification of the Angel of God with God Himself in very many passages (*e.g.* Genesis xxxii. 24, comp. vv. 28, 30; Hosea xii. 3, 4; Genesis xvi. 10, 13, xlviii. 15, 16; Joshua v. 14, vi. 2; Judges ii. 1, xiii. 22; Isaiah vi. 1; cf. John xiii. 41; Isaiah lxiii. 9), leads markedly to the conclusion, that God spake to man by an Angel or Messenger, and yet that that Angel or Messenger was Himself God. No man saw God at any time, but the only-begotten Son, who was in the Bosom of the Father, declared Him. He, who was the Word of God, the Voice of God to His creatures, was yet in the beginning with God, and He was God.

(Genesis xxii. 2.) "*The Angel of the Lord.*

"Up to this verse we have only the name Elohim, God. Now that the Divine intervention to save Isaac and to accept a ransom for his life is related, we find the name Jehovah, the great covenant name, frequently made use of, though the name Elohim occurs again in the next verse. The being here called 'the Angel of Jehovah,' who speaks as with Divine, supreme authority, is doubtless the Angel of the covenant (Malachi iii. 1), the everlasting Son of the Father, who alone 'hath declared Him' (John i. 18).'

It seems strange to find Dr. Pusey wavering on this question, and almost deserting the guidance of the Greek Fathers. The passages here selected from his most valuable work on Daniel will both exhibit and explain his vacillation :—

"But chiefly there was one, designated as '*the* Angel of the Lord,' in whom God accustomed His creatures to the thought of beholding Himself in human form. Whether it were God the Son, who so manifested Himself beforehand, (His Godhead invisible, as in the days of the flesh,) or no, yet there was one, known as *the Angel of the Lord;* therefore the Lord, whether the Father or the Son or the Holy Ghost, was present with Him, and spake by Him; He is called, not as an epithet, but as a description of His being *the Angel of the Lord;* therefore it seems to me most probable, that He was a created Angel. It seems most probable, that the word *Angel* describes His actual nature, not the higher Nature which spoke or was adored in Him. God spake by *the Angel of the Lord* to Hagar, *I will multiply thy seed exceedingly; and she called the Name of the Lord that spake unto her, Thou, God, seest me.* The Angel of the Lord arrested Abraham in doing that which God had bidden him to do, to offer Isaac his son. God in him accepted the obedience, as having been done to Himself. *Now I know that thou fearest God, seeing that thou hast not withheld thy son, thine only son, from Me.* Angels of God's host met Jacob; but it was one, to whom *he made supplication,* and who *blessed him,* and who, Hosea says, was *the Lord of hosts,* of whom Jacob said, *I have seen God, face to face.* The Angel of the Lord withstood Balaam, *because* God says by him, *thy way is perverse before Me, the word that I shall speak unto thee, that thou shalt speak,* the self-same words which God had said to him in vision before; those words, which were the turning-point of his next subsequent history. Of this Angel God says, *My Name is in Him;* in Him were manifested the Divine attributes; He was the minister of God's justice who would *not pardon* their transgressions; to Him God required obedience to be paid. His speaking was God's speaking in Him; for God says, *If thou shalt indeed obey His voice and do all that I command you.* And since He was not present by any visible presence, there was no way of obeying *Him,* except in obeying what God commanded to Moses. Since God was present in Him, God uses as equivalent terms, the words, *The Angel of His Presence, or My Presence.* And when the time of fulfilment came, of which God had said, *Mine Angel shall go before thee, and bring thee in unto the Amorites, &c., and I will cut them off,* it is still one Angel in human form, who says to Joshua, *As Captain of the Lord's host am I come,* in whom Joshua worshipped God, and by whom God required the same tokens of reverence as He had from Moses. By *the Angel of the Lord* God upbraided Israel in the time of the Judges; *I made you to go up out of Egypt, and have brought you unto the land which I sware unto your fathers, and I said, I will never break My covenant with you. Wherefore also I said, I will not drive them out from before you.* The Angel of the Lord pronounced the curse upon Meroz for unfaithfulness ; and it disappears from history. In the Mission of Gideon, the titles, *the Angel of the Lord*, and *the Lord*, interchanged. Yet both are evidently one. God promised by him what God only can promise, and accepted the sacrifice.

"In the revelation to Manoah and his wife, the wife, ignorant, at first, who He was, yet speaks of the *Angel of the Lord* as a being known to them. *His countenance was like the countenance of the Angel of God, very terrible.* To offer sacrifice unto the Lord and to the Angel of the Lord, was one. His name was *wonderful.* No mention having been made of an *Angel* previously, *the Angel* of the *Lord* is not 'the Angel,' i.e. he who had been spoken of, but He who was known as 'the Angel of the Lord.'

"Of this Angel, and of others with Him, it seems to be said, *The Angel of the Lord encampeth round about them that fear Him, and delivereth them.* The word, *encampeth*, probably alludes to that appearance to Jacob on his return from Mesopotamia, when he saw *God's host*, and from it called the name of the place Mahanaim, 'Two-camps,' and, after that, saw the Angel of the Lord, who tried his strength and blessed him. The captain of the host is said to 'encamp,' but he 'encamps *around*,' through the army of which he is the head. On account of this image, and the mention of 'the chariots of God,' as a title for the angels present at His manifestations of Himself, it seems not improbable that the *horses of fire and chariots of fire* round about Elisha, and those which carried up Elijah to heaven, were symbols of angelic presence.

"This same Angel, I think, was meant by Elihu, the *Angel-interpreter, one of a thousand, who showeth unto man his righteousness,* i.e. how he may be righteous in God's sight, *and is gracious unto him, and saith, Rele m him from going down to the pit, I have found a ransom.* For it is the office of no mere created angel, but it is anticipative of His who came, at once to redeem and to justify; as S. Gregory says, 'It is as though the Mediator of God and men said, "Since there hath been no man, who might appear a righteous intercessor for man, I made Myself man to make propitiation for man."'

"This then, in itself, involves a distinction among the heavenly beings, so far at least that, in the earliest books as well as in Daniel, we hear of one Angel, above those ordinarily spoken of.

"In the Seraphim (probably, *fiery* spirits,) in Isaiah, and the Cherubim, we have other orders of spirits in near relation to God. Of these, the Cherubim are not mentioned to have any office of ministry to man, but, having been placed, with symbols of terror, to forbid his return to Paradise, were objects of awe. The Seraphim are spoken of, as engaged in ceaseless praise in great nearness to God, yet as concerned also about us below ; for part of their song was, *The earth is full of His glory.* One of them also was sent to Isaiah with the symbolic burning coal, which was to cleanse his iniquity and fit him for the Seraphic mission of bringing good tidings to man. . . . . .

"Such gradation then of heavenly beings, as is implied in Daniel, is in harmony with what had been revealed before. He sees one in great majesty, whom he describes in language of Ezekiel, probably that same Angel of the Lord, who had appeared to those before him. This Angel gives directions even to Gabriel. It seems also that among those exalted intelligences, some know more of the Divine purposes than others, and communicate that knowledge to others. Twice, in these visions, an angel inquireth of that exalted Angel, (who yet himself is a creature, for he swears by the living God,) and receives an answer.

"Both these relations of that one great Angel, his special office for the people and his superiority to other angels, are mentioned in one of the prophets after the Captivity, Zechariah. There, other angels whom God had *sent to walk to and fro upon the earth*, give account of their mission to *the Angel of the Lord*, and he himself intercedes with the Lord. He stands as judge, surrounded by angels who fulfil his commands, hears the accusations of Satan, pronounces forgiveness to Joshua the high-priest, and, in him, to the people whom he represents. It is probably '*the* Angel of the Lord,' certainly it is a superior angel, who, in another vision, directs another angel to instruct Zechariah. Again, God speaks of *the Angel of the Lord*, as having a glory like His own."—Pusey's *Lectures on Daniel the Prophet*, p. 519 *seq.*

How could "Divine attributes be manifested" in a created angel? And how could the term angel "describe his actual nature" and at the same time take "human form?" And, lastly, why is the language of the prophet Hosea emptied in spirit of all the meaning which in word is assigned to it? By his strength he had *power* with God; yea, he had power over the angel. . . . "He found him in Beth-el, and there he spake with us; EVEN THE LORD GOD OF HOSTS; THE LORD IS HIS MEMORIAL." (Hosea xii. 4, 5.)

NOTE XXI., p. 121.—*THE SON OF GOD IN THE GOSPELS.*

The question as to the identity of the Son of God and Messiah in the gospels is one of great importance. Many passages seem to look that way. But a thorough investigation proves that the former title was both distinct from and superior to the latter.

Wilson's *Illustration of the Method of Explaining the New Testament by the early Opinions of Jews and Christians concerning Christ* has set the matter at rest. The following extracts will give some idea of the manner in which the subject is handled. They are given only as specimens without any particular connection :—

"The object of the trial would therefore be to establish the falsehood of one claim by the supposed blasphemy of the other. They would at once satisfy themselves and the people that He was a false Christ, and merited death ; because, in declaring Himself the Son of God, they conceived Him to have claimed Divinity, and on that account, and that only, to be convicted of blasphemy.

"On this supposition, that unison in their conduct and sentiment in different ages is observable which in Jews might be expected. In modern times, they accuse Christians of blasphemy and idolatry for denominating their Christ the Son of God : in the seventh century, they urged the same accusation : in the fifth century, they urged the first commandment in the decalogue against Christians : in the fourth, Eusebius of Cæsarea relates that they would not admit the possibility of the existence of a Son of God : in the beginning of the third century, according to Origen, who had conversed very extensively with Jews on this particular subject, they refused to admit the application of the term Son of God to the Messiah ; and, as it has been somewhere observed by Basnage, the compiler of the Misna indirectly attacks Christians on the same account in the treatise of which Maimonides has given us a paraphrase : in the middle of the second century, the fictitious Jew of Celsus continually attacks Christ for calling Himself God, and Son of God ; and ridicules the Christians for believing His claims : in the beginning of the second century, the Jew in Justin Martyr objects against the Divinity of the Messiah, as a doctrine peculiar to Christians, and repugnant to the notions of his countrymen : and a century before, the Jews, at different times, attempted to stone Jesus for alluding to His Divinity and preexistence, and actually condemned Him to death for declaring Himself the Son of God.

"A further consistency, in the conduct of the Jews towards Christ and Christians in different ages, may also be observed. When they only appealed to their own law, the authority of which was acknowledged by Christians as well as themselves, they have urged the charge of blasphemy and idolatry ; and they condemned Jesus to death for the crime of blasphemy, in declaring Himself the Son of God. But, when they addressed themselves to the Roman Emperors before the time of Constantine, they accused Christians of a species of treason, in acknowledging and expecting a great King, called Christ, to overthrow the Roman Empire and to rule the whole earth ; and they accused our Saviour, to the Roman governor of Judæa, because He made Himself Christ, a King, and therefore spoke against Cæsar."—p. 15.

"There is also strong negative evidence in the New Testament, that it was not accounted blasphemy by the Jewish magistrates, to acknowledge Jesus as the Christ. If He blasphemed, in the eyes of the Jews, by indirectly declaring Himself Christ, the same guilt must have attached on others, who honoured Him with that invidious title; whereas, when the two blind men cry out, 'Jesus, Thou Son of David!' they are simply rebuked, not stoned as blasphemers. At one time, five thousand men affirm Jesus to be that prophet who should come into the world; at another, the multitude hails Him with Hosannas into Jerusalem as the Messiah; yet none of these are stigmatized with the name, or suffer the severe penalty annexed to blasphemy.

"Let all the different significations of the phrase 'Son of God' be enumerated: it is only in one of them that the application of it to any individual could amount (in the opinion of the ancient Jews) to the crime for which Jesus suffered. But if, according to its most obvious meaning, it be thought to imply Divinity, the Jews, it may easily be supposed, would pronounce Jesus a blasphemer for claiming a property which they admitted in the one Jehovah only."

After giving Limborch's luminous statement of the evidence on the opposite side—*manifesto indicio, Messiam seu Christum, et Filium Dei esse, idem plane significasse*—the writer goes on :—

"Notwithstanding the subtilty with which this evidence is stated by a professed disputant—on attending to the several arguments, they will be found to fall short of the object which they are brought to establish. They, in fact, prove only that Jesus had declared Himself Messiah, the Son of David, and that He had also been announced under this title by John the Baptist; but from them no inference can be drawn relating to the only point in question, the popular use of the phrase 'Son of God,' as a title of the Jewish Messiah. As great stress, however, continues to be laid on these arguments by several men of learning, a separate examination of each may be necessary.

"i. And first, with respect to the two questions of the Jewish Sanhedrim, to our Saviour, recorded in St. Luke : to affirm that one of these is a mere repetition of the other, that they are the *same question (eandem quæstionem repetentes)* in different words, is taking for granted all that the learned writer is attempting to prove. I have endeavoured to show in the preceding chapters, in opposition to this gratuitous supposition, that the two questions must have been essentially different (as they are supposed to be by many others); and that Jesus was not condemned for simply professing to be the Christ, either in direct or indirect terms.

"But, according to S. Matthew and Mark, the high priest asked our Saviour, 'Art Thou the Messiah, the Son of God?' and the question, it is contended, proves that custom had set apart both these terms to denote the same idea. Not to mention that this, which, in the abridged accounts of Matthew and Mark, appears as one question, was in fact two; as may be inferred from S. Luke's narrative; it is sufficient to observe, that the questions of the Sanhedrim would be regulated by the accounts that they had received of the nature of our Saviour's claims, not by their own opinions on the subject of their Messiah: nor would their questions be confined to *language*, which custom had sanctioned; when their only object was to discover what terms Jesus had actually applied to Himself, whether custom had justified their use or not. They would ask Him about *His* doctrines, not about language which he had applied to Himself, not about language which they thought applicable to their Messiah: and the only inference from their questions is, that Jesus had previously professed to be the Christ the Son of God, instead of Christ the Son of David, and that the high priest had received information of the circumstance; but, whether these titles had ever been combined, or used synonymously, in that age, except by Christ Himself, by John the Baptist, who first announced His nature and office, and by their disciples and followers, by no means appears from these questions.

"ii. When Nathanael acknowledged Jesus as the Son of God and King of Israel, before he became a disciple, it is concluded that these must have been the established titles of the Messiah among the Jews of that age. Two contending classes of theologians have united in insisting strongly on this point. On examining the whole account, however, it is found that Nathanael uttered this declaration two days after our Saviour had been announced as the Messiah and Son of God, at the baptism of John; he seems also to have been near the place, and to have had the means of being informed of the circumstances attending the baptism, from one of John's disciples: and a knowledge of these circumstances, acquired in this manner, combined with the proof, which our Lord immediately gave, of a foresight more than human, probably induced him to exclaim—'Thou *art* the Son of God, Thou *art* the King of Israel.' Thou art really possessed of the Divine nature, and invested with the royal office, which John has just proclaimed. The application of the first of these titles to the Messiah, by a disciple or follower of John or of Jesus, after the former had appeared to prepare the way for the new economy, affords not the slightest proof that the title was acknowledged among the Jews at large.

"To remove old prejudices, and to prepare the minds of some of his hearers for the reception of new and sublime truths, would be the great objects of the preaching of John. And if the prejudices of the great body of the Jews were always alarmed whenever our Saviour professed to be the Son of God, the aversion to His claims and doctrines might have been universal, had not some of them been previously informed by John that the Messiah, whose kingdom was at hand, was to be in some very eminent and peculiar manner the Son of God, and not a mere descendant of David.

"iii. When 'they that were in the ship came and worshipped Him, saying, Of a truth Thou art the Son of God ;' when Martha declared, 'Lord, I believe that Thou art the Messiah, the Son of God, which should come into the world ;' and when the Eunuch of Candace answered Philip, 'I believe that Jesus Messiah is the Son of God ;' these persons must have known that Jesus had assumed these titles which they admitted ; but from this no inference can be drawn in favour of the general prevalence of this sort of language in the Jewish nation. Their answers amount only to this : 'Jesus is really the being which He professes to be.'

"iv. The accounts of Peter's answer in the first three Evangelists, at first sight, seem to prove something more. In S. Matthew, Peter says, 'Thou art the Messiah, the Son of the living God ;' in S. Mark, 'Thou art the Christ ;' in S. Luke, 'Thou art the Christ of God.' When these answers, separated from their respective contexts, are compared together, it might seem that the terms Messiah and Son of God were used synonymously by the Apostles in the early part of Christ's ministry ; and the probable inference would be, that they were so used by the Jews at large. This conclusion would be inevitable, were it true that the same subject matter is always to be found in all the Evangelists, set forth only in different language. If one Evangelist never omitted to relate what is mentioned by another, the words of Peter, as described by S. Matthew, would unquestionably convey no further meaning than his answer, as it is found in S. Mark. But, on comparing the three Gospels, it is found that several material circumstances, in the conferences of Christ with His disciples, are mentioned at length by S. Matthew, which are either wholly or partially omitted in the others.

"By what reasons the Evangelists were sometimes led to omit the recital of some of the words and actions of our Saviour and the Apostles, can now only be a matter of mere conjecture. In the present instance, the case might possibly be thus. During our Saviour's ministry, and before it, the terms Messiah and Son of God had not been generally used by the Jews in the same sense ; but after He had applied both these titles to Himself, they would in a few years be used by Christians indifferently the one for the other, as they are at present. S. Luke and S. Mark, who wrote principally for the information of Greek and Roman Christians about A.D. 59 and 65, would think it superfluous to employ both terms, when custom had brought one to be implied in the other, when to be acknowledged as the Christ was to be acknowledged as the Son of God. But S. Matthew, who wrote his Gospel for the use of Jewish Christians, only a very few years after our Saviour's crucifixion, might judge it necessary to impress on their minds a truth of which they had but lately been informed. It was necessary to teach them that their Messiah was not merely a descendant of David, but the Son of God.

"None of these indirect testimonies (and no others, I believe, can be produced) tend to prove that the Jewish Messiah was commonly described under the appellation of the Son of God in our Saviour's age. The evidence against this opinion will perhaps be thought conclusive."— P. 62.

NOTE XXII., p. 122.—*THE SON OF MAN.*

All that need be added on this subject is found in the following passages from Dr. Pusey's *Daniel.* The reader should study the lecture of which this is a fragment:—

"Such was the aspect of the successive kingdoms, such their outline. But the chief object of interest, that chiefly expanded, as in Nebuchadnezzar's dream, is that in which they should end, the kingdom of God victorious over the evil of the world. One verse is assigned to each of the first three kingdoms; one verse contains the explanation of them all; the rest of the vision and the explanation is occupied with that great conflict. We see, on earth, *the little horn with eyes like the eyes of a man,* man's intellectual acuteness, *and the mouth speaking great things,* setting himself *over against God,* destroying the saints of the Most High, *essaying to change* worship *and law;* and all is, for the allotted time, given into his hand. On the other side, heaven is opened to us; we see the Throne of God, and the Eternal God, and the judgment set, and the books opened, the records of man's deeds and misdeeds; and *one like a Son of Man* in Heaven; like man, but not a mere man; man, but more than man; in the clouds of heaven, to whom, as man, *is given power and glory and kingdom; all peoples* should *serve Him, and His dominion* should last for ever. It is a sublime picture; man, with his keen intellect, a look more stout than his fellows, overthrowing kings, doing his own will, speaking against God, placing himself over against Him as His antagonist, having, for a set time, all things in his hands; and above, out of his sight, God, enthroned in the serenity of His Majesty, surrounded by the thousands of thousands of heavenly beings who serve Him; and near Him One in human form, born of a human birth, yet, like God, above in the clouds of heaven, the darkness shrouding Him from human eye, but reigning and to reign for ever, His kingdom neither to *pass away* by decay nor to be *destroyed* by violence. 'God is patient because He is eternal.' . . .

"The King of this kingdom was to be of human birth, *like a son of mortal man*, and therefore not a mere man ; accompanied by angels to the throne of God, in that majesty which had, before Daniel in this place, been spoken of God only, *coming with the clouds of heaven.*

"Even before our Lord came, the description was recognised as relating to the Messiah. The passage was cited in the book of Enoch, when affirming the preexistence of the Messiah 'before the creation of the world and for ever,' that He was the Revealer to man, the Object of prayer, and would be to all nations the stay, the light of nations ; the hope of the troubled ; the righteous Judge, with whom the saints should dwell for ever. 'Anani,' 'He of the clouds,' continued to be a name of the Messiah, and the Jews, unable to distinguish beforehand His first and His second coming, reconciled the account of His humiliation and His glory by the well-known solution : 'It is written of King Messiah, *and see with the clouds of heaven One like a son of man* came ; and it is written, *meek and riding upon an ass.* Be they [Israel] worthy, *with the clouds of heaven ;* be they not worthy, *meek and riding upon an ass.*' Caiaphas understood it and all which it claimed for Him, his Judge, who was arraigned before Him, and whom He had *adjured by the living God* to say whether He were *the Christ, the Son of God. Thou hast said ; nevertheless I say unto you, Hereafter ye shall see the Son of Man sitting on the Right Hand of Power, and coming in the clouds of Heaven.* Caiaphas understood, and thereon condemned Him for blasphemy. Once more our Lord applied the words of Daniel to Himself. *All power is given unto Me in heaven and in earth.* The title, *the Son of Man*, as employed by our Lord, is the more remarkable, in that He always uses it of Himself as to His work for us on earth ; no one ventures to use it of Him, except that S. Stephen points to the commenced fulfilment of His prophecy to Caiaphas, *I see the heavens opened and the Son of Man standing at the Right Hand of God.* Our Lord called Himself 'the Son of Man,' *i. e.* He who was foretold under that name in Daniel.

"Daniel foretold, not a kingdom in Israel only, not a conversion of the heathen only, but that He who sat above, in a form like a son of man, should be *worshipped by all peoples, nations, and languages,* and that this His kingdom should not pass away. And to whom have peoples, nations, and languages throughout the world, millions on millions, and hundred millions on hundred millions in successive generations, looked to and worshipped as their King, hereafter to come to be their Judge ; whom have they confessed in their Creeds all these centuries since any questioned it, as Him 'whose kingdom shall have no end,' save Him who came in the form of a servant, like a Son of Man, in Judæa?"

NOTE XXIII., p. 152.—*ST. PAUL'S ANTITHESIS OF THE TWO NATURES.*

The view taken of St. Paul's testimony in the Romans is not generally received. It may be interesting to see it fairly contrasted with the other current views. The question is treated thus by Philippi in his elaborate Commentary on the Romans : a work from which a considerable extract will be taken, as it does not seem likely that it will be translated. The Greek is retained only where necessary to the sense :—

(Ver. 3.) "*Concerning His Son.*

"According to the order and grammar this is to be connected with ' promised before,' not with ' gospel ' (ver. 1), though certainly the object of the latter is really given here. Ver. 2 therefore is not to be put into a parenthesis. The υἱὸς θεοῦ is not to be regarded as a mere Messianic official name : it always indicates in our apostle a metaphysical relation of Christ to the Father. It is the same as the υἱὸς μονογενὴς παρὰ πατρός (John i. 14), and the υἱὸς ἴδιος of Romans viii. 32. As such preeminently He must be *demonstrated* (ver. 4). We have here the same contrast of the Manhood and Godhead of Jesus Christ as in Romans ix. 5, which place in itself is decisive as to the meaning of 'Son of God' in the present passage : comp., in Colossians i. 13—17, the representation given of 'the Son of His love.'

"*Which was made of the Seed of David.*

"He was born the Son of David according to the promises of the prophets ; only as such is He a γενόμενος, One born in time, One who 'became or was made' according to Galatians iv. 4: for as Son of God He is eternally existent. Nevertheless, this eternally existent Son of God became a Son of David : not by any change in His unchangeable Godhead—it must not be forgotten that only in Pantheistic systems has the Infinite becoming finite any place and sense—but through the assumption and taking up of the heavenly into the unity of His Divine Person. The Incarnate Son of God is only One : therefore the expression is allowable that the Son of God was born of the seed of David. But, as the seed of David, He was born of the Virgin Mary, the daughter of David. Thus the seed of David was at the same time the seed of the Woman promised in the Protevangelium. To ascribe to the apostle the idea of the metaphysical Divine Sonship, and to deny to him a faith in the birth of the Son of God of the Virgin, is to attribute to Him a dogmatic unmeaning.

"κατὰ σάρκα.

"σάρξ signifies here the sum of human nature, constituted of σῶμα and of the higher and lower ψυχή, which is described according to the characteristic marks of its visible, sensible manifestation. In the same meaning it is in John i. 14 'the Word was made flesh,' and is not essentially different from 'God became man:' comp. Romans ix. 5. The ethical element of the sinfulness of the flesh is absent here, for Christ did not appear 'in the flesh of sin,' only 'in the likeness of sinful flesh;' but the infirmity and mortality of the flesh is made prominent, although the dissolvable human nature 'of the seed of David' is glorified.

(Ver. 4.) "*And declared to be the Son of God with power, according to the Spirit of holiness, by the resurrection from the dead.*

"By the Asyndeton, which leaves the clauses without link, the second member of the parallel is made emphatic. Ὁρίζειν τινά τι is to determine or fix, to declare or appoint, one to anything, *constituere, creare*, so in all the New-Testament passages, Luke xxii. 22; Acts ii. 23, x. 42, xi. 29, xvii. 26, 31; Hebrews iv. 7. The interpretation of Chrysostom and Theophylact, exhibited, confirmed, adjudged, gives rather the sense than the meaning of the words. Christ is proved and demonstrated to be the Son of God because He was *before men*, or in the conviction of men, appointed as such through the resurrection. Acts xiii. 33 is quite parallel.

"As 'according to the Spirit of holiness' is manifestly the antithesis of 'according to the flesh,' it is unnatural to coordinate 'with power,' 'according to the Spirit,' and 'by the resurrection,' and make them all the threefold opposite to 'the flesh,' as if Christ was demonstrated to be the Son of God in these three senses at once. The current antithesis of flesh and spirit rather requires us to explain it as the Son of David according to the flesh, the Son of God according to the Spirit. The words 'with power' must be connected either with 'declared' or with 'Son of God.' If, taking the former, we interpret 'by the power of God,' we find 'of God' wanting (comp. 2 Corinthians xiii. 4; 1 Corinthians vi. 14), or such an expression as 'by the glory of the Father' (Romans vi. 4, 6). If 'with power' is adverbially taken, as 'mightily' or 'abundantly,' we should expect another order in the words. Hence we prefer the connection with 'Son of God:' *id est*, says Melanchthon, 'declaratus est esse Filius Dei potens.' 'Who was established and approved as a Son of God in power.' If then the 'flesh' defined the lower, human nature, the 'Spirit' must define the higher, Divine principle, in Christ. (So Greg. Naz., *Orat.* xxxix. 13, xxxviii. 13, sees the distinction of the Divine and human natures here. And Cyprian, *De Idolorum Vanitate*, says of the incarnation: 'Carnem Spiritus Sanctus induit.') It is not therefore the 'Holy Spirit' which is the dogmatic term for the Third Person in the Trinity: neither as He who spake through the prophets and declared the Divine Sonship of Christ; nor as Christ Himself was anointed with that Spirit without measure; nor inasmuch as after the resurrection He poured out the Spirit on His disciples. The Holy Spirit is never in the New Testament called the Spirit of holiness; and this last must needs be the higher, heavenly, Divine nature of Christ, according to which or in which He is the Son of God. There is here attributed to the Son of God a pneumatic or spiritual essence; for John iv. 24, 'God is a Spirit,' refers to Him also, and in 2 Corinthians iii. 17 He is called 'Spirit,' and in Hebrews ix. 14 He offered Himself by the Eternal Spirit. 'Of holiness' is the *gen. qualitatis* and defines the nature of the Spirit. Ἁγιωσύνη is distinguished from ἁγιασμός; it is holiness (comp. 2 Corinthians vii. 1; 1 Thessalonians iii. 13), and not sanctification or making holy. But the reason why the apostle calls Him Son of God in power and His higher nature a Spirit of holiness, seems no other than this, that with the 'flesh,' the human nature, ascribed to Him there is connected the notion of frailty and sinfulness, although the latter, as we have seen, is not here in the word. Now the Son of God had in fact subjected Himself to the 'weakness of flesh,' and appeared 'in the likeness of the flesh of sin;' nevertheless, He was and continued to be the Son of God in power according to the Spirit of holiness; and it was in His resurrection, as the victory over death and sin, that He proved Himself to be the Almighty living and holy Son of God, to whom all power in heaven and earth was given, that He should give eternal life to as many as the Father had given Him (Matthew xxviii. 18; John xvii. 2). Moreover, we may compare with our passage the similar thought of 1 Timothy iii. 16: 'God was manifest in the flesh, justified in the Spirit;' as also the antithesis of flesh and Spirit in 1 Peter iii. 18.

"*By the resurrection from the dead.*

"The ἐκ may be a particle of time or of cause (comp. James ii. 18): *since* or *through* the resurrection has Christ been approved to be the Son of God. The causal signification is to be preferred; for apostolical preaching everywhere exhibits the resurrection of Christ as the ground of faith in His Divine Sonship: comp. Acts ii. 24, xiii. 30, xvii. 3—31, xxvi. 23. It actually gave this demonstration of the Divine Sonship according to John ii. 19, x. 11. It confirmed the testimony of Christ concerning Himself, the substance of which was the Divine Sonship. 'Resurrection of the dead' cannot be grammatically identical with 'resurrection from the dead.' But it is not the future resurrection that is spoken of; Christ's resurrection is the resurrection of the dead itself, inasmuch as in His resurrection ours is included, and His resurrection exhibits in a concrete instance the universal resurrection; Acts iv. 2, xxvi. 8; 1 Corinthians xv. 12. 'Jesus Christ our Lord' is not, with the Itala and Vulgate, to be connected with 'by the resurrection of the dead;' it is in apposition with 'Son of God.' This Son of David and Son of God is the historical Person Jesus Christ, the Man Jesus, the Messiah (Christ), the one and common Lord of the Church."

With this may be compared the remarks of Dr. Vaughan, in his Commentary on the Romans :—

"*According to the Spirit of holiness.*
"There is an evident contrast between κατὰ σάρκα and κατὰ πνεῦμα here, *as regards flesh*, and *as regards spirit*, as in 1 Timothy iii. 16 ; 1 Peter iii. 18. But the *nature* of the contrast must be defined by the context. Here the sense seems to be : *As regards flesh, Christ was born of the seed of David ; but as regards spirit, that which was in Him a spirit of holiness was a soul perfectly pervaded and animated by the Holy Spirit, who was given to Him not by measure* (John iii. 34), *in whom all His works were done* (Acts x. 38), *and by whose quickening He was at last raised again from death (*compare viii. 11). *He was conclusively proved to be the Son of God by the one decisive sign of resurrection from the dead.* The humiliation of Christ consisted in this, that He laid aside the inherent powers of the Godhead (Philippians ii. 6, 7), and consented to act within the limits of a human soul perfectly possessed and actuated by the indwelling Spirit of God. That soul, indwelt by the Holy Ghost, is the *Spirit of holiness* here spoken of."

It seems hard to understand what difference there is between this view and that of the modern Depotentiation theories, which regard the Son of God as having condescended to become a power or potency of the Godhead in human nature : which is Apollinarianism, or Entychianism, according to circumstances. Surely it cannot be right to affirm that the Son of God "laid aside the inherent powers of the Godhead :" He could not lay them aside, though He might veil their exercise. Nor did He "act within the limits of a human soul :" He made a human soul the organ of His manifestation, but constantly declared that He was not limited to its range of faculties. But with that question we have not to do. Suffice that such an exposition entirely excludes the higher and Divine nature from the passage. The same may be said of the note of Dr. Wordsworth, who represents a more current opinion :—

"*According to the Spirit of holiness* which was in Him, by which He was anointed (Luke iv. 18 ; John x. 36 ; Acts iv. 29, x. 38; Hebrews i. 9), and by which He was declared to be the Messiah, the Son of God, and by which Spirit He worked (Matthew xii. 28 ; Acts xi. 22), and overcame the spirits of darkness ; and by which He offered Himself (Hebrews ix. 14), and which *Spirit of holiness* being in Him, rendered it impossible that He, the *Holy One* of God, should be holden by the *bands of death* and the grave, and *see corruption* (comp. Acts xi. 24—29).

"Therefore, as the *first birth* of Jesus, namely, that from the womb of His Virgin Mother, was by the operation of the Holy Ghost (Luke i. 35), so likewise His *second birth*, that from the tomb, by which He was the *firstborn* of the dead (Colossians i. 18 ; Rev. i. 5), was due to the energy of the same Divine Person, the Holy Ghost (comp. chap. viii. 11).

That the Holy Spirit was the Spirit of the Incarnate Christ there can be no doubt. But it is exceedingly important to draw a clear line of distinction between the agency of the Holy Ghost in the work of redemption and the essential agency of the Divine nature of the Redeemer. Surely the sacrifice of the Incarnate Person was offered by the Divinity in Him, not by the Holy Ghost. He offered Himself in virtue of His eternal Godhead. It was His Divinity in which He was justified as God manifest in the flesh. But, apart from this theological point, Dr. Wordsworth's exposition, in common with all others taking the same view, entirely renounces the striking antithesis between the two natures which it was obviously St. Paul's purpose to exhibit.

On the two central passages of the epistle the following is the comment of Philippi :—

(Chap. viii. 3.) "*God sending His own Son in the likeness of sinful flesh.*

"The act of God's love is made very prominent by the words which take the lead : τὸν ἑαυτοῦ υἱόν. This, like the ἴδιος υἱός of ver. 32, makes the Son-relation a metaphysical one ; and by 'sending' the personality of Christ is shown to have preexisted. But Christ did not appear 'in the flesh of sin,' which is the Ebionite view ; nor in 'the likeness of flesh,' which is the Docetic ; but 'in the likeness of the flesh of sin,' which is the Biblical-Pauline teaching. 'Flesh' is evidently the entire nature of man, as in John i. 14 ; Romans i. 3; 1 John iv. 2, including body and soul. But this flesh is, as chap. vii. shows, a flesh of sin. Now Christ could indeed come in 'flesh,' but not in the 'flesh of sin ;' for He must be 'without sin' (Hebrews iv. 15), in order to be capable of 'condemning sin in the flesh.' Therefore He appeared ἐν ὁμοιώματι, 'in the likeness' of the flesh of sin : comp. Philippians ii. 7, 'in the likeness of men.'

(Chap. viii. 32.) "*His own Son.*

"The word ἴδιος is seldom in the New Testament used instead of the possessive pronoun without emphasis : comp. Matthew xxii 5, xxv. 14. In far the greater number of cases there is in it an open or concealed antithesis : comp. Acts ii. 6 ; Romans xi. 24, xiv. 4 ; Titus i. 12. So it is here. The antithesis to the ἴδιος υἱός is the υἱοὶ θετοί, the sons by adoption. The 'own son' is the only and peculiar Son : comp. John v. 18, πατέρα ἴδιον, *His own Father, making Himself equal with God.* 'His Son,' therefore, is His Son by nature in contrast with sons by adoption : He who is the 'Only-begotten' (John iii. 16) and the 'First-begotten.' The connection expresses this interpretation. For this is the supreme demonstration of Divine love, that God gave His *own* Son.

"*Spared not.*

"Deus paterno suo amori quasi vim adhibuit (Bengel). Comp. Sept. Genesis xxii. 12 : καὶ οὐκ ἐφείσω τοῦ υἱοῦ σου τοῦ ἀγαπητοῦ. The coincidence here is scarcely fortuitous. God has Himself accomplished that which in the example of Abraham He showed to be the highest demonstration of love. Comp. also the τὸν μονογενῆ προσέφερεν, Heb. ii. 17."

The exposition of Romans ix. 5 is a most elaborate vindication of the antithesis of the Divine and human natures in that passage. It will be necessary somewhat to abridge ; but nothing essential is omitted, and the reader must weigh well what is here written :—

"*Of whom Christ came according to the flesh.*

"The last and highest prerogative of Israel. 'Of whom :' not 'to whom belongs,' but 'out of whom sprang,' as the insertion of ἐξ shows. τὸ κατὰ σάρκα, 'as to what concerns the human nature,' limits the 'springing from the Jews,' and excludes the notion that Christ is *only* man. *Who is over all, God blessed for ever.*

'Ο ὤν is equal to ὅς ἐστι : comp. John i. 18, iii. 13,‘xii. 17 (where ὁ ὤν is equal to ὅς ἦν) ; 2 Corinthians xi. 31. 'Over all' is 'over all things,' not 'over all men ;' for Christ is to be represented, in contrast with the weakness of the flesh, as 'God ruling over all.' The article not being before θεός must not suggest a Philonic or Origenist distinction between θεός and ὁ θεός ; as if the latter were the absolute God, the former only a relative God, God in a subordinate sense. The Monotheism of the New Testament, which is not less rigorous than that of the Old Testament, forbids such a distinction between God and an under-God. The God who will not give His honour to another knows no distinction between God and not-God. Reason and Revelation are here in beautiful harmony. On the standpoint of an emanistic Pantheism, such as Philo's, this distinction may have an intelligible meaning. But He who is 'over all' cannot be subordinated to another. The article could not be inserted because θεός is a predicate: it was the being 'God' which was to be asserted of Christ, not the being 'the God,' which would have been erroneous, as He is not ὁ θεός, that is, God the Father, or the Three-One God, but God. It could not be said that Christ was 'the God,' because He whose being God was to be asserted could not be described as the God *already known*. The same holds good of John i. 1: καὶ θεὸς ἦν ὁ λόγος. The predicate comes first for emphasis; and the addition of the article would have confused the sentence. For, as 'the Word was with God' immediately precedes, the article in the immediately following clause would have suggested that ὁ λόγος was the predicate. But, here, the addition 'who is God over all' is quite in its place, because only by the fact that He who sprang from Israel after the flesh is God over all the glorious prerogative of Israel appears in its richest light. By the obvious and natural Doxology the Apostle opposes, with devout solemnity, the blasphemous denial, on the part of the Jews, of the Deity of Jesus (comp. Matthew xii. 24; John viii. 48), according to the canon of John v. 23. This explanation of the Doxology is also absolutely necessary. Since 'according to the flesh' obviously demands an antithesis, it is most natural that when, as here, it is inserted, the clause representing it should be an expression of that antithesis. Otherwise, the counterpart of 'according to the flesh' would vanish, and must be supplied in thought (comp. chap. xii. 18; 1 Corinthians i. 26; Colossians iii. 22). But neither the absence, nor the mental insertion, of the antithesis can be tolerated where the thesis is stated for the very sake of it. 'According to the flesh' is mentioned only on account of the following 'God over all.' Without this antithesis there would be an undesigned diminution of the advantages of Israel. The Apostle would then have written only 'of whom came the Christ.' For, that the Messiah sprang from the Jews would have been a higher prerogative of theirs than that He only sprang from them according to the flesh. But that *He* sprang from them according to the flesh who is God over all, that is the highest conceivable prerogative.

"The objections urged against the reference of this clause to Christ are, to all who simply adhere to Scripture, irrelevant.

"It is said, for instance, that 'according to the flesh' demands 'according to the Spirit' as its counterpart. But this would be the case only if it were said here, as in chap. i. 3, 4, *what* Christ 'according to the flesh' and *what* He 'according to the Spirit' was: that is, 'the Son of David' or 'Son of Man' in the one case, and 'Son of God' or 'God over all' in the other. But here it is not stated that the Christ who sprang from the Jews, in His lower nature Man, is God in His higher nature; but that the Christ who is God over all sprang from the Jews, obviously in the only possible sense, that is according to His human nature. The order of the clause is therefore unimpeachable; and 'according to the Spirit' not only may be dispensed with, but would have been disturbing if inserted.

"But the main objection is based upon the Pauline Christology. It is said that the Apostle never uses so strong an expression elsewhere, that he has no Doxology to Him, that he does not attribute to Him the predicate 'God,' which, if he had once done, his reverence would have disposed him often to do. But, first of all, it is certain that Paul almost always, we might say, when he mentions Christ and predicates anything of Him, describes Him indirectly as God, and thought of Him as God even when he did not directly term Him God. For He to whom Divine perfections, such as eternity (Colossians i. 15, 17), omnipresence (Ephesians i. 23, iv. 10), and grace (Romans i. 7), Divine works, such as creation and preservation of the world (Colossians i. 16, 17), and judgment (Romans xiv. 10 ; 2 Corinthians v. 10), and Divine honour Romans x. 13 ; Philippians ii. 10, 11), belong, must be Himself God. On another supposition the Apostle would have laid himself open to the charge, urged by the Jews against the Christians, of deifying the creature. It is hard to understand how his expositors can think that he avoided calling Christ God in the interests of Monotheism. The early church, in an opposite sense, opposed that Arianism and Semi-Arianism which is thus attributed to St. Paul because they endangered Monotheism. Appeal is made, however, to 1 Corinthians viii. 6 ; Ephesians iv. 4—6. But in vain ; for the 'One God the Father' is opposed to the 'gods many' of the heathen, and the 'one Lord Jesus Christ' to their 'lords many.' That the Apostle would not hesitate, in another connection, to declare this 'Lord' to be 'God' is evident from the fact that, while of the 'one God' it is said that 'of Him are all things, and we for Him,' it is also said of the 'one Lord' that 'by Him are all things and we by Him.' Origen rightly said : 'Non animadvertunt, quod sicut Dominum Jesum Christum non ita unum Dominum esse dixit, ut ex hoc Deus pater Dominus non dicatur, ita et Deum patrem non ita dixit esse unum Deum, ut Deus filius non credatur.' And, in fact, the denominations of 'Son,' 'Image of God,' 'Firstbegotten,' and 'Lord' (the Sept. translation of JEHOVAH) which are so common in Paul are equivalent to the appellation 'God,' and serve to characterize specifically the Second Person in the Godhead, as well as the position of the God-man in relation to the church redeemed to His service. If Paul thought of Christ as God he would call Him God, and this passage shows that he did. If he did so nowhere else, there are *hapax legomena*, both verbal and real, and this would be one of the former. Necessary occasion to call Christ God would occur only as in this passage, when the prominence was to be given in definite antithetical terms to the fact that the Messiah was not merely man, but God. We could not wonder if the expression were not elsewhere used : the other equivalent terms were the more descriptive ; he needed not the *word* to show his honour to Christ, his Divine Lord, and he did not write in the prospect of the acuteness of his expositors in the eighteenth and nineteenth centuries, who with such hairsplitting keenness distinguish between properties, works, and essence, between 'God' and 'the God,' that the Apostle must needs have met them by defining the locus of Christ's Divinity in the strictest Athanasian and Augustinian phraseology. And then he would only have fallen under the censure that the *Symbolum Quicunque* receives.

"But, in fact, the designation of Christ as God occurs oftener than his interpreters will have it. Not only does he say, (2 Corinthians v. 19) 'God was in Christ,' (Colossians ii. 9) 'In Him dwelleth all the fulness of the Godhead bodily,' (1 Timothy iii. 16) 'God was manifest in the flesh,' and of the Man Jesus (Philippians ii. 6) that 'He was in the form of God' and 'equal with God,' which are identical with 'God became Man,' but he expressly names Him God in Ephesians v. 5, 'of Christ and God,' as in Titus ii. 13, where the one article necessitates the one Subject, Jesus Christ: 'the Great God and our Saviour.' Winer does not contend against the grammatical possibility of this, only against its dogmatic propriety and its grammatical necessity. But the grammatical propriety of the opposite view is instanced only by doubtful arguments; and the 'manifestation of glory' is in Paul's doctrine more appropriate to Christ than to the Father; while the epithet 'Great God' applied to the Father specifically is strange and almost unmeaning. The dogmatic argument is a *petitio principii*. But, on account of 1 Timothy i. 1, ii. 3, iv. 10; Titus ii. 10, iii. 4, we lay no great stress on this passage. We must mention the reading of Colossians ii. 2, 'of the God Christ,' as also the relation in which Christ, Lord, and God stand to each other in Romans xiv. 10. These passages, however doubtful, weaken the force of the argument drawn from the unfrequent use of 'God' as a predicate.

"For the same reason that the predicate 'God' is seldom absolutely necessary, the Doxology to Christ is infrequent. But we find it again in 2 Timothy iv. 18; comp. Romans xvi. 17; 2 Thessalonians i. 12; Hebrews xiii. 21. Here, as in the use of the term 'God,' St. Paul is supported by the other writers: comp. 2 Peter iii. 18; Apocalypse v. 12; 1 Peter iv. 11. In the Jewish Theology the Messiah bears the names of Jehovah, the Holy One, blessed be He! although in later books, which however does not affect the question. We need not mention the Socinian *coup de désespoir*, 'to whom the God over all, blessed for ever, belongs.' The new punctuation, introduced by Erasmus, would make the Doxology of Christ a Doxology of God the Father: 'The God over all be blessed for ever!' But it should be well weighed that a Doxology to God the Father would be here out of place: sadness fills the heart of the Apostle, in his thought of the people's dishonour to God. And the habitual phraseology of the Hebrew, Septuagint, and Apocrypha, as of the New Testament (Matthew xx. 1, 9; Luke i. 68; 2 Corinthians i. 3), would demand that the predicate 'Blessed' should precede and not follow. The only exception is Psalm lxvii. 20. This exception confirms the rule; for the twice repeated

'Blessed,' the weaker form following the stronger, has a designed rhetorical emphasis. We may conclude with Calvin: 'Qui hoc membrum abrumpunt a reliquo contextu, ut Christo eripiant tam præclarum Divinitatis testimonium, nimis impudenter in plena luce tenebras obducere conantur. Plusquam enim aperta sunt verba: CHRISTUS EX JUDÆIS SECUNDUM CARNEM, QUI DEUS EST IN SŒCULA BENEDICTUS.'"

www.ingramcontent.com/pod-product-compliance
Lightning Source LLC
Chambersburg PA
CBHW030755230426
43667CB00007B/982